A FOOL FOR A CLIENT

A FOOL FOR A CLIENT

by

Will R. Wilson, Sr.

EAKIN PRESS Austin, Texas

FIRST EDITION

Published in the United States of America
By Eakin Press
A Division of Sunbelt Media, Inc.
P.O. Drawer 90159 Austin, Texas 78709-0159
email: eakinpub@sig.net
website: www.eakinpress.com

1 2 3 4 5 6 7 8 9

ISBN 1-57168-395-X

For CIP information, please access:
www.loc.gov

Dedicated to my wife,
Marjorie Ashcroft Wilson,
my daughter, Lou Loving,
and my son,
Will Wilson, Jr.

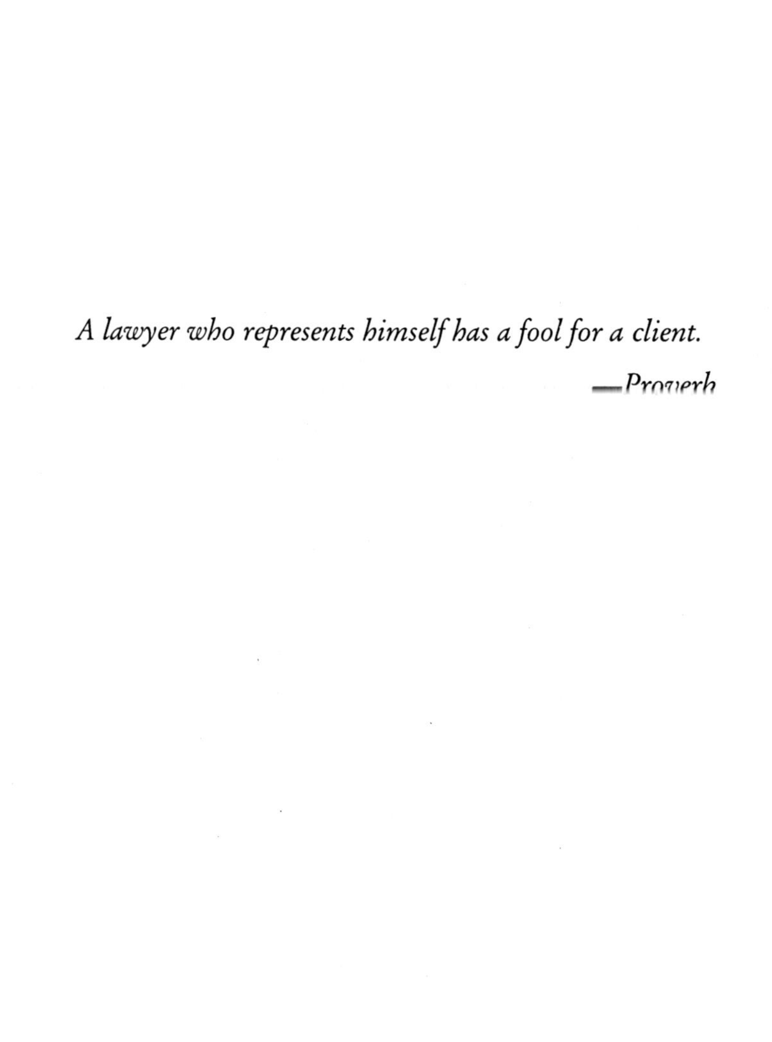

A lawyer who represents himself has a fool for a client.

—*Proverb*

Contents

Acknowledgments

I am grateful to Betty Wilke Cox, my editor and researcher, not only for four years of hard work but also for being a delightful literary companion and steady source of encouragement. Also, I want to thank Judith Blackwell for her thorough and solid research, and Bill Crawford for his counsel in structuring the book.

Will R. Wilson as chief of the Criminal Division, Department of Justice, during the Nixon administration.

— Author's Collection

Introduction

This is a judgmental book.

In order to appraise the validity of these judgments, you should know something about my credentials.

I graduated from Oklahoma University in 1934 with a bachelor of science degree in geology. I spent a year as a member of a geophysical surveying team for a company now known as Mobile Oil. I then decided on a career in law.

After graduating from Southern Methodist University Law School in 1937, I practiced civil law for five years, working in a Dallas corporate law firm by the name of Turner, Rodgers and Winn. Then, under Texas Attorney General Gerald C. Mann, for a year and a half I was an assistant attorney general in the Land Division, trying land lawsuits. During World War II, I served in the army for three years with twenty-seven months in New Guinea and the Philippine Islands in the Inspector General's Department and then as a combat artillery officer.

When I returned from the army, I rejoined the Texas Attorney General's Office briefly. While in the army I had decided upon a career in public service. So in 1946 I ran for and was elected district attorney of Dallas County, Texas, on a strict law-enforcement platform. While serving two terms, for a total of four years, I took slot machines out of all the clubs and labor union halls in Dallas and shut down gambling casinos and numbers lotteries.

After the election, Benny Binion, the boss of the gambling rackets in Dallas, recognizing that his game and his time were over, moved to Las Vegas, Nevada, with a suitcase full of money and opened his Golden Horseshoe Casino, known today as the

Horseshoe Hotel and Casino. On New Year's Eve of 1946—which marked the change of administration in the Dallas District Attorney's Office—some twenty-seven gambling joints closed in downtown Dallas, never to reopen.

However, the absentee Binion did not close his policy games, which continued to operate. After taking office, I made cases on Binion's Harlem Queen and other policy wheels. Binion and his associates were indicted in Dallas, but the Governor's Office of Nevada prevented Binion's extradition from that state to Dallas. Subsequently, the federal government brought Binion back to Texas and convicted him of income tax evasion on data I had furnished plus additional evidence secured by my successor, Henry Wade. Binion served three years in the federal penitentiary in Leavenworth, Kansas.

There followed lifelong public relations attacks on me by Binion, with Binion firing occasional bursts of publicity from Las Vegas. I never met the man nor saw him face to face.

In 1950 I was elected an associate justice of the Texas Supreme Court. I moved my young family from Dallas to Austin, which has remained our home.

After serving for five and a half years on the Texas Supreme Court, I resigned from the bench and was elected attorney general of Texas. Just as I had promised ten years earlier to clean up Dallas, I promised to clean up Texas, starting with flagrantly open gambling in Galveston. As Texas attorney general, I won the second Tidelands case which was tried as an original case in the U.S. Supreme Court. I served three terms, a total of six years, in that office. During that time, my goals were accomplished.

When Lyndon Johnson was sworn into office as vice president, his Senate seat became vacant. I ran for that office in a 1961 special election but was defeated. In 1962 I ran for governor of Texas but was defeated by Lyndon Johnson's political protégé, John Connally.

Those two unsuccessful campaigns ended my public service on the local and state level and also ended my friendship with Lyndon Johnson. I spent six years in private law practice in Austin with Wilson, Kendall, Koch and Randall, and formally switched my party allegiance from Democrat to Republican.

In 1969 I was invited to Washington by President Richard Nixon and served from 1969 through 1971 as chief of the Criminal

Division, a subcabinet post under Attorney General John Mitchell in the Justice Department.

In Texas, what became known as the Sharpstown scandal erupted. The scandal involved Frank Sharp, a Houston entrepreneur and land developer whom I had previously represented while practicing law in Austin. I was never implicated, never investigated, and never indicted in the scandal. But as a result of guilt by association, my ability to continue work in the Criminal Division was seriously impaired.

Richard Kleindienst, with whom I had worked closely, summed up my feelings when he said: "That he found it necessary to resign his position of assistant attorney general . . . has to be the most agonizing experience in an otherwise illustrious career." (Kleindienst, *Justice: The Memoirs of an Attorney General,* Ottawa, Illinois: Jameson Books, p. 139)

I resigned in November 1971, left the Nixon Administration, and returned to my home in Austin—just six months before the Watergate break-in occurred in June 1972.

My long experience in law enforcement, my personal experience in the dynamic of the U.S. Justice Department, and my intimate acquaintance with the actors in Watergate should yield a new perspective on why it happened, how it happened, and what it cost the American people.

CHAPTER 1

Working in the White House

"John Dean created an ambush for Nixon from which the only exit turned out to be his *resignation."*

ONE SUNDAY MIDSUMMER morning in 1972, my wife Margie and I were enjoying a leisurely breakfast at our home in West Austin. We were sitting with a great view looking down on Lake Austin and out over the countryside.

"He can't do that," I said.

The *American-Statesman*'s lead story covered the Watergate burglars who were still in jail. Attorney General Richard Kleindienst issued a statement about the prosecution of the burglars, saying: "Let the chips fall . . ." In effect, President Richard Nixon washed his hands of the whole affair.

"He can't do that," I repeated. "They were his people. They were doing it for him. He can't throw them to the wolves. If he tries that, it will destroy him."

He did—and he was destroyed.

And that is what this book is about.

John W. Dean, III . . . Marine Lt. Col. Oliver North . . . and Monica Lewinsky. What do they have in common? All were inconspicuous employees on a White House staff. All severely compromised their president. Under threat of criminal prosecution, all testified against their president.

Impeachment problems of three presidents—Richard Nixon, Ronald Reagan, and Bill Clinton—originated with the malfunction of the White House staff. All three presidencies were endangered by inconspicuous employees working at the White House.

As I left the Nixon Justice Department in November 1971, I remember thinking that the principal danger to President Richard Nixon came not from outside, but from inside—from his free-wheeling staff. While it is true that the fundamental and first cause of both Nixon's and Clinton's problems lay in their own character flaws, still, the immediate trigger for Nixon was a malfunction of the White House legal staff.

With Nixon, it was G. Gordon Liddy's compulsion to do political intelligence which produced the illegal break-in and illegal wire-tapping of the Democratic National Headquarters in Washington.

Nixon was out of Washington when the Watergate burglars were arrested in the early hours of Saturday, June 17, 1972. The president returned Monday evening. The whole circumstance should have alerted him to the fact that the Watergate break-in was a stupid thing, probably planned and carried out by his campaign staff. The president easily could have gotten all of the facts from G. Gordon Liddy, Jeb Stuart Magruder, and Maurice Stans. He then could have fired everyone responsible, including Attorney General John Mitchell. Since these people were acting not for themselves but for Nixon, he could have immediately pardoned those guilty of a federal violation. Then he could have laid out all the facts publicly and apologized to his political opponent, Democratic candidate George McGovern, who could not possibly have defeated Nixon. There would have been a firestorm of bad publicity, but it would have passed.

Instead of coming to grips with the break-in, Nixon made a fatal decision to contain the whole matter until after the election. He then made an even worse decision: He took the control of the Watergate investigation out of the hands of the Justice Department and placed John W. Dean—his inexperienced but fast-moving and eager young presidential counselor—in charge of containing publicity concerning the Watergate raid until after the campaign and election were over.

John Dean's lack of legal experience took over and, without consulting a lawyer experienced in criminal law or anyone else, Dean used hush money, grand jury perjury, and public lies to accomplish a news cover-up. This—while successful for the period of the Nixon vs. McGovern campaign—eventually collapsed into what became known as Watergate. John Dean created an ambush for Nixon from which the only exit turned out to be *his* resignation.

Events need not have ended that way. Had John Dean known how to do it, he could have accomplished by legal procedures most of what he did do by illegal means. Had he followed legal procedures, there would have been no cover-up. Without John Dean's testimony connecting Nixon to the cover-up—and Alexander Butterfield's testimony which almost accidentally revealed the existence of White House tapes—the incident would have been too thin for an impeachment trial.

In the Reagan and Clinton presidencies, advisers who claimed to have "learned the lessons of Watergate" nevertheless went through some degree of the old familiar maneuvers: initial cover-up of the incident, denial of prior knowledge, willingness to sacrifice lower-level White House employees, bypassing the Justice Department, bringing in personal legal counsel, testimony by the president's men under threat of prosecution or in exchange for grants of immunity, and finally the question of presidential pardon.

During the Reagan Administration, Lt. Col. Oliver North and Adm. John Poindexter, by their activities in the arms-for-hostages affair with Iran and by the diversion of moneys to the contras of Central America, brought both President Reagan and Vice President Bush under intense investigation by independent prosecutor Lawrence E. Walsh.

Reagan's secretary of state, George Schultz, was "concerned that the attempts to cover up a bad policy could lead to more legal troubles than the original policy." Schultz warned: "It's Watergate all over again."

The White House counsel knew that North and Poindexter "almost certainly would be forced to testify before Congress soon under grants of immunity." (Bob Woodward, *Shadow: Five Presidents and the Legacy of Watergate*, New York: Simon & Schuster, 1999, p. 135) North appeared before the joint congressional investigating committee "in his Marine olive uniform, his chest covered with medals. . . ."

North, born in Texas and the son of a lieutenant colonel who had served under Gen. George S. Patton in World War II, maintained that his only crimes "had been zeal and resourcefulness in following the orders" of his president. Under a grant of limited immunity, North testified that he had kept "his immediate superiors fully informed of his actions at all times," and believed that the president had indeed authorized such activity. (*Current Biography Yearbook*, 1992, pp. 419-422)

Oliver North captured the sympathy of the American television audience in a way that G. Gordon Liddy never had.

Nancy Reagan, the First Lady, "suggested they hire Nixon's lawyer, Jack Miller. . . . [Chief of Staff Don] Regan thought that was a terrible suggestion. Appointing a famous criminal attorney to defend the president would send absolutely the wrong message to the press and the public." (Woodward, *Shadow*, pp. 100, 102, 105)

When Reagan considered pardons for North and Poindexter, he asked his counsel for advice. If the president pardoned Poindexter or North, his counsel said, people would never believe that the president did not know about the diversion of funds in advance. It would be a taint on the presidency. (Woodward, *Shadow*, p. 138)

The Iran-contra investigation continued even after Reagan's successor, George Bush, took office.

Once again Walsh questioned Reagan. But the former president's slide into Alzheimer's disease had progressed too far. He could not remember anything about the Iran-contra affair. "I'm very embarrassed. I'm sorry. . . . It's like I wasn't president at all." (Woodward, *Shadow*, p. 162)

In discussing the possibility of testimony before the Ervin Committee or the grand jury, Nixon had told his men: "But you can say I don't remember. You can say I can't recall. I can't give an answer to that that I can't recall." (Staff of the *Washington Post, The Presidential Transcripts*, New York: Dell, 1974, p. 132) But in Reagan's case, loss of memory was not a legalistic ploy. It was literal truth.

Walsh then focused on Bush, who claimed he had been "out of the loop" while he was vice president. Bush clearly believed that the prosecutor and the press, by keeping the investigation in the spotlight of public attention, had cost him his re-election bid. Bush's attorney general, William Barr, considered dismissing Walsh. But such an action would ignite "a new firestorm [and] trigger a reaction like the Saturday Night Massacre." (Woodward, *Shadow*, p. 206)

The suggestion of a presidential pardon was trotted out like the tired old war horse it had become. Attorney General Barr "recommended pardons for Caspar Weinberger, former CIA officials, and the former State Department assistant secretary Elliot Abrams. . . ." On Christmas Eve of 1992, in the closing days of his administration, President Bush signed an executive order pardoning five men, including Weinberger and Abrams. (Woodward, *Shadow*, pp. 212, 214)

The new Democratic president, Bill Clinton, and First Lady Hillary Rodham Clinton came into the White House with an apparent understanding of Watergate and its political legacy. Ironically Hillary Rodham, as a twenty-six-year-old lawyer just graduated from Yale University, had been invited by John Doar, special counsel to the House Judiciary Committee, to come to Washington in January 1974. In charge of legislative research, she was one of only three women on a team of some forty-three lawyers. Nixon would later point out in a conversation with Monica Crowley (Monica Crowley, *Nixon Off the Record*, New York: Random House, 1996, p. 64): "As far as Hillary is concerned . . . she was on the goddamned committee to impeach me."

The Clintons had enough knowledge about Watergate to be alert to potential problems, as Clinton's White House counselor, Bernie Nussbaum, described: "Small problems which can be handled properly and should be handled properly [can] mushroom into huge political problems. . . . It seems that every president since Nixon has had their problems—this theme of legal problems becoming huge political problems that debilitate the president. . . . My job will be to look out for those things so they don't explode."

But, unfortunately for Bill and Hillary Clinton, almost immediately after the president's inauguration things *did* explode. The events began with a few quiet pops like a string of small firecrackers going off and eventually culminated in the skyrocket display of a presidential impeachment.

Two of Clinton's first nominations—one for attorney general and one for the Civil Rights Division in the Justice Department—seemed unlikely to win Senate approval. Clinton withdrew the names in spite of Nussbaum's warning: "When you abandon your people, you send a message that you can be rolled."

Next came a charge of mismanagement in the White House Travel Office, the apparent suicide of the deputy counsel, Vince

Foster, the rumors of the Clintons' involvement in some Arkansas investments, and stories of Clinton's alleged sexual liaisons while governor of Arkansas.

Nixon followed the news of the Clintons' growing problems with the interest of one who had himself been vulnerable. If investigators wanted to know what was going on, Nixon said, "They should interview Nussbaum. They can't hide behind attorney-client privilege because [John] Dean knocked that out with Watergate." (Crowley, *Nixon off the Record*, p. 193)

Attorney General Janet Reno, acting on a request from the president and transmitted to the Justice Department by Nussbaum, moved to appoint a special counsel. The first special counsel, Robert B. Fiske, Jr., was replaced by Judge Kenneth W. Starr, a Republican conservative.

While previous allegations against the president were under investigation, Bill Clinton faced new problems. Monica Lewinsky, a female intern, used her position behind the White House barricades to establish an emotional and sexual relationship with an older married man—namely, the president. She flirted, exposed her underwear, and used other feminine allurements to exploit Clinton's vulnerability. It is somewhat ironic that a president who had emerged as a champion of the feminist movement should be enticed into political embarrassment by an aggressive female.

When the president was asked if he had ever been alone with Monica Lewinsky in the Oval Office, Clinton replied: "I don't recall." Had he ever given Monica Lewinsky gifts? His reply: "I don't recall."

In June 1998 Monica Lewinsky went to the office of Plato Cacheris. Lewinsky's mother had asked that Cacheris replace William Ginsberg, Monica's earlier lawyer. Monica "provided what seemed almost frightening detail" about her relationship with the president. In an earlier era, the intimate details would have been shocking. As it turned out, the relationship became an object of ridicule and crude jokes.

Shortly after Clinton's first election, Nixon commented, "[T]he country's willingness to elect someone like Clinton . . . shows we are on the way down. . . . The president is a womanizer? So what? . . . the people elected Clinton because they're surrounded by immortality." (Crowley, *Nixon in Winter*, pp. 321-322)

One might wonder why such employees as John Dean, Oliver North, and Monica Lewinsky were working in the White House anyway.

Before President Franklin D. Roosevelt took the oath of office in March 1933, the White House staff consisted of the domestic help plus only a small staff of presidential aides. The existence of an enlarged White House staff, many of them operating out of the First Family's living quarters, originated with Roosevelt.

When Roosevelt appointed his good friend and longtime political adviser, Louis McHenry Howe, as his chief secretary (an early equivalent of today's chief of staff), Howe moved into the White House. He lived there until shortly before his death. Roosevelt's personal secretary, Marguerite "Missy" LeHand, also lived in the White House, as did two of Eleanor Roosevelt's loyal friends and aides. With almost every available space in use, the family quarters began to look like a boardinghouse or college dormitory. (Franklin D. Roosevelt, *FDR: His Personal Letters, 1928-1945*, Vol. 1, New York: Duell, Sloan and Pearce, 1950)

Both the president's personality and his physical condition contributed to this unusual domestic arrangement. He loved to be with people, but his bout in 1921 with infantile paralysis—poliomyelitis, as it is now known—left him unable to stand up without assistance. The president's military and naval aides also lived in the White House during their tours of duty.

For political reasons, knowledge of the president's disability had been kept from the public. But both Howe and LeHand had known Roosevelt for many years. They were devoted to him. In the evenings after work, his live-in close friends and a few carefully selected, discreet guests gathered around him, enjoyed a drink, and shared lively conversation.

President Roosevelt had only a few Cabinet seats to fill, and this he did quickly. His appointments, "if not actually haphazard, had no overall design." (Kenneth S. Davis, *FDR: The New York Years, 1928-1933*, New York: Random House, 1985, 1979, p. 422) Some of his Cabinet members thought of themselves in the roles of deputy presidents who would function much as viceroys might in a monarchy.

Early in his administration, tension arose between Roosevelt and individual Cabinet members as a result of competition for publicity and a scramble for public credit. Some Cabinet members were not shy when it came to garnering the limelight. One was Secretary of the Interior Harold L. Ickes, whose grandson later served as deputy chief of staff in the Clinton White House.

The attitudes of some Cabinet members caused jealousy and presidential frustration within the chain of command. Another source of Roosevelt's frustration was that many of the federal bureaucrats had been Republican appointees protected by civil service. If Roosevelt were to succeed in pushing through his radical ideas for solving the nation's Great Depression, he needed the help of young, enthusiastic idealists. He installed in the White House eight young men—specifically ones who possessed "a passion for anonymity"—and used them as a personal staff to get things done.

The new president also turned to Felix Frankfurter, a law professor at Harvard, who for some years had encouraged bright young graduates to enter the government's service. (One of them, Erwin N. Griswold, later became solicitor general. He was my friend and colleague when I worked in the Nixon Justice Department.) Frankfurter declined Roosevelt's offer of the solicitor general's post, but he responded to Roosevelt's request to recruit staff to fill the many New Deal or "alphabet soup" offices. Because the men were recruited by Frankfurter, they were dubbed the "Happy Hot Dogs" by the press. (Leonard Baker, *Brandeis and Frankfurter: A Dual Biography*, New York: Harper & Row, 1984, pp. 284-287) They were absolutely dedicated to the president's New Deal with much the same fervor as Robert Kennedy's Band of Brothers two decades later in the 1960s Justice Department.

Through the years, this group of personal assistants expanded into the present number of White House staff who now inhabit the Executive Office Building.

President Nixon would bemoan the difficulty of finding people for government service. Employees needed to have "judgment, character, loyalty, patriotism. Most lack at least two of these, especially the Eastern intellectuals." (H. R. Haldeman, *The Haldeman Diaries*, New York: Putnam's, 1994, p. 145)

When I was in Washington, the White House staff were employed directly by the president without an FBI personnel check. At first they were mostly campaign aides—such as H. R. "Bob" Haldeman and John Ehrlichman—who moved directly from the winning campaign headquarters to offices in the White House. Haldeman and Ehrlichman were "not your conventional political operatives," Leonard Garment observed. (Leonard Garment, *Crazy Rhythm*, New York: Times Books, 1997, pp. 151-152) They were "formidably intelligent and [bristling] with energy and self-confidence."

Nixon's original staff also included people like Henry Kissinger, Arthur Burns, and Daniel Patrick Moynihan, who were employed for their special expertise. All were ambitious to establish their own reputations. This staff had unlimited perks, such as passes through the White House security system, meals in the White House staff dining room, pampering by the battery of skilled White House telephone operators, use of the White House stationery, use of the government motor pool, and so on.

Attorney General John Mitchell warned me of this situation when I first went to work at the Justice Department. He gave me specific instructions not to let any member of the White House staff participate in decisions of the Criminal Division.

It was only natural for the White House staff to expand the scope and importance of its work. A good example of this under Nixon was the way in which Henry Kissinger turned the position of the White House national security adviser into an operating unit conducting foreign policy directly out of the White House. This was done for the express purpose of bypassing the State Department.

Shrill complaints by Kissinger about news leaks led to the creation of the Plumbers Investigative Unit operating out of the basement of the White House. From the start, this secret unit was underground in more ways than its purely architectural connotation. The Plumbers were created because of dissatisfaction with the FBI and soon got Nixon into trouble by conducting a wild, illegal, and unnecessary raid on the office of Dr. Fielding, Daniel Ellsberg's psychiatrist.

There was no real supervision or control of the Plumbers by anyone. The Criminal Division had no communication with them. They were free as birds to use the prestige of the White House and fly wherever they wanted. After the fiasco of the Fielding break-in, it became necessary to get the Plumbers out of the White House. They were transferred to the Committee to Re-elect the President. Here they were allotted a budget of a half million dollars—but they were still unsupervised. They soon got into trouble again by raiding and wiretapping the Democratic National Committee headquarters in the Watergate building.

When Nixon first entered the Oval Office, his former law partner, Leonard Garment, had hoped—perhaps expected—to be named counsel to the president. He resented seeing the job handed to John Ehrlichman, "a campaign advance man." When Ehrlichman switched jobs, Len Garment was sounded out, but Ehrlichman aides Egil "Bud" Krogh and Jeb Magruder recommended John Dean—who was to report not to the president but to Haldeman.

"In this capacity [White House counsel]," Nixon wrote in his *Memoirs* (Vol. 2, p. 640), "Dean had the responsibility for keeping track of and attending to any legal problems affecting the President or the White House." But the president's appointment of John Dean as White House counsel proved that Nixon did not want a mature, experienced, battle-tested lawyer. He still thought of his aides as political campaign men. He wanted a smooth and likable runner. This is what he got in John Dean.

Nixon did not make up for the gap in his staff's experience. In fact, Watergate occurred because of his lack of executive experience.

When President Dwight D. "Ike" Eisenhower took office as president, he had executive experience as the commander of the Allied Armies in Europe throughout World War II. But unlike Eisenhower, when President Nixon took command of the federal government, he had very little managerial or command experience anywhere. As a congressman, senator, and vice president he had not exercised command. Most of the managerial experience he did have was gained in political campaigns.

Nixon had not run a large law office, a district attorney's office, or a governor's office. President Eisenhower actually kept Vice President Nixon out of the country much of the time. This gave him an excellent background in foreign affairs but no executive experience.

Nixon's White House aides also lacked executive experience. Haldeman's career had been as an advertising professional. Ehrlichman had been a condemnation lawyer with his father. Charles "Chuck" Colson had practiced law in Boston. Jeb Magruder had been in advertising. Henry Kissinger, Arthur Burns, and Daniel Patrick Moynihan were all academics. From the start, the Nixon White House was thin on executive or managerial experience.

The true executive work of his administration was carried out by subordinates such as Haldeman and John Mitchell. The Committee to Re-elect the President was set up for the second term to take the Nixon vs. McGovern campaign away from the Republican party and run it. This committee was supposed to be supervised by Mitchell, but he was so distracted by a personal crisis that it received no supervision.

After the raid on the Democratic National Headquarters occurred, Nixon acted as his own lawyer. The old saying that a lawyer who represents himself has a fool for a client is still true. From the start of Watergate, Nixon needed the close legal guidance of a lawyer skilled in criminal practice and dedicated to saving the Nixon presidency. This he did not have. He made his own legal decisions without having a background in criminal law.

At the very beginning President Nixon turned the whole Watergate matter over to John Dean, who was incompetent in both law enforcement procedure and in criminal law. In handling Watergate, Dean made one mistake or serious blunder after another which eventually brought about the disgrace and resignation of President Nixon in the face of impeachment.

Nixon would not have fallen if he had relied on an experienced criminal defense lawyer. Such a lawyer could have advised him that the Committee to Re-elect could legally extend financial aid to its employees charged in a criminal case—especially so when the employees were on an authorized mission. The Committee could have obtained the burglars' release from jail without violating the law, could have paid for bail bond premiums, and could have paid attorneys' fees, travel and living expenses, and other necessary support.

John Dean committed a lawyer's ultimate betrayal. Under threat of imprisonment, Dean traded his testimony to the prosecutors for release from prison and became an enthusiastic cooperating witness against Nixon.

Nixon's Watergate troubles grew with his efforts to protect John Mitchell and other staff members. However, time and events separated them, and toward the end Nixon did not remain completely loyal to Mitchell. On the other hand, Mitchell remained Nixon's knight in shining armor of loyalty to the bitter end. He offered to sacrifice himself to save Nixon, but his offer was refused by the special prosecutor. Nixon's Faustian bargain with John Dean that Dean would testify only against Nixon's aides and not against Nixon himself did not stand the test of prosecution—as any good criminal defense lawyer would have advised him it could not. Neither could it survive any definition of loyalty.

The Watergate burglars were employees of the Committee to Re-elect. They thought they were doing the break-in and wiretapping for Nixon and that he would back them up. Nixon's lawyers should have known in their bones that under these circumstances President Nixon did not have the option of prosecuting the Watergate burglars without bringing about his own destruction.

On August 9, 1974—almost three years after I had left the Justice Department—President Nixon resigned in disgrace in the face of impeachment charges. John Mitchell became the first former attorney general in our nation's history to serve time in a federal prison. Others of Nixon's top aides also were tried, convicted, and sentenced to prison terms. This brought about a series of conflicting loyalties which makes a fascinating study.

Former President Nixon's death in April 1994—four months shy of the twentieth anniversary of his resignation—brought my own memories flooding back. In addition, a large number of biographies, autobiographies, transcripts, memoirs, and other analyses are now available. Together with the Nixon tapes, these constitute rich resource materials.

Nixon had a grand vision of a peaceful and orderly world. If Watergate had not cut him down when he was beginning a second term after winning a landslide re-election, he could have ended the cold war many years ahead of when it did end. He could have saved the United States the accumulation of debt caused by many years of military buildup and perhaps saved the Soviet Union from disintegration and bankruptcy. I believe he would have. Some form of sanction less than impeachment of Nixon would have been far better for our nation.

During Watergate, the legal and ethical mistakes and conflicting loyalties of the president's advisers—both in the Justice Department and within Nixon's own White House inner circle—compounded rather than concealed a pattern of strategic mistakes. The turning of John Dean by the Washington, D.C. prosecutors brought on a swearing match between Nixon and Dean as to what Nixon knew about the cover-up and when he knew it. The foul language revealed on tapes of the president's unguarded conversations shocked the nation.

Every experienced trial lawyer knows that—even when you start with a good case—if the opposition can expose one of your principal witnesses in a big fat lie, you will probably lose that jury.

Nixon was caught in a big fat lie when he was exposed by one of his own tapes ("the smoking gun") about an attempt to use the CIA to stop an FBI investigation into money laundering of campaign funds in Mexico. The tapes and the impeachment cut short Nixon's presidency, which might have delivered a new world order of peace and prosperity—all to our great loss.

President Nixon never had his day in court. That was his fault. In pointing out the president's desperate need for the skills and talents of the best possible criminal lawyers *from the very beginning* of the Watergate crisis, I am not arguing his innocence. But neither did President Clinton's lawyers argue Clinton's innocence in defending him in his Senate impeachment trial.

Nixon was crushed because of bad lawyering. Clinton survived because of good lawyering.

There is an old parable concerning a Russian nobleman who is traveling with his family and several servants during winter in Siberia. They are in a sleigh pulled by a troika of horses. A pack of wolves attacks them in a deep forest, lunges at the horses, and attempts to make them stumble. The nobleman orders one of his servants thrown off the back of the sleigh. While the wolves close in on the unfortunate servant, the sleigh escapes to the safety of the next village.

In law enforcement, the expression "thrown to the wolves" is used every day all over the United States.

In the beginning of the Nixon Administration, very few of the bright young Republicans who had come from around the nation to work in the glamorous White House visualized themselves as riding in a sleigh pursued by a pack of hungry wolves. And least of all did President Nixon, in the flush of confidence and pride following his inauguration, see himself deciding which of his staff to throw to the wolves.

Many years ago, a great-granddaughter of former President Calvin Coolidge told me that after Coolidge finished a day in the Oval Office he liked to sit for an hour before dinner in a rocking chair on the front porch of the White House and think things over—among them, the Teapot Dome scandal left over from the administration of the late President Warren G. Harding. It might be that future presidents should eliminate much of the White House staff and replace them with a rocking chair where they, too, can think about things.

Maybe Silent Cal had the right idea.

At least one lesson was learned from Watergate. President Clinton employed knowledgeable and skilled lawyers and, after he created a mess, followed their advice. He was not ousted from office.

In Watergate, many Republican congressmen and senators put principle ahead of party and did not unite behind Nixon and support him in his fight against impeachment. In Monica-gate, the Democrat senators *did* put party ahead of principle and defended the presidency while not condoning the president's conduct.

CHAPTER 2

The Failed Impeachment of Justice William O. Douglas

"We are the Supreme Court and we can do what we want."
— Chief Justice Warren E. Burger

IN DECEMBER 1969, when I was asked to go to Washington to head the Criminal Division, I had no idea my office would be called upon to investigate two sitting justices of the U.S. Supreme Court. The result would be the resignation of Justice Abe Fortas and a failed impeachment proceeding in Congress against Justice William O. Douglas. Little did I know that these events were to be prophetic of a dark fate lying in ambush for the Nixon Administration.

The Fortas resignation and the Douglas impeachment proceedings, both of which were handled by my office in the Justice Department, helped create an atmosphere of implacable hostility in the House of Representatives which culminated three years later in a bipartisan committee's vote for Nixon's impeachment.

In late April or early May of my first year at the Justice Department, Bill Bittman came to see me. He had been one of Robert Kennedy's bright young prosecutors in the Attorney General's Office and a member of the "get-Hoffa" squad.

When Bittman visited my office he represented Louis Wolfson, a former financier who had had trouble with the Securities and Exchange Commission. Wolfson had begun serving time in a federal prison in Elgin, Florida, and additional untried cases were pending against him as a result of his security sales on Wall Street. Naturally, he wanted out of the penitentiary, but first he had to dispose of the pending cases. In exchange, he offered to become a witness for the government. In other words, he was willing to throw his former associates to the wolves—including a sitting justice, Abe Fortas.

Bittman had startling information to offer on behalf of his client. In January 1966 the Wolfson Family Foundation had paid Supreme Court Justice Abe Fortas $20,000 as a supplement to his federal judicial salary.

This was most interesting news. To understand why, you need to know something of Fortas's background.

Abe Fortas had a long history as a Washington lawyer. Much of his work had been as a lobbyist. One of his principal clients was Lyndon Johnson. When Johnson later became president, he rewarded his old friend and attorney Abe Fortas by nominating him in 1965 to the Supreme Court. After going on the high Court, Fortas continued as an adviser to President Johnson and Louis Wolfson—in violation of the convention that a justice "takes the veil."

Chief Justice Earl Warren had announced his plans to retire in 1968 near the end of Johnson's last term. Johnson nominated Justice Fortas as chief justice to replace Justice Warren. Although he was certainly bright and capable enough, Fortas's background did not qualify him to be on the Supreme Court, much less to be chief justice.

Fortas's known liberalism, his years as a political lawyer in Washington, and his advisory relationship to LBJ—plus the fact that the nomination came from a lame-duck president—all worked against him. His service as lead counsel for Johnson in the infamous Box 13 vote fraud case—a turning point in Johnson's career—made the nomination questionable. The nomination failed to receive Senate confirmation, but of course Fortas retained his position as an associate justice on the high bench. Chief Justice Warren delayed his retirement until early in the Nixon Administration.

When I learned from Bill Bittman the connection between Louis Wolfson and the sitting Justice Fortas, and of Wolfson's intense desire to get out of the penitentiary, I took the situation up with Attorney General John Mitchell. Mitchell told me to follow up and get the facts. I went to Director J. Edgar Hoover and asked him to appoint two of his top FBI special agents to go with me to the federal prison in Florida to interview Wolfson. At the prison, I waited in a nearby room while an FBI agent took Wolfson's statements.

According to Wolfson, on the day in 1966 that Abe Fortas was sworn in as an associate justice of the U.S. Supreme Court, Wolfson had been invited to a small dinner party given in Fortas's honor at the Georgetown home of Justice Douglas. During the course of the evening's conversation, Wolfson learned that Justice Fortas would be taking a big cut in income to serve on the Court. Members of the Supreme Court were paid a generous salary, which in 1965 was $39,500 annually. But as a successful Washington attorney, Fortas had been earning several times that amount.

At the dinner party, Wolfson—in a spirit of public service, as he explained it—offered to supplement Justice Fortas's salary by $20,000 a year and to continue that arrangement to his widow even after the justice's death.

No doubt Wolfson acted in a burst of generosity, and no doubt Justice Fortas accepted the offer in that spirit. Justice Douglas told them that he had such an arrangement with the Parvin-Dohrman Foundation, which permitted Justice Douglas to do much of the travel and mountain climbing for which he was famous. At one time Fortas had actively represented Wolfson, so he had been accepting money from him for some time—but not an ongoing, annual payment.

As things worked out, from the time Fortas was sworn in as a Supreme Court associate justice, he had placed himself in hostage to Wolfson's conduct. When Wolfson's trouble with the SEC surfaced, payments to Fortas were discontinued. Fortas then returned $20,000 to Wolfson in December 1966 and severed his connection with the Wolfson foundation.

I could hardly believe that justices of the Supreme Court were accepting retainers from outsiders to supplement their federal salaries.

After we had taken the statement from Wolfson in Florida, I telephoned General Mitchell's deputy, Richard "Dick" Kleindienst, who was visiting President Nixon at his Key Biscayne residence. I gave him a resumé of the statement and said that in my opinion there was no choice—Justice Fortas would have to resign his seat on the Supreme Court.

A few days later a writer for *Life* magazine, William Lambert, came to my office to see me. He told me that he had been investigating the Fortas-Wolfson connection.

"I want to ask you, Mr. Wilson," Lambert said, "if you can confirm the information I've gathered."

"Tell me what you have," I replied.

He laid out his story for me. After I had listened to everything he had, I said, "Yes, that's correct."

The procedure was not unusual; in fact, it was quite common. An investigative reporter might dig around through public records and interview people "on background," but whenever possible a reputable newspaper or newsmagazine always sought confirmation from legitimate sources.

The following week (May 9, 1969) *Life* magazine came out with its story about the Fortas-Wolfson relationship. The outside cover headline was:

A NEW CHARGE
JUSTICE FORTAS AND
THE $20,000 CHECK

The inside story was headlined "Fortas of the Supreme Court: A Question of Ethics," with Lambert's byline. Full-page facing photographs showed Fortas appearing very judicial in his black robes and Wolfson as a distinguished-looking capitalist. In captions beneath the photographs, *Life* asked: "Why would a man of [Fortas's] legal brilliance and high position do business with Louis Wolfson, a well-known corporate stock manipulator known to be under federal investigation?"

The allegation was that Fortas, while a justice, was rendering legal service to Wolfson. Fortas denied this. He telephoned Attorney General Mitchell and asked for a conference.

John called me. "What shall I do, Will?" he asked.

"Don't have the conference," I advised him. "Tell Justice Fortas that you will furnish the Wolfson material to Chief Justice Warren. Justice Fortas can take the matter up with the chief justice."

A few days later, May 14, Justice Fortas resigned. He was the only justice to step down from the U.S. Supreme Court under pressure of public criticism. (An earlier justice, Samuel Chase, was impeached in 1802, tried before the Senate, and acquitted.)

Justice Douglas set out his own version of the Wolfson-Fortas affair in his autobiography (*The Court Years, 1939–1975: The Autobiography of William O. Douglas*, New York: Random House, 1980, p. 357):

> Chance played into Nixon's hands . . .
>
> In charge of the Criminal Division of the Department of Justice was Will Wilson, the man who soon was forced to resign because of scandals in his Texas practice. In 1969, Wilson rummaged through the files on Wolfson and found papers which an evil mind would say implicated Abe Fortas. These papers were certainly no evidence of Abe's involvement in any criminal matter. Nevertheless, Wilson leaked this privileged information to the press as he was later to leak unsubstantiated material on me to Gerald Ford when Ford was working to have me impeached.

Justice Douglas saw in me the malevolence of an Iago in bringing about the destruction of Otello in Verdi's opera. I saw myself as ridding the Supreme Court of a man who never should have been on the Court.

Justice Douglas used the wrong word: *privileged*. Obviously, the attorney/client privilege would not prevent the publication of the Wolfson-Fortas relationship since the client (Wolfson) had released the material himself. In addition, Justice Fortas was denying the existence of an attorney/client relationship after he joined the court. Justice Douglas probably meant "confidential," but Wolfson, bargaining to reduce his prison term, did not place any restrictions upon the use of the material. Therefore, this was not a "leak" on my part. In practice, when we had not issued an official publicity release, the Justice Department—usually acting through Henry Petersen—often confirmed an investigative reporter's stories in order to ensure more accurate news coverage. I do not know where or how Lambert got his facts, but he had them when he came to me. I did confirm to Lambert that the facts he had were accurate.

Douglas continued:

> . . . the disclosure in *Life* of the fee paid by Wolfson, the long delay returning it, and the fact that Wolfson was in deep trouble with the Federal government all brought matters to a head and gave Nixon the opportunity to free another Court seat.

Fortas knew why he resigned. While on the court, he had been helping Wolfson with his legal difficulties. The *Life* magazine story was enough to drive Fortas from the high bench.

As far as I ever knew, President Nixon personally had nothing to do with the Fortas resignation. John Mitchell and I handled the whole thing as part of our duties at the Justice Department.

The weekend after the Fortas resignation, Nixon decided the time was ripe to choose his new chief justice. The president had instructed Mitchell to initiate the necessary background check of Warren Burger. When Burger (described as "middle-class, middle-aged, middle-of-the-road and middle-Western") checked out satisfactorily, Nixon followed his custom of making a surprise announcement. He arranged for Burger and his family to be smuggled into the White House and announced the news on national television on May 21, 1969.

Burger was quickly confirmed by the Senate.

Nixon gave up on trying to get a Southern conservative confirmed by the Senate as it was then constituted and turned to Harry A. Blackmun. A lifelong friend of Warren Burger, Blackmun had been "house counsel" to the Mayo Clinic before serving on the U.S. Court of Appeals for the Eighth District from 1959 to 1970.

Vice President Spiro Agnew rushed in with his sharp tongue in a fixed-bayonet position. He blamed certain political lobbies for the failure of G. Harrold Carswell to win confirmation to the Supreme Court. The vice president predicted a public outcry if Judge Blackmun were also rejected.

At last the Senate had a nominee they liked. Blackmun was confirmed May 12, 1970, without a single negative vote.

The impeachment move against Douglas quite possibly was prompted by Nixon's anger at failing to win confirmation of either Haynsworth or Carswell. Ehrlichman wrote: "Nixon decided, perhaps we should be going after one of theirs." The president instructed him to "talk to Jerry Ford" and that Ford should "move to impeach that sitting Justice who has been charged."

This was not the first move to impeach Douglas.

In 1953 Justice Douglas—acting alone and completely without legal authority—granted a stay of execution to the husband-and-wife pair, Julius and Ethel Rosenberg. The Rosenbergs had been convicted of espionage and sentenced to die in the electric chair. The Supreme Court as a body quickly overturned Justice Douglas's unilateral stay and the Rosenbergs were executed at Sing Sing prison on June 19, 1953. The nation was in the grip of McCarthyism and anti-Communism hysteria. A drive was launched to impeach Douglas but the attempt was unsuccessful.

Justice Douglas had long been thought by members of law enforcement to be hostile to law enforcement. As a member of the Supreme Court, he was the administrative judge for the Ninth Circuit, which included Las Vegas, Nevada. This was a sensitive position. It gave him initial control of motions and writs in the Supreme Court for that circuit. Las Vegas had always been a difficult place for law enforcement and was rapidly becoming a money center for the rackets by reason of skim from the casinos. The combination of President Lyndon Johnson's prohibition of wiretapping in Las Vegas and Justice Douglas's open contempt of conventional law enforcement were very frustrating to run-of-the-mill law enforcement officials. There can be no doubt that this contributed to Richard Nixon's victory in 1968.

So it is not surprising that we at the Nixon Justice Department were already aware of Justice Douglas's relationship with the Parvin Foundation and had been compiling a file on its activities.

This foundation had been started in 1960 by Albert Parvin, a Los Angeles businessman, with profits of nearly $3 million from the sale of the Flamingo Hotel and gambling casino in Las Vegas. The foundation's largest stock holdings were in the Parvin-Dohrman Company, which owned three hotels and casinos in Las Vegas. Furthermore, Parvin had been named as an alleged co-conspirator in securities fraud charges against Wolfson. And then there was the fact that Douglas, while a sitting justice, had received $85,000 over a seven-year period as the only paid official of the Parvin-Dohrman Foundation, which drew its principal income from Las Vegas gambling casinos.

At President Nixon's urging, John Mitchell directed me to turn our Douglas file over to Congressman Gerald Ford, who was then minority leader in Congress. According to my appointment log, I met with Congressman Ford on December 12, 1969, in his House office.

I remember thinking that with his blond hair, blue eyes, and broad, open face he was a sharp contrast to the dark, brooding Nixon. I also noted he had maintained his athletic strong build and appeared to be in top physical condition. He listened courteously and asked knowledgeable questions about the Justice Department's role in the investigation.

I gave him the files as I had been instructed to do, but I cautioned Congressman Ford that the data were raw and that the entire matter needed much more time and a more thorough investigation.

I thought Ford would begin a legislative investigation of the Parvin-Dohrman Foundation and this would complete the investigation.

Again, Douglas had a different view of my activities. He said I had "leak[ed] unsubstantiated material . . . to Gerald Ford when Ford was working to have me impeached." This was not a leak, but my response to direct instructions from Attorney General Mitchell. And there was nothing unsubstantiated about Justice Douglas receiving $85,000 from the Parvin-Dohrman Foundation.

No matter what one's initial political position, officeholders often move more toward the center as they mature. Not Justice Douglas. Through the years he continued to hold the most extreme of liberal political views. Overstating Douglas's popularity with the nation's young liberals would be as difficult as understating his popularity within the law enforcement community.

Douglas's own advanced age (he was seventy-two in 1970) notwithstanding, the young liberals regarded him as one of their own. They viewed him with much the same adulation usually reserved for rock stars. Some of his popularity was due to his rugged outdoor lifestyle and some perhaps to his tendency to marry attractive young women.

While most justices were pictured in their solemn black judicial robes, Douglas was photographed climbing mountains with a pack on his back and with the fourth Mrs. Douglas, Cathleen Heffernan, at his side. He had married Cathy in 1965, when she was twenty-three and he was sixty-eight.

His books on travel and conservation brought him attention as well as income. The idea of conservation of our natural resources was beginning to emerge, and Douglas was in step with the times. He was so connected to ecology that in a dissenting Court opinion in 1972 he argued that legal standing should be accorded to trees and rivers.

One of Douglas's briefing attorneys summed up Douglas's attitude toward Nixon when he said, "When you put the devil in the White House, almost anything can happen."

Congressman Ford himself already had put together a great deal of material. He decided to go ahead immediately with an attempt to impeach Justice Douglas, but the effort was not successful. A special House judiciary subcommittee, controlled by the Democrats, cleared Douglas of all allegations on December 15,

1970, and declared there were no grounds for impeachment. Ford called the report a "whitewash." He later said that he regretted initiating the Douglas impeachment as the major mistake of his political career. I think the major mistake was in not waiting until we had a completed FBI investigation of the Parvin–Dohrman Foundation.

The lesson to be learned from the whole unfortunate matter is that an impeachment proceeding in Congress should not begin until the facts are down cold. The Douglas impeachment should never have begun until there was a strong and provable case.

What should have been done in the Douglas matter was to defer even considering impeachment proceedings against Justice Douglas until after we at the Justice Department had completed a thorough investigation of the activities of Albert Parvin and thereby gained more solid grounds against Douglas—if we ever got that far. I wish now that when John Mitchell instructed me to turn the Douglas file over to Congressman Ford, I had persuaded the attorney general to delay delivery of the file until we had completed the investigation. I feel sure Mitchell could have restrained President Nixon, and that going slow on attacking Justice Douglas until we had better facts would have been better for President Nixon.

Impeachment is deadly warfare. When Mexican General Santa Anna attacked the Alamo during the Texas revolution, he flew a red flag—the traditional signal that he would take no prisoners. When you start an impeachment, you raise a red flag. You had better know your facts. When the Nixon Administration placed its hands on Douglas's throat by trying to impeach him, I believe a mind-set of hostility was implanted in many Democrats and many Democratic congressmen.

Once the word *impeachment* was out, there was no way it could be stuffed back. If an administration could attempt to impeach an associate justice of the Supreme Court, the presidency itself no longer seemed beyond reach to some of the Democrats. Some in Congress watched the developments of Watergate and bided their time from then on.

In any event, the Fortas resignation and the Douglas-Parvin matter were certain to add kerosene to the fires which later were to consume so many in Watergate.

CHAPTER 3

Strike Forces: A Score and More

"One of the notable triumphs in law enforcement was the conviction of Al Capone."
—President Herbert Hoover

SOME OF THE WORK done in the Nixon Justice Department under my supervision may have contributed to the extreme hostility of Democratic congressmen toward the president. The efforts of the strike forces to investigate organized crime were bound to have triggered the animosity of the Mafia all over the United States. I feel quite sure that whatever influences the Mafia may have had in Congress were used against Nixon in the impeachment build-up.

The origin of the strike force concept can be traced back to the era of Prohibition following World War I. The United States had hit a high moral plane in 1917 when it followed President Woodrow Wilson into "a war to save the world for democracy." After the armistice treaty, the United States responded to years of entreaty by the Women's Temperance League and other anti-liquor organizations by passing the Eighteenth Amendment to the Constitution. The beverage amendment became effective in January 1919. Thus began the "noble experiment" called Prohibition. Gambling had already been made illegal. With the closing of the saloons, the sites for open and visible gambling also disappeared.

This caused a general revolt, in what would be known as the Flapper Age or the Roaring Twenties, characterized by bobbed hairstyles and short skirts for women, energetic new dance crazes such as the Charleston, supper clubs, gambling, and a great thirst for alcohol.

But in 1920, law enforcement was completely decentralized. As a consequence the Mafia and other criminal organizations flourished. There was no FBI or Narcotics Bureau. The Internal Revenue Service—only ten years old at the time—was still a very small affair. County sheriffs and constables, completely autonomous, were the main law enforcement. As cities developed, city police departments took over within their incorporated city area, but with no jurisdiction outside city limits.

In rural areas sheriffs carried the whole workload with an overlapping jurisdiction in the cities. In most states sheriffs had long ceased doing any real police work in cities. In Texas they furnished bailiffs for the state courts and operated a jail which housed both city and county prisoners. During racial turbulence following World War I, Dallas County had to call out units of the city fire department equipped with pumps and high-powered hoses to protect prisoners in the county jails. By that time the county constables had become primarily process servers.

After World War I, the number of automobiles on the roads increased steadily and state highway patrols developed. A few states had the remnants of a central police unit which had originally been set up by governors as defense against hostile Indians, but many of those units had withered away by 1920. In Texas there was still a Ranger force with indistinct lines of jurisdiction. The often quoted myth of "one riot, one Ranger" was romantic fiction. The Rangers were under the command of the governor, but most governors used the Ranger force seldom or not at all.

Under this Balkanized and highly decentralized law enforcement structure—each unit jealous of its own turf—there could be no central planning nor effective intelligence gathering. It was an ideal situation for the expansion of the Mafia.

The Volstead Act, the enforcement law of the Eighteenth Amendment, went into effect January 16, 1920, and the liquor business was no longer either legal or legitimate. This act created a new federal police force—to be commonly called G-men (for government men)—which would enforce Prohibition. Criminals immediately began to find ways to turn the law to their own profit—and the most profitable was not homemade "bathtub gin" or rotgut whiskey but rumrunning. Rumrunners brought good whiskey into this country from England, the Bahamas, or Canada, creating an ideal market for what the Mafia had to offer.

The Volstead Act had several unintended results, one of which was the widespread corruption of many law enforcement officials who accepted payoffs to look the other way. Rumrunners were the wholesalers. Bootleggers were the retailers. Rumrunners having good connections with European or Canadian distillers and selling name-brand liquor became very rich men—far beyond what the average bank robber or burglar could hope to achieve in a lifetime. And because the law itself was unpopular with thirsty Americans, bootleggers were patronized by a high level of society and often became local celebrities.

Worst of all, from the standpoint of honest law enforcement, as illegal liquor was transported from city to city, gangsters began to cooperate and deal with one another across city and state lines. The illegal liquor business provided on-the-job training for careers in illegal gambling, prostitution, loan sharking, union corruption, extortion, violence, and murder. In large cities, this proved fertile ground for the Mafia.

In Chicago, competing hoodlum organizations engaged in open warfare for turf. A criminal named Alphonse "Scarface" Capone, a bootlegger, mobster, and ruthless killer, was born in Naples, Italy, and grew up in Brooklyn. In 1919 he became a brothel keeper and soon moved into a variety of liquor businesses. He paid off the authorities, opened gambling establishments, and stepped into the vacuum created by the folding of breweries, wholesale liquor companies, and their distribution systems.

Turf wars erupted. Gangsters killed gangsters who had elaborate funerals, often attended by judges and high-ranking elected officials.

By 1929 both the morale and the esprit de corps of most big city police departments had broken down. The St. Valentine's Day murder of seven men by hoodlums, some disguised as policemen, shocked Chicago and the nation. No one doubted Capone was to blame. Mob bosses in the East warned Capone to behave.

The situation was so bad after the Valentine massacre that on March 1, 1929, a group of Chicago citizens called on President Herbert Hoover for federal help. President Hoover recorded in his *Memoirs of Herbert Hoover: The Cabinet and the Presidency*, New York: Macmillan, 1952, pp. 276-277):

They gave chapter and verse for their statement that Chicago was

> in the hands of gangs, that the police and the magistrates were completely under their control, that the governor of the state was futile, that the Federal government was the only force by which the city's ability to govern itself could be restored. At once I directed that all the Federal agencies concentrate upon Mr. Capone and his allies. Our authority was limited to violations of income tax and prohibition laws. It was ironic that a man guilty of inciting hundreds of murders, in some of which he took a personal hand, had to be punished merely for failure to pay taxes on the money he had made by murder. The Attorney General [William DeWitt Mitchell] set up a special Deputy Attorney General [William J. Froelich] and equipped him with the best men from every bureau of investigation in the government. It required two years to assemble the evidence and conduct the trials, but in the end we restored the freedom of Chicago.

In uniting federal law enforcement agencies to bring one known criminal to justice, President Hoover deserves credit for being the first to conceptualize what later became known as the strike force, or headhunting.

Since that time much of the popular media credit for convicting Al Capone has gone to Elliot Ness. For years Capone had been the target of a special team of federal investigators led by Ness. The lawmen were dubbed the "Untouchables" because they refused to be bought off. In the popular television series with Ness portrayed by Robert Stack, and the 1987 movie starring Kevin Costner, Ness is given the lion's share of the credit.

The true story is much more complex if perhaps less glamorous. Much of the working credit should go to Special Agent Frank Wilson, an accountant, and his team of investigators who gathered evidence of income tax violations by Al Capone. That was a rap Capone could not beat. He was convicted on charges by the Internal Revenue Service and in May 1932 was sent to federal prison on Alcatraz Island in San Francisco Bay.

President Hoover made no further effort against the Mafia in other big cities. Apparently, he was too busy with problems arising from the nation's worsening economic depression and his own bid for re-election. He lost to the Democratic candidate, Franklin Delano Roosevelt.

After the conviction of Capone, nothing much happened in the fight against organized crime for a long time. During the fourteen years of President Roosevelt's administration, no concerted effort against the Mafia was attempted.

In February 1950, Roosevelt's successor, President Harry Truman, asked his attorney general, J. Howard McGrath, to call together in Washington, D.C. a small conference to consider organized crime problems. Former Senator McGrath of Rhode Island had become attorney general in August 1949, when President Truman named Attorney General Tom Clark to the Supreme Court.

This first conference on organized crime was an outgrowth of the annual conference of United States attorneys. I was one of the few state district attorneys invited. Others invited were District Attorney Pat Brown of Oakland, California (later governor of California); Mayor Quigg Newton of Denver; Attorney General Alan H. Bible of Nevada (later senator from Nevada); Mayor David L. Lawrence of Pittsburgh; John L. McGrath, corporate counsel of New York City; and several others. It was a small group.

President Truman gave a brief introductory talk on the theme that the nation's wars had always been followed by periods of lawlessness. At the conference, Attorney General McGrath reminded us all that "the mobsters of the 1930s" had not been entirely eliminated—an understatement I was prepared to believe from my own law enforcement experience.

For me one of the high points of the conference was the subcommittee on gambling and its relation to organized crime. DeLesseps Morrison, then mayor of New Orleans, talked about problems resulting from his city's slot machines controlled by the "czar of slot machines," New York mobster Frank Costello. Morrison added that racing wire services, essential to organized gambling rackets, were largely controlled by members of the old Capone gang.

Morrison made a good point when he said that nothing is accomplished when cities and states simply push gamblers and mobsters to other locations. What was needed, Morrison said, was federal legislation; for example, transporting slot machines across state lines should be prohibited under interstate commerce legislation.

One of the most positive things to come out of the conference was the organization of the National District Attorneys Association.

That same year Senator Estes Kefauver (D.–Tennessee), chairman of the Senate Special Committee to Investigate Organized

Crime in Interstate Commerce, began a valiant effort to expose criminals through televised hearings. He helped throw some light into the dark corners of suspected mob activities in the United States. The Kefauver committee "paraded a host of hoods before microphones and photographers . . . [and] entertained the public by forcing the grouchy, surly hoods into the open. . . ." (William Brashler, *The Don: The Life and Death of Sam Giancana*, New York: Harper and Row, 1977, p. 122) The television audience became accustomed to hearing the mumbled pat phrase: "On the advice of my attorney and under the protection guaranteed to me by the Fifth Amendment, I respectfully decline to answer."

Television was still relatively new, and the American people were riveted by the revelation of criminal wrongdoing day by day.

The yearlong hearings may have had little lasting effect on organized criminal activities, but they did give a push to Kefauver's political career. "Estes believed that Democratic bosses, embarrassed by his crime probe, put the skids under him at the [1952] convention." (H. H. Martin, "The Mystery of Kefauver," *Saturday Evening Post*, June 2, 1956) Four years later Kefauver's popularity was enough to earn him the Democratic vice-presidential nomination on the ticket with Adlai E. Stevenson.

Next came the Senate Select Committee on Improper Activities in the Labor or Management Field, chaired by Senator John L. McClellan (D.–Arkansas), investigating the link between organized labor and racketeering. The most significant thing about this committee is that in 1957 Robert F. Kennedy, just out of law school, was employed as chief counsel for the McClellan Committee and received an introduction to the murky world of Mafia crime.

The leader of the International Brotherhood of Teamsters union, Jimmy Hoffa, became Bobby Kennedy's main target. Arthur M. Schlesinger *(Robert Kennedy and His Times*, Boston: Houghton Mifflin, 1978, p. 306) suggested that RFK's idea for the "get-Hoffa" squad owed something to President Herbert Hoover's "get-Capone" squad of 1929.

The chain of title of the federal strike forces extends from President Herbert Hoover to Bobby Kennedy to Ramsey Clark to Richard Nixon.

Attorney General Ramsey Clark set up a strike force in Buffalo, New York, in November 1966. Henry Petersen, dubbed by

Time (May 2, 1969) "the Justice Department's chief racket buster," sent a team of twelve men, headed by Thomas Kennelly, to break up the organized crime family headed by Stefano Maggadino. Maggadino had brought his only son, Peter A. Maggadino, into the family businesses. When the FBI and local law enforcers raided Peter's house on November 26, 1968, they searched and found an old suitcase stuffed with bills totaling about $500,000 in cash as well as some weapons.

The Buffalo strike force was soon followed by a second strike force, this one in Detroit, Michigan. Before Ramsey Clark left office in 1969, additional strike forces were in operation in Brooklyn, Chicago, Miami, Newark and Philadelphia—seven in all.

The idea of a strike force did not enjoy universal popularity. From the start, the concept was controversial inside the federal government. Even some of the participating departments gave it only a token nod of approval. Some people on the outside actively opposed the idea, calling it unconstitutional if not downright un-American.

The strike forces were composed of specialists from all of the federal enforcement agencies. With FBI agents working closely in the same room with Customs, Narcotics, Internal Revenue, and a number of the other strike force members, greater teamwork became possible.

At first I myself was uncomfortable with the strike force type of law enforcement. Something about it seemed unfair. I also had reservations about widespread use of turned witnesses. But this is actually what happens in police work all over the United States. Each detective has his own sources—sometimes called stooges or snitches—who will feed the detective information and thus allow them to solve major crimes. In exchange, the detective often looks the other way when his stooge commits a minor crime or negotiates a plea to get his charge reduced.

I soon came to realize the Justice Department and the other investigating agencies were so mammoth and unwieldy—and organized crime so widespread, pervasive, and deeply entrenched—that the strike forces constituted a very effective method for achieving focus in intelligence-gathering operations against organized crime. They were necessary in obtaining convictions of the top people.

One morning soon after I arrived, Henry Petersen came into

my office for a meeting with me. I gladly shoved aside my bundles of administrative papers to hear him out.

Petersen's heavy facial features, his dark hair and thick dark eyebrows, gave him an appearance of brooding intensity. He had a little bit of bulldog in him; once he clamped down on something, he would not let go.

Lighting one Camel cigarette after another, Petersen explained, in his customary hoarse and raspy voice, the practical details of how the strike force concept worked. He was one hundred percent sold on the idea and set about selling me on it as well. He recommended that we not only retain the program but expand it to cover most of the known centers of organized criminal activity in the United States.

I took the expanded strike force program to Attorney General Mitchell. I found him not in his large ceremonial office but busy at his somewhat cluttered desk in his smaller "working" office. Most of us in Washington had smaller offices where we could to some extent isolate ourselves and concentrate on our paperwork and many administrative tasks. Even President Nixon often left the Oval Office for his hideaway office in the Executive Office Building.

Much of Mitchell's own time at the department was absorbed by civil unrest and school desegregation issues. The president telephoned him frequently, depending on his close friend to handle a number of issues not directly related to his job as attorney general. I have no idea how much Mitchell told the president about the everyday routine work of the department, but Mitchell was so taciturn it was probably not much.

Despite his heavy workload, never once while I was at Justice did I ever know John Mitchell to pull back from our sustained drive against organized crime. When I took up a problem with him, he almost invariably gave me a ruling during the conference. That day he tamped his favorite Bond Street tobacco into the bowl of his pipe and puffed small bursts of aromatic smoke into the air as he listened closely to my proposal. He asked a few questions in a voice surprisingly light for a man of such physical bulk. I gained his approval on strike force expansion at once.

I set up a series of meetings among executives of the various federal departments to introduce them to the strike force concept and to sell them on its expansion. Usually the Cabinet or sub-

Cabinet officials from each of the departments attended those meetings—but never FBI Director J. Edgar Hoover.

The FBI director was arguably the most skillful and accomplished bureaucrat in the entire federal government. (I use the term *bureaucrat* to mean a government professional who remains in position regardless of the political party in power. Although the word often is used in a derogatory sense—and certainly President Nixon had nothing good to say about bureaucrats—they are the people who keep the government functioning day by day, year after year.)

In May 1969 we set up the eighth strike force, the first of our new administration. Edward F. Harrington, a lawyer with eight years at the Justice Department, headed the Boston force. We followed with strike forces in New York in July and Cleveland in November.

The operation of the New York joint strike force was particularly noteworthy in the development of the strike force concept. The New York unit was a combined federal-state-city operation directed by a council whose members represented the Department of Justice, New York state and local law enforcement agencies, and the Manhattan and Bronx district attorneys' offices. The combination permitted the free flow of intelligence across jurisdictional lines and closer cooperation among the agencies.

The joint New York strike force, headed by Daniel P. Hollman, brought together Bill Lynch and Robert Morgenthau, along with the New York state attorney general, the Bronx district attorney, the New York police commissioner, the director of the Waterfront Commission, the director of the Office of Labor Management, a chief postal inspector, the superintendent of the State Police, the FBI, the IRS, the Bureau of Customs, the assistant secretary for law enforcement of the Treasury Department, and a special assistant from the Treasury Department. That's a tremendous amount of knowledge, experience, excitement, energy, and determination to bring to bear on a criminal investigation. The wide-reaching investigation probed union corruption, waterfront crime, pornography, and loan-sharking, but the main emphasis was on illegal gambling.

Hollman requested a special federal grand jury in October 1969. Using court-approved wiretaps to gather leads and information, the strike force had made seventeen arrests and was ready to present evidence on the criminal activities of four alleged Mafia "families": Carlo Gambino, Joseph Bonano, the Luchese family run by Carmine Tramuti, and the Genovese family run by Gerry Catena.

The success of this New York strike force led to converting the Newark strike force to a coordinated federal-state joint strike force to attack organized crime in New Jersey.

In 1970 we set up strike forces in Los Angeles, St. Louis, New Orleans, Pittsburgh, Baltimore, and San Francisco. By the end of the year we had seventeen. On the table of organization I was listed as chairman of the task force's council.

Eventually the IRS sent one of their top men around behind me in an apparent attempt to slow down the strike force program. But by that time the strike forces had gained such momentum and had demonstrated such tangible results that even those top bureaucrats could not halt the project.

Hoffa had been convicted as a result of Bobby Kennedy's single-minded determination. The old Kennedy hands still working in the Justice Department regarded Hoffa as an icon of the martyred Bobby Kennedy. But Hoffa had behaved himself in federal prison and was legally eligible for parole. He very much wanted out.

Hoffa had given generously to Nixon's unsuccessful campaign against John Kennedy in 1960. The Teamsters also were rumored to have contributed $100,000 to Nixon's 1968 campaign. When Nixon came to the Oval Office, John Ehrlichman suggested that a presidential pardon for Jimmy Hoffa would be an affront to the Kennedy people—an idea having some appeal to Nixon.

I became tangentially involved in the Hoffa affair. Mrs. Josephine Hoffa quite naturally was eager to secure her husband's release from prison. She requested an appointment with Attorney General Mitchell, who did not want to see her. Mitchell asked me to give her an audience.

In August 1971 Mrs. Hoffa and her son, James P. Hoffa, often referred to as Jimmy, Jr., came by my office for their first appointment. They were accompanied by William Loeb, publisher of the *Manchester* (New Hampshire) *Union Leader*, and Mrs. Loeb. Loeb himself was a political conservative and active in the Republican party. His *Union Leader* newspaper had a reputation for its conservative viewpoint, and Loeb had been critical of the Teamsters in the past. Although it may not have influenced him, after he received a rumored $2 million loan from Teamster funds his criticism vanished, and he became devoted to helping get Hoffa paroled.

The Criminal Division had nothing to do with granting paroles and pardons. That was handled through the office of the pardon attorney, Lawrence M. Traylor. All I could do was listen courteously to what Mrs. Hoffa had to say about her husband's pardon and pass on anything new to Attorney General John Mitchell.

Henry Petersen had worked closely with Kennedy's "get-Hoffa" squad. When I discussed the meeting with him he was quick to express his opinion that Hoffa should not be paroled. Mike Epstein, who had been a member of the "get-Hoffa" squad, also was very much against the pardon. I made no recommendation to Attorney General Mitchell and he did not ask me for one.

Meanwhile my office, through our strike force teams, continued efforts against known criminal kingpins, organized crime and criminals.

All over the country we began to bring down the Mafia leadership of organized crime. During fiscal year 1970 alone, indictments of 1,012 defendants were returned. The 389 convictions secured of members and associates of the organized crime syndicates throughout the nation included some of the top bosses.

The effort was off to a good start, but to our dismay there was an unexpected side effect—by taking out the top-level crime bosses, we had unintentionally triggered a retirement-and-promotion program. As the old-style bosses—the Mustache Petes, as they were sometimes called—were indicted, tried, and convicted, the way was opened for younger, smarter, better educated criminals to move up to top management positions. Another side effect was that independents scrambled for the protection offered by the crime families.

The close association in the media between organized crime and "men whose names ended in vowels" began to create friction in some quarters. Joseph Colombo, head of the Profaci organized crime family, initially may have become miffed when his son, Joseph Colombo, Jr., was arrested on charges of counterfeiting. But the elder Colombo also began to resent what he regarded as ethnic slurs. He founded the Italian-American Civil Rights League and picketed the FBI headquarters in New York.

In the spring and summer of 1970, a series of protests and demonstrations took place in New York City as Italian-Americans, many of them members of the league, protested the widespread presumption that Italians dominated organized crime. Demonstrators carried signs, one of which read: "President Nixon—Why Only Italian Americans Involved in Organized Crime?"

On orders from the White House, Mitchell directed that the terms "Mafia" and "La Cosa Nostra" were no longer to be used because they implied a relationship between ethnicity and organized crime and "a good many Americans of Italian descent are offended."

"Spokesmen for President Nixon's administration," wrote Ianni (Frances A. and Elizabeth Ianni, *A Family Business: Kinship and Social Control in Organized Crime*, New York: Russell Sage Foundation, 1972, p. 4) "insisted that the decision was in no way related to the demonstrations, which were of course attributed to the Mafia itself, but was the result of sensitivity to the argument that large segments of organized crime are not Italian-dominate." There was certainly some truth in that. Both Irish and Jewish gangs had established their own turf in Boston and were as vicious as the Mafia.

So although the terms we used changed, our targets did not.

Joe Colombo may have felt he was doing a good thing to try to separate ethnic Italians from the stigma of Cosa Nostra, but organized crime families believed that the best publicity is no publicity at all. Colombo's Annual Unity Day stirred up too much attention. On the second Unity Day, June 28, 1971, Colombo was shot down—presumably on orders from one or more of the Mafia families. He was not killed but remained paralyzed the rest of his life.

In Washington, Nixon was still trying to decide the best way to handle the Hoffa problem.

Chuck Colson received a memo, dated September 8, 1970, from Haldeman: "The President wants you to take on the responsibility for working on developing our strength with the labor unions and union leadership." The vice president of the Teamsters Union, Frank Fitzsimmons, visited the White House, the memo continued, "and the President found that he is extremely friendly and that we should move ahead to cultivate him politically in any way we can." (Richard M. Nixon, *From: The President: Richard Nixon's Secret Files*, Bruce Oudes, editor, New York: Harper and Row, 1989, pp. 157-158)

According to Oudes (p. 155), "The Mafia was especially cozy with Fitzsimmons, finding him easier to manipulate than the strong-willed Hoffa. . . . Fitzsimmons was regarded by organized crime as a man who could be counted on always to be looking the other way."

Mrs. Hoffa tirelessly kept up her efforts on behalf of her husband until she was hospitalized with a heart ailment. Hoffa was released from prison on April 1, 1971, on a temporary furlough to go to her.

While Hoffa was out of prison he had an opportunity to visit with Fitzsimmons, vice president and (during Hoffa's absence) acting president of the Teamsters. Although he was bitterly opposed to doing so, in June Hoffa resigned from all his positions in the union, retired as president, and received his Teamsters' pension in a lump sum.

Shortly after I had left the Justice Department, in late December 1971 Hoffa did receive a presidential commutation. Theodore H. White (*The Making of the President 1972*, New York: Atheneum, 1973, p. 305) wrote: "The President had paid a fee to indecency by releasing from Federal prison the convicted former chief of the Teamsters, James Hoffa, two days before Christmas; and a few months later [Nixon] was to receive the endorsement of the 2,500,000-member Teamster union."

Colson was instrumental in getting the pardon, which was delayed long enough for an election: Fitzsimmons took over as president of the union. Leo Rangell (*The Mind of Watergate: An Exploration of the Compromise of Integrity*, New York: Norton, 1980, p. 287) observed a chilling connection between the Hoffa pardon and Watergate: "*Time* magazine reports that Nixon received one million dollars in cash in early 1973 from Teamsters Union president Frank Fitzsimmons in exchange for barring Jimmy Hoffa from seeking elective office in that union [before 1980]. The courier for Nixon in this transaction was White House aide Charles Colson, the magazine claims." In his book, *Born Again* (Old Tappan, New Jersey: Spire Books, Fleming H. Revell Co., 1977), Colson is silent on the subject.

The *Time* article further suggested that the amount could have been the same million dollars Nixon referred to in his conversation of March 21, 1973, with John Dean: "We could get that. . . . You could get a million dollars. You could get it in cash. I know where it could be gotten." *(The Presidential Transcripts*, p. 110)

The criminal elements within the Teamsters had sound business reasons for not wanting Hoffa to take up where he had left off: "A return to power by Hoffa would lead inevitably to further FBI surveillance of union activities—which was hardly conducive to tranquil mob operation." (Oudes, *From: The President,* p. 155)

Hoffa's enemies decided not to give him time or opportunity to regain his strength among the rank-and-file. "I knew the guy," said Anthony "Tony" Delsanter of the Cleveland crime family. (Ovid Demaris, *The Last Mafioso: The Treacherous World of Jimmy Fratianno*, New York: Times Books, 1981, p. 296) "He was a good man but he was hard of hearing. Detroit [crime family] told him to cool it. . . . Still, you know, he kept right on coming, making his move against Fitzsimmons."

Hoffa vanished on July 31, 1975, from outside the Manchus Fox restaurant in a Detroit suburb. His disappearance triggered rumors that he had been murdered—as he almost certainly had been—by order of the Detroit mobsters.

No trace of his body has ever been found.

CHAPTER 4

EVEN A LITTLE POWER

". . . the activities of syndicated criminals mesh gears with those of crooked politicians, policemen, merchants and business executives."

—Steve Allen, *Ripoff*

ACCORDING TO THE axiom, power tends to corrupt and absolute power corrupts absolutely. But even a little power can tempt a person to extend his hand and to violate his public trust.

Much of our work in the Criminal Division added to the hostility building in Congress. We had a file containing allegations of bribery against Otto Kerner, a former Democratic governor (1961-1968) of Illinois and at the time a sitting judge on the U.S. Court of Appeals. He had been chairman of the Kerner Commission (National Commission on Civil Disorders) and had such a splendid reputation he was called "Mr. Clean of Illinois."

While Kerner was governor, he owned stock in a firm called Chicago Thoroughbred Enterprises. The principal stockholder was Mrs. Marjorie Everett. The bribery case came out of Kerner's alleged influence on the Illinois Harness Racing Commission's setting of race track dates and helping to prolong the season in a way that greatly benefited Mrs. Everett's income.

Internal Revenue Service agents had also uncovered evidence of income tax violations. In December 1971 the IRS agents became so impatient they leaked the story to the *Chicago Tribune*.

The file reached my office in Justice after the staff had performed a detailed review of the evidence. I authorized the indictments. My office issued a statement that approval of indictments had been held up because we moved very cautiously in prosecuting a sitting federal appellate judge. Then I assigned one of the best trial men we had in the department as a special prosecutor on the case to help William Thompson, then U.S. attorney for Chicago. Otto Kerner was convicted on counts of bribery, conspiracy, income tax evasion, mail fraud, and perjury. He was sentenced to prison.

Judge Kerner was a well-established and entrenched Illinois Democrat with a national reputation as a liberal leader. I'm sure he had many friends in Congress who remembered his case while considering whether to hold the president of the United States to the same high standards of law enforcement we had imposed on Judge Kerner.

One strike force case often unexpectedly led to another.

In investigating a housing project in Maryland, we exposed a colorful "rainmaking" operation. In Washington parlance, a rainmaker is a person who purports to sell influence but who in fact may not have any influence to sell.

Nathan P. Voloshen was a seventy-three-year-old lawyer and lobbyist in New York City. He was also a longtime friend to Speaker of the House John W. McCormack (D.–Massachusetts). Voloshen was in close cahoots with the Speaker's chief aide, Martin Sweig. Working together, Voloshen and Sweig sold appointments with high-ranking public officials.

This is the way the scam worked.

Let's say you were a businessman and you wanted an appointment with a Cabinet officer, such as the Secretary of the Interior. You would call Voloshen and ask him to make the appointment for you, which he would agree to do for a modest fee of—oh, say, $10,000 ought to cover it.

It was a full-service scam.

Voloshen would invite you to meet him in the Speaker's office. There Sweig, appearing to act on behalf of the Speaker, collected the money, made the appointment and even arranged transportation in the Speaker's official limousine with official flags flying on the front fenders. Voloshen often accompanied you to your appointment, made the introductions, waited, and rode back with you. If the Speaker was available, you were invited to lunch with him in the private dining room in the Capitol building. I'm sure most businessmen who could afford the fee and who got this royal treatment felt they had received their money's worth.

The Criminal Division set up an intensive investigation into this influence-peddling scheme. An investigator dressed as an electrician set up his ladder and tools right outside the Speaker's office. One afternoon, as the client left after lunch, two men approached the front door of the Speaker's reception room. The investigator heard a male voice in the Speaker's office.

"Have you got the money?" the man asked.

Unfortunately, the investigator was outside the open door and could not see the two men. We had no way of proving the identity of the questioner.

Voloshen and Sweig were indicted by a federal grand jury in January 1970. In May, Voloshen pleaded guilty and the following month Sweig was tried and found guilty. The Sweig case established a legal precedent that would reappear in Watergate.

But back to the original case: Speaker McCormack denied any involvement in the influence-peddling scam, but he did give a deposition in the case. After forty-three years in Congress and almost a decade as Speaker, McCormack left at the expiration of his term.

Speaker McCormack was from Massachusetts and had been a very powerful man in Congress. He had introduced Thomas P. "Tip" O'Neill into former Speaker Sam Rayburn's "Board of Education." (Texas Congressman Sam Rayburn was Speaker from 1949 to 1953. Rayburn met regularly with his circle of congressional insiders, his "Board of Education.")

McCormack had been O'Neill's mentor. When McCormack resigned the speakership and left Congress, Tip O'Neill was selected as the Democratic whip.

An FBI file reached my desk involving campaign donations to the Hubert Humphrey campaign in his 1968 presidential race against Nixon. The file arose from the conviction and sentencing of officers of a failed Western bank. Both the bank president and the vice president had been indicted on numerous counts of theft and fraud against the bank. When the time for trial arrived, the Justice Department reduced the bank president's counts to one; the bank official pleaded to some type of probated sentence.

The bank vice president received a much higher sentence. While serving his term, the former bank vice president contacted the FBI and bargained for a reduction of sentence. In exchange for a reduction of his own sentence, the bank official offered to testify that a reduction of the counts and the sentence of the bank president had been made in exchange for a big donation to Hubert Humphrey's campaign against Nixon.

A conviction in this file depended on the testimony of the bank vice president. There was enough additional evidence to make these charges serious. An obstruction charge arose from a difference in sentencing between the bank president and the bank vice president. A bribery charge arose from a large campaign donation made on behalf of the bank president, who received the lighter sentence.

Probably we would have indicted a U.S. attorney on the same facts. We almost certainly would have offered the ex-bank vice president a reduction of sentence and then followed the facts wherever they led, but for the fact that former Vice President Humphrey might be involved.

If the circumstances were true as they were presented to us, this was a blatant and ugly case which I did not want to decide without first consulting the attorney general. During Mitchell's absence, the deputy attorney general, Dick Kleindienst, was in charge. I directed the query to him.

Kleindienst's decision was immediate: "We are not going to indict a former presidential opponent of President Nixon. Close the file."

I followed orders. I closed the file.

Looking back through the twenty-five years that have passed since then and thinking about that file, I still do not know whether that was the right thing to do.

As far as I know, President Nixon was never informed of nor consulted about that file. Since then, I have wondered what President Nixon might have done with the bank case had it reached him. He was a believer in the imperial presidency—I imagine he would have approved Kleindienst's ruling.

Not exploring charges against Hubert Humphrey, President Nixon's former opponent, was more nearly a political decision than a legal one. Such a decision might be regarded as an act of self-defense on the part of the Nixon Administration. For one thing, in a fast-moving presidential campaign it is probable that Humphrey himself knew little if anything about this decision. However, had we developed a case and returned an indictment, you can imagine the resulting uproar and the inevitable charge that President Nixon was a vile, vindictive, mean-spirited man governed by personal hatred and jealously. No disclaimer would have mollified the Nixon critics nor calmed the partisan passions.

Is it hypocritical to indict the former governor of Illinois for bribery and yet not indict a former vice president of the United States simply because he *was* a former vice president? What makes such a case different?

The indictment of a vice president—whether sitting or former—carries with it elements of an act of national self-destruction. However, Raoul Berger's *Impeachment: The Constitutional Problems* (Cambridge: Harvard University Press, 1978, p. 316) contends that a sitting president may be indicted at any time without regard to impeachment:

> No special dispensation is required to allow prosecution of a citizen; nor is there a scrap of evidence that the Framers were minded to clothe an ex-President in any immunity whatsoever. On the contrary, immunity was denied to him as President. It follows that the President is criminally triable while in office, because no special provision is required for trial of an ex-President.

Apparently, there are some things that one does not do in American government. One of those is that you do not indict a former political opponent if you can avoid it. The Colorado bank case might have been handled by a special prosecutor—especially so, had that special prosecutor been a Democrat. At the time, we did not consider that option nor did we have available the present statute on the subject. In the days of Watergate, we would see just how tense and divisive an indictment or impeachment situation could become. Several administrations later, we saw the same thing in the debate about the impeachment of President Clinton.

In his political campaign of 1968, Nixon had pledged to be a law-and-order president. During his first term in office, the Justice Department's expanded strike forces program proved to be an important weapon against both organized criminal activity and corruption among some government officials—enabling the president to keep his promise.

But an investigation of organized crime almost always leads to local public officials.

CHAPTER 5

Nixon and His Gatekeeper

"What gave Haldeman such overwhelming power was that he served as a sentinel for a President who chose to sequester himself behind a wall of 'Do Not Disturb' signs."
—Dan Rather, *The Palace Guards*

ALTHOUGH THE PRESIDENT is called the nation's chief executive, we as a nation often elect men who bring almost no executive experience to the job. Richard Nixon had little or no executive experience, but he knew exactly how he wanted to conduct himself when he got to the White House's Oval Office.

He intended to withdraw behind the palace gates and rule through his hand-picked staff.

Surrounded by a nest of compliant yes-men, Nixon used the full power of the presidency. He lived in the height of luxury in the White House. He enjoyed the use of Camp David, *Air Force One,* and the presidential yacht, *Sequoia.* When he chose to get away from Washington, he had two luxurious homes: one in California and one in Florida.

With all that he had at his disposal, why did Nixon choose self-imposed isolation?

Every man is both the author and the product of his career. From his career he forms an internal definition of loyalty and integrity and establishes his own methods of dealing with people and problems. That certainly held true for Richard Nixon.

Looking at his childhood and his early family life, one can begin to see some of the influences at work which later were to dominate his crisis decisions.

He was born in Yorba Linda, a small farming community near Los Angeles, and grew up in Whittier, California. In the predominantly Quaker town of about 8,000, his mother's family, the Milhouses, were among the oldest settlers.

Nixon said he grew up in a strict environment centered on religion. As Quakers, his family did not practice outward expressions of affection or approval.

His mother, Hannah, a practicing Quaker of Irish descent, was austere, disciplined, and devout in her faith. She selflessly nursed two of her sons, Arthur and Harold, who later died of tuberculosis. In 1974, when Nixon was going through the agony of resignation from the presidency, he said of Hannah: "My mother was a saint."

There was said to exist a quiet feeling in the Milhous family that Hannah had married beneath herself.

Nixon's father, Frank Nixon, was a rough-hewn Irish maverick who had been forced to drop out of school after the sixth grade to help support his family. He found whatever work he could, moving from job to job. Of him Richard Nixon said: "My father had an Irish quickness both to anger and to mirth. It was his temper that impressed me most as a small child. . . . He was a strict and stern disciplinarian, and I tried to follow my mother's example of not crossing him when he was in a bad mood." (Richard Nixon, *RN, The Memoirs of Richard Nixon,* New York: Grosset & Dunlap, 1975, Vol. 1, p. 6) Nixon's tendency to avoid tight situations rather than facing them squarely may well have originated as a coping device when he was a child to avoid his father's anger.

A boy growing up under the domination of an intemperate father might be expected to develop an insecurity coupled with an inability to fully trust the good nature of other people. Such a boy might turn into a loner incapable of exchanging complete loyalty with other people.

Frank Nixon was an underdog "who tried to better himself through work" all his life. He was against the "haves" and for the "have-nots"—and so, I believe, was Richard, who was against the "entrenched" and the people who possessed the "fortresses."

Young Richard likened life and politics to combat and frequently used the terminology of battle, an un-Quakerlike attitude. In the history of warfare, those who take to the open fields of maneuver usually prevail against those who rely on fortifications and fortresses. All of his life Nixon chose to fight in open fields—until he became president. Then, in the worst crisis of his life, he attempted to make a fortress out of the presidency. His scheme failed.

Young Richard grew up "bone poor," working in the Nixon Market, a mom-and-pop grocery store and small filling station in Whittier. The family's straitened circumstances clearly shaped the man he would become. "Poverty curdles character as well as strengthening it," Theodore White wrote (*Breach of Faith: The Fall of Richard Nixon*, New York: Atheneum, 1975, p. 60). "Poverty soiled Nixon, he grew up to be hard—and vulnerable—so vulnerable, the instinct for control, control of one's circumstances and perimeter of dignity, would grow."

Nixon's grades at Whittier High School were good enough to make possible a scholarship at Harvard. Although he "had dreamed of going to college in the East," the family's financial situation, worsened by the 1929 depression, made it impossible for him to realize his dream. Instead he continued to live at home and attended Whittier College, a small Quaker institution in his hometown. He became a leader of the "barbs"—the barbarians, or non-Greek fraternity students—and was active on the debating team. "I learned an invaluable lesson," Nixon wrote (*In the Arena: A Memoir of Victory, Defeat and Renewal,* New York: Simon & Schuster, 1990, p. 81), "that the best tactic in a debate is always to concentrate on one fundamentally strong argument rather than to scatter your fire over a broad area." The skill was one which Nixon retained and used to his advantage all of his life, but his debating coach later recalled there was always "something mean in him." (White, *Breach of Faith*, p. 59)

At the end of his third year, Nixon ran for president of the student body. He based his campaign on the question of dancing on campus—a hot issue at the Quaker college, as it was in other church colleges across the nation. "I had no personal stake," Nixon later recalled. "My argument was strictly pragmatic." *(Memoirs,* Vol. 1, p. 18) He was not on the religious side of the dancing issue, but he was never a party boy. He won the election.

Nixon went to Duke University Law School in Durham, North Carolina, on a very modest scholarship. The young man from Whittier was captivated by the Duke campus, comparing it to a "medieval cathedral town" with "spires, towers and stained glass everywhere." (Nixon, *Memoirs,* Vol. 1, p. 24) Duke was an eye-opening experience after the plainness and simplicity of Quaker life—an intellectual experience free from parental control.

At Duke, Nixon continued to be hard-working and frugal but did find time to take part in campus activities. He was elected president of the Student Bar Association. One of his teachers at Duke saw in him "qualities of statesmanship" and recommended that the young Nixon return to California after graduation and enter politics.

Nixon applied for the position of special agent with the Federal Bureau of Investigation. His application was approved, but he chose not to accept appointment. If he had joined the FBI and stayed with it, he might have been just one of J. Edgar Hoover's many employees—instead of becoming president and therefore Hoover's boss.

Nixon chose to return to Whittier and sit for the California bar exam. He joined Wingert and Bewley, the oldest law firm in town. Within a year Nixon was a partner. He practiced law there for four years. One of the law partners recalled, "Dick was a better politician than he was a lawyer." (Roger Morris, *Richard Milhous Nixon: The Rise of an American Politician,* New York: Henry Holt & Company, 1990, p. 203)

During that period, Nixon met a young high school teacher, Thelma "Pat" Ryan. The couple married June 21, 1940, and Pat continued to teach.

In early December 1941, Nixon gained appointment to the Office of Price Administration. The Japanese attack on Pearl Harbor occurred on December 7; the job in Washington was to begin January 1942. When Nixon and Pat loaded into their car they drove across the country to a Washington that was now the capital of a nation at war. Nixon worked eight months as an assistant attorney for the rationing coordination section. The job gave him some firsthand knowledge of the inside workings of a federal bureaucracy. As a P-3 earning $3,200 a year, Nixon was puzzled as he watched newer, less qualified appointees come in at higher classifications and higher pay. "Build a staff," he was advised. "Hire two or three people and then we can raise you to P-5."

His dislike and distrust of bureaucrats may have originated during the time of his OPA job.

His staff position in OPA plus his religious convictions as a

Quaker might well have enabled Nixon to claim conscientious objector status and avoid military service during World War II. "But the problem with Quaker pacifism," Nixon wrote, "is that it could only work if one were fighting a civilized, compassionate enemy." *(Memoirs,* Vol. 1, p. 27) In politics his treatment of his enemies was neither civilized nor compassionate.

He chose to enter the U.S. Navy and reported to the naval officer indoctrination school at Quonset Point, Rhode Island, in August 1942. Assigned to a specialized supply unit, the South Pacific Combat Air Transport Command, he served as a lieutenant junior grade. From his own brief description of his service in his *Memoirs,* it is difficult to tell how much command experience he had. One of his biographers, Fawn Brodie *(Richard Nixon: The Shaping of his Character,* New York: Norton, 1981) wrote that "Of his forty-five months in the Navy, Nixon spent thirty-one in the United States, fourteen in the South Pacific, and only six in 'that kind of command.'"

For a short while he was officer in charge of a SCAT detachment supporting the invasion of Green Island. The Japanese had retreated except for a few snipers.

In the navy, Nixon came into contact for perhaps the first time with men who used rough language, smoked, drank, and gambled—the complete antithesis of his Quaker background. He became a skilled poker player. "I learned that the people who have the cards are usually the ones who talk the least," Nixon wrote. "Those who are bluffing tend to talk loudly and give themselves away." *(Memoirs,* Vol. 1, p. 29) He came out of the navy far more sophisticated and streetwise than when he entered. This is probably when he picked up his use of profanity.

Returning home after the war with a substantial pot of money from his winnings, he set about becoming a politician.

In two-party California there were two ways to enter politics —as a Democrat or as a Republican. From Nixon's standpoint, the clear and open path was as a Republican—and this despite his basic emotional tilt toward non-fraternity barbs and the underdog.

A committee of Republican leaders, looking for a candidate to unseat a fifth-term liberal incumbent in the Twelfth District congressional seat, found in Nixon a feisty young lawyer who seemed like a natural.

"The greatest advantage I had in 1946 was that the national

trend that year was Republican," Nixon wrote. (*Memoirs,* Vol. 1, p. 46)

Nixon ran against Democrat Jerry Voorhis. Before the California election Nixon visited House Minority Leader Joseph W. Martin, Jr. (R.–Massachusetts) in the Capitol to introduce himself. He was that sure of winning. His campaign against Voorhis was one long seek-and-destroy mission against a high-powered, high-minded Democratic incumbent.

"To be perfectly fair to Mr. Nixon," Voorhis later wrote (Jerry Voorhis, *The Strange Case of Richard Milhous Nixon*, New York: Eriksson, 1972, pp. 4-5), "it should be stated that the tactics he employed were not his own discovery. They were, and still are, the product of the facile brain of a once obscure Los Angeles lawyer—now a major White House official—by the name of Murray Chotiner."

To his regret, Jerry Voorhis had found himself in an excellent position to observe the Chotiner method firsthand. Chotiner's was a one-two-three knockout punch:

One, discredit the opponent.

Two, associate the opponent with something unpopular—such as communism, for example.

Three, attack, attack, attack. Never defend.

Nixon and Chotiner bonded early. Chotiner would remain with Nixon from the Voorhis campaign all the way to the Oval Office. He left the White House in 1971, before Watergate, and began the practice of law in Washington.

As a young congressman on the House Un-American Activities Committee, Nixon gained national attention for the Whitaker Chambers and Alger Hiss investigations. Some twenty-five years later, Bud Krogh would say that the Watergate Plumbers' first job was patterned after the account of the Alger Hiss case in Nixon's book, *Six Crises* (New York: Doubleday, 1962, 1969).

In addition to serving on the Un-American Activities Committee, Nixon was chosen for the House Select Committee on Foreign Aid. (Morris, *Richard Milhous Nixon*, pp. 362-363) Numerous junkets to a Europe still shattered by the recent war undoubtedly presented Nixon with lessons in the need for peaceful settlement of international disputes through diplomacy. These trips also polished his persona as a citizen of the world.

In 1949, a year before the election, Nixon announced his candidacy for a Senate seat. Congresswoman Helen Gahagan Douglas was Nixon's Democratic opponent, and the campaign was a particularly vicious one. It was his third campaign against communism. He attacked Douglas by calling her "the pink lady," among other things, frequently adding that she was "pink all the way to her underwear."

Nixon won the election, but his malicious attacks on the popular Democratic congresswoman had earned him the enmity of newspapers in New York and Washington. Helen Gahagan Douglas withdrew from politics, but she left a lasting legacy: it was she who coined the phrase "Tricky Dick."

Joan Hoff, in her scholarly re-examination of Nixon (*Nixon Reconsidered*, New York: Basic Books, 1994, p. 2) wrote: "From the beginning of his political career, there was a nastiness about Nixon that served both as a public stimulus for his support and as a private motivation for his determination to succeed against all odds."

Nixon's experience as a member of Congress was from 1947 to 1952. But it wasn't managerial training ground. A congressman has a relatively small staff. Any manager of a Sears store gets more executive experience than is gained by being either a congressman or a senator, although both of those jobs can provide an excellent education in the structure and operation of Congress and the federal government.

Nixon went to the Republican National Convention in Chicago on July 7, 1952, as leader of the California delegation. He was a supporter of Ohio Senator Robert Taft. At a crucial point in the convention Nixon switched the California delegation to Dwight Eisenhower, which ensured Eisenhower's getting the nomination. No doubt this was a major cause of Nixon's being selected for the vice-presidential nomination.

In January 1953 Nixon took the oath of office as vice president with little personal exposure to executive experience except in running his two campaigns. And his campaigns were not examples of a smooth political executive at work building political consensus and unifying contending factions behind him. He must have spent at least one-third of his professional career in active political campaigning. Lyndon Johnson called him a "chronic campaigner."

Nixon described himself as a politician—which he was. (Nixon, *In the Arena*, p. 118) He knew well that politics "is the riskiest of professions. You risk losing when you run the first time. Even when you win, you can never be sure that you will win the next time." In his political lifetime he campaigned for Congress, for the Senate, for governor, for vice president, and for president. He was good at his profession of campaigner.

The vice president's job is constitutionally almost devoid of content except that which is expressly assigned by the president. President Eisenhower assigned Nixon very few domestic duties of the sort which would have brought him into contact with the vast federal bureaucracy of the United States. Instead, Eisenhower sent Nixon overseas to attend state funerals and other formalities. If there were not some formal function, Nixon was scheduled on state goodwill trips that kept him moving in foreign countries. In the late spring of 1953 the president sent Nixon and Pat on a major two-month tour of Asia and the Far East. There the Nixons were treated like royalty. In Sukarno they ate off gold plates. But Nixon also insisted on visiting Vietnamese soldiers near the front lines.

"The 1953 trip had a tremendously important effect on my thinking and on my career," Nixon observed in his *Memoirs* (Vol. 1, p. 134). "It established my foreign policy experience and expertise." But none of his foreign travels gave him any executive experience.

In the 1954 congressional election, Nixon continued to campaign right up to the wire. "In the seven weeks between September 15 and November 2, I flew nearly 26,000 miles to visit 95 cities in 30 states, campaigning on behalf of 186 House, Senate, and gubernatorial candidates." (Nixon, *Memoirs*, Vol. 1, p. 198) His heroic efforts were unsuccessful, and Eisenhower was faced with a Democratic Congress for the rest of his presidency.

If the earlier Asian trip had been a diplomatic success, Nixon's 1958 trip to Latin America was very nearly an international incident. The vice president and his wife were the targets of rocks, rotten fruit, raucous catcalls, and cries of "¡*Fuera*, Nixon!" Pat Nixon handled the threatening situation with gracious forbearance. Nixon had to be restrained from leaping out of the diplomatic car and weighing into the fray.

Besides travel, Nixon's main vice-presidential duties consisted of handling the controversy surrounding the anti-Communist activities of Senator Joseph R. McCarthy (R.–Wisconsin), being host to visiting foreign dignitaries, and campaigning in the Republican midterm congressional elections. Still, none of it gave him the executive experience he needed to be president.

"Off-year elections for the Senate, House, and state houses are often even more bitter and divisive than presidential elections," Nixon wrote in his *Memoirs* (Vol. 1, p. 245). "This was particularly true in 1958. . . . Eisenhower, always reluctant to involve himself in partisan politics, would be able to do even less than in 1954 because of his health."

Several times President Eisenhower expressed reservations about Nixon's ability to follow him as president. Tom Wicker (in *One of Us*, New York: Random House, 1972, p. 196) quoted Eisenhower as saying he had "watched Dick a long time, and he just hasn't grown. So I just haven't honestly been able to believe that he is Presidential timber."

When Eisenhower began thinking about the ticket for his second-term race, he considered many alternatives to Nixon. Wicker (*One of Us*, p. 196) referred to the reservations about Nixon: "Eisenhower told Bryce Harlow that he wanted the vice president to move to the Cabinet because he hadn't run anything or even been a corps commander."

Even in his second term as vice president, Nixon showed little grasp of executive precepts. Wicker (*One of Us*, pp. 177-178) related Arthur Burns's comment on Nixon's use and supervision of the vice president's staff:

> Arthur Burns also tagged Nixon as a "poor administrator." As late as 1957, the vice president had a staff of only eight people—half what the junior senator from California had rated in 1951—crowded into inadequate quarters in the old (now the Russell) Senate Office Building. Even with such a reduced work force, Burns observed:
>
> "He could not handle them efficiently. . . . I would write him a letter and then I might get two replies to the same letter, sometimes no reply and sometimes a reply that had nothing to do with me or what I had written about. Friends of mine who corresponded with Nixon had similar experiences. . . . So I kept wondering, if Nixon couldn't manage an office of eight or ten properly, how could he possibly manage our enormous government where the President needs to have superb managerial skills?"

This was a very shrewd observation by Arthur Burns. Many

major mistakes leading to Watergate can be traced to Nixon's lack of executive experience. I think President Eisenhower can be faulted for selecting Nixon for his vice president and then not giving him the opportunity to participate in running the country. Eisenhower was an experienced executive who could have taught Nixon a great deal, but he did not do so.

Nixon won the top slot on the Republican national ticket in 1960 in spite of a subdued suspicion seeping from the White House that maybe President Eisenhower did not really like Nixon. During the campaign, a reporter asked President Eisenhower what major decisions Nixon had made as vice president. "If you give me about a week, I might think of one," Ike answered. He later said he had been joking. When asked how Nixon won the nomination in 1968, Lyndon Johnson made a very similar retort.

Unknown to Nixon, his career was being avidly followed by a young graduate of the University of California at Los Angeles—Bob Haldeman. By then pursuing a successful career in advertising, Haldeman was one of the many volunteers working on Nixon's behalf in the 1956 campaign. Haldeman's advertising and managerial skills as well as his personal commitment to the candidate attracted the attention of Nixon's key advisers. Haldeman was taken on officially as one of Nixon's advance men.

Haldeman, then a successful advertising executive, became "custodian of the body" in the political jargon (White, *Breach of Faith*, p. 97) and "the most devoted personal manager Nixon had ever known." He set about selling his candidate as he would have sold shampoo, deodorant, or laundry detergent. He mapped out a strategy to minimize Nixon's public appearances. Nixon had a marked tendency to tire himself out, and Haldeman wanted the candidate to appear rested and to remain remote from all but the friendliest of tame audiences.

That was all sound political practice.

Here we see Bob Haldeman emerging as the true executive of the Nixon campaign. Later we will see him as the executive of the Nixon presidential administration. It is just too bad that Bob Haldeman had no governmental experience—except in campaigning—and no background in federal, state, or local government. And most of all, when Watergate happened, it is too bad that he had no experience or knowledge of criminal law and particularly of the way the criminal processes work.

Nixon suffered a narrow defeat by John Fitzgerald Kennedy—a mere 113,000 votes, with returns from Texas and Illinois open to question. He lost partly because he lacked administrative experience, partly because of the threat of another recession, and finally, because his undoubted debating skills were no match for Kennedy's eloquence and clean-cut all-American boy good looks on television.

Nixon realized he had made a serious mistake by running his own campaign. Leonard Garment (in *Crazy Rhythm*, p. 116) wrote: "It demoralized his nominal managers, sent confusing signals to his organization, and exhausted Nixon himself." As Nixon's chief advance man, Haldeman made note of the campaign's many errors and vowed never to repeat them.

In the same election year, a young man named Charles "Chuck" Colson successfully managed the re-election campaign of Leverett Saltonstall, the Republican senator from Massachusetts—a state considered to be a Kennedy stronghold. Nixon was to remember both Haldeman and Colson.

Following the 1960 defeat, Haldeman continued to serve Nixon in any way he could. Mostly he just listened to the sourly disappointed Nixon, but he did speak up and strongly advised against the race for governor of California in 1962. Nixon ignored the advice and lost the gubernatorial election to Edmund G. "Pat" Brown.

Angry and embarrassed by his defeat, Nixon lashed out at the press, uttering his memorable line: "You won't have Richard Nixon to kick around anymore." He may have hoped—and even believed—that would be the end of it. As events developed, the fight was to go several more rounds before one side scored a knockout.

Bitter and disheartened, Nixon moved to New York. He joined the firm of Mudge, Rose, which at the time "didn't have what most large firms should have—a public partner." (Gerald S. and Deborah Hart Strober, *Nixon: An Oral History of His Presidency*, New York: HarperCollins, 1994, p. 5) Leonard Garment, the firm's litigating partner, described Nixon as "a man of real size and significance—a major figure in American history" who attracted attention to the firm.

For the six years he practiced law there, Nixon was known primarily as the firm's revenue getter—that is, he brought in the business but seldom handled the cases himself. On one occasion in

1966, Nixon and Garment worked together against *Life* magazine on a suit involving their clients' right to privacy. The two fought the case all the way to the Supreme Court. They lost on a 5-4 decision, but they gained considerable experience and recognition.

In this case, Nixon did his homework well. Of his argument before the Court, Garment (Garment, *Crazy Rhythm*, p. 87) wrote:

> This was Nixon's first argument in any appellate court, but he sounded like a polished professional of the bar—his footing confident, his language lawyerlike, his organization clear. He had true "bottom," responding to dozens of tough questions. . . . Bruce Allen Murphy's biography of Abe Fortas notes that soon after the argument, Fortas said that Nixon had made "one of the best arguments that he had heard since he had been on the Court" and that, with work, he could be "one of the great advocates of our time."

That may well have been the case mentioned by Justice William O. Douglas in *The Court Years, 1939-1975*. Douglas complimented Nixon on an argument he made before the Supreme Court, saying it was "a creditable performance."

Pat Nixon was glad to get away from politics and enjoyed the six years in New York—until she saw the unmistakable signs that Nixon was busy laying the base for yet another campaign. When he gauged the time was right, he marshaled his loyal supporters around him and began building his team for the 1968 presidential election. Maurice Stans and Peter Flanigan got busy raising the necessary funds. Nixon called on his law partner, John Mitchell, to plan campaign strategy in the states. As a bond lawyer, Mitchell's experiences with state and local governments and with local bond houses were an advantage. Bond dealers frequently have close contacts with the city civic leaders in passing bond issues.

Nixon summoned his former advance man, Bob Haldeman, as campaign manager. Garment wrote that Haldeman and Ehrlichman "refused to join until they were convinced that Nixon had kicked the habit of grabbing the controls at critical moments." (Garment, *Crazy Rhythm*, p. 117)

"At the end of April," Kleindienst recalled (White, *Breach of Faith*, p. 97), "Mitchell called us in the Park Avenue offices and gave us the change of concept. Haldeman was going to be the personal chief of staff, to give Nixon time for the big issues, and if we had problems, don't bother Nixon, take it to Haldeman."

Nixon's successful campaign for president in 1968 was given a tremendous boost by the debacle of the Democratic Convention in Chicago. Many voters were stunned by the violence they saw on television and re-examined their political positions. But the Democratic nominee, Hubert Humphrey, steadily gained on Nixon and might have overtaken him if the campaign had lasted longer.

As it was, Nixon's margin of victory in the election was slim. He was a minority president, elected by only 43.6 percent of the vote.

He knew he faced an unpopular war, a hostile Congress, a press that disliked him, and increasingly vocal and violent civil protest groups. If ever the nation needed the steadying reassurance of a wise, strong, and experienced administration in the White House, that time was January 1969.

In the main, Nixon, instead of looking for proven public officials and statesmen, turned to the men he trusted the most, his campaign team: Bob Haldeman, John Mitchell, Robert Finch, Herbert Klein, Charles Colson, John Ehrlichman, Leonard Garment, Richard Kleindienst, Maurice Stans, and Fred Larue. They would move on with him to the White House to create—and destroy—the Nixon Administration.

Nixon wrote (*In the Arena*, p. 276) that "A freshman congressman today [1990] has a larger staff than I had as Vice President. . . . When a congressman is handed $415,000 for a staff, it is tempting to let them write speeches, prepare questions to be asked at hearings, and write out answers for press conferences. But the danger is that the staff will end up making the decisions rather than sticking to their correct role of carrying out the member's decisions. *The more a staff does for a leader, the less he does for himself, and he inevitably becomes weaker in the process.*" (Emphasis added.)

This is not the attitude of a sure-footed executive. Such an executive cannot do it all and must work through other people. He has to lay out the work, delegate, and follow up. He cannot be a detail man himself.

Haldeman foresaw his job as guarding the president's time and strength from frequent, frivolous, or unnecessary interruptions. The rule extended even to Nixon's loyal and longtime secretary, Rose Mary Woods. She had met Nixon when he was a young congressman on the House Select Committee for Foreign Aid (Morris, *Richard Milhous Nixon*, p. 365), and she devoted "the rest of her career to being his personal secretary."

But once they reached the Oval Office, "Nixon himself explained to her that there must be only one gatekeeper: Haldeman. Her reaction of 'grief-stricken fury' was predictable, but she continued to serve Nixon with dedication and undivided loyalty." (William Safire, *Before the Fall: An Inside View of the Pre-Watergate White House*, New York: Doubleday, 1975, p. 113) In the White House Haldeman moved Woods's office from the traditional personal secretary's place next to the Oval Office and excluded her from important meetings. (Herbert G. Klein, *Making It Perfectly Clear*, New York: Doubleday, 1980, pp. 144-145)

Haldeman brought with him his friend and former college buddy, John Ehrlichman, as presidential counselor. Before accepting Nixon's appointment as his chief legal counsel, Ehrlichman had practiced law for eighteen years with his father in Washington state. Theirs was a condemnation practice, a specialized form of civil trial work. Ehrlichman had tried many civil cases but, as far as I know, no criminal cases.

Congressman John B. Anderson (R.–Illinois) concisely summed it up: "John Ehrlichman was a very intelligent, capable man, but he had no knowledge of politics. . . . [He] might as well have been on another planet."

Soon Ehrlichman became an assistant to Haldeman. Ehrlichman's job evolved into an administrative one, carrying out specific tasks for the president as assigned by Haldeman, but not as a practicing lawyer advising the president on legal matters nor guarding the president against legal mistakes. Ehrlichman recognized he could not do both, and so John Dean was brought in as presidential counsel.

Due in some measure to overprotection from the president's closest advisers—but also to Nixon's own strong tendency toward secrecy and withdrawal—the barrier between Nixon and the rest of his people grew higher and less penetrable. During the time I was at the Justice Department, I thought some of the rift was caused by John Mitchell's possessiveness toward Nixon. Mitchell often referred to himself as "the president's lawyer" and to Nixon as his "client." In a law firm, possessiveness is referred to as being jealous of a client.

Haldeman saw his job as protecting Nixon and particularly his public image from Nixon himself. By this time Nixon had become an extraordinarily self-disciplined public official who suppressed and controlled an internal volcano of hatred and malice against anyone who opposed him. Haldeman saw his job as concealing and correcting for Nixon's anger.

Friction grew between Mitchell and Haldeman as each man sought in his own way to shield and protect the president. For his part, Nixon said he would rather solve problems than choose personnel, so he left that up to Mitchell and Haldeman. Each brought in men upon whom they believed they could depend for personal loyalty.

Haldeman's unabashed hero worship, his total loyalty to Nixon, his willingness to work around the clock, and his ability to say "no" firmly to men Nixon wanted to avoid—all made him the perfect gatekeeper from Nixon's point of view. Haldeman's willing subordination to Nixon and his absolute dedication to Nixon's cause became for the president a crutch which in the end contributed to his downfall.

Almost as soon as he entered the White House, President Nixon ordered the removal of former President Lyndon Johnson's bank of telephones with their numerous buttons, along with LBJ's system for taping conversations, a wire-service teletype, and his much-publicized three White House television sets. On one of Johnson's many visits to the Nixon White House he remarked on the changes. He was clearly puzzled: How could a president fail to watch all three major news networks and still expect to keep up with the mindset of the American people? How could a man govern the country if he couldn't pick up a phone and be directly connected to anyone he wanted?

"If I wanted to get hold of somebody," Lyndon said, "all I had to do was mash a button."

Right there lay a big difference between President Johnson and President Nixon. No gatekeeper could isolate Lyndon Johnson. He was quick with a remembered name, a personal phone call, a vigorous handshake, a pat on the back. He had been a very public man, often working behind glass on *Air Force One* so that he could be *seen* working.

Nixon was just the opposite. An obsessively private man, he did not want personal contact. He did not reach out to other people. He wanted to be left alone. He sought and soon obtained isolation. Nixon was never comfortable while on display. He ordered the president's official plane reconfigured. He maintained a ceremonial reception area but preferred to squirrel himself away in a tiny cubicle not much larger than a train's sleeping compartment.

Instead of following the news himself, Nixon assigned the task to his staff. He expected brief written reports by 8:15 each morning. Yet Nixon was very concerned about the public's conception of him as a working president. In one of his frequent memos to Haldeman, Nixon wrote: "We apparently have not been getting across the theme which I have been emphasizing to you for four or five months—the long hours, hard-working image which we deserve. . . . there is an urgent need for a more effective job to be done on this score. . . . [Press Secretary Ron] Ziegler just can't get across what we do day by day. . . . that the President is working hard, even though he may be at Camp David, Florida or California." (Oudes, *From: The President*, pp. 58-59)

Dan Rather wrote, "In 1969 . . . [Nixon] was away from 1600 Pennsylvania Avenue as many days as he was there. . . . he likes to be left alone, and getting out of Washington sometimes is the only way he can be alone, really alone." (Dan Rather and Gary Paul Gates, *The Palace Guards*, New York: Harper & Row, 1974, p. 28)

Julie Nixon Eisenhower explained: "My father is the kind of man who needs to get away, where he can think." (Safire, *Before the Fall*, p. 270)

One of the places Nixon liked to get away and think was Camp David, the Maryland presidential retreat that dated back to FDR's Administration in 1942, when it had been called Shangri-la. In 1945 President Harry Truman made it an official presidential retreat, but it was President Eisenhower who named it Camp David for his grandson (who had become Nixon's son-in-law in December 1968 when Julie Nixon and David Eisenhower married).

Nixon made 117 trips to Camp David during his first term. Only a half-hour from Washington by helicopter, Camp David could accommodate up to twenty-four invited guests of the president. Meals were served by the White House kitchen staff.

Nixon loved to watch movies at Camp David. In April 1969 Haldeman wrote a memo outlining the need for up-to-date projection equipment and a varied selection of recent films. One of Nixon's favorites, *Patton*, starred George C. Scott as the blood-and-guts World War II tank commander. Perhaps Nixon enjoyed watching the rogue general whom even his old boss, Gen. Ike Eisenhower, had been unable to subdue completely. Nixon saw the film repeatedly, insisting that his family, friends, guests, and staff remain and see it with him.

"If I have to watch *Patton* one more time," John Mitchell grumbled to his wife Martha, "I'll resign!" (Winzola McLendon, *Martha: The Life of Martha Mitchell,* New York: Random House, 1979, p. 76)

Another Nixon favorite was *Friendly Persuasion*, a 1956 motion picture starring Gary Cooper and Dorothy McGuire. The movie was made from the novel of the same name written by Nixon's cousin, Jessamyn West, and portrayed Quaker principles of nonviolence. *Patton* and *Friendly Persuasion* were polar opposites, yet Nixon enjoyed them both and could watch them over and over again.

Nixon liked to talk to his aides. His staff were all good listeners, and they were all good yes-men. The recorded conversations with his staff indicate Nixon usually did most of the talking and often gave lengthy, rambling monologues. When he talked informally, his sentences were disjointed and incomplete with long pauses while he thought something through. His speeches and his documents were often long, involved, and detailed. To say the least, Nixon was a wordy person.

On his periodic late-night prowls through the White House halls, he enjoyed dropping in on those staffers who were still at their desks. One of those men was Daniel Patrick Moynihan. Nixon, whose family background, like Moynihan's, was Irish, enjoyed Pat's company. The two often spent hours in conversation, and Nixon adopted many of Pat's proposals.

During my first two years in the Justice Department, I visited Pat in his crowded office in the basement of the White House near Henry Kissinger's office. I never saw Dr. Kissinger scurrying through the halls—or if I did, I failed to recognize him.

Basement offices may not sound very grand, but as I remember, it was not an unattractive workplace. I recall wide corridors and white- or light-colored walls.

A loyal Democrat and a strong supporter of both John Kennedy and LBJ, Moynihan had campaigned actively for Robert Kennedy. Depressed after Robert Kennedy's assassination in 1968, Moynihan returned to his Harvard University faculty post. He certainly had no idea of serving under a Republican president.

Moynihan had been recommended to the president by Nixon's former law partner, Leonard Garment. Garment had been impressed by a speech Moynihan had made, urging "liberal Democrats to recognize their responsibility for dealing with the national crises of stability and to make alliances with political conservatives who shared this concern." (Garment, *Crazy Rhythm*, p. 123) In November 1968 Nixon selected Moynihan as a resident White House intellectual and brought him into the administration as adviser to the president for urban affairs and director of the Cabinet-level Urban Affairs Council. His position was roughly analogous to Henry Kissinger's role as foreign policy adviser.

As domestic adviser, Moynihan was vitally interested in crime legislation and therefore in the work of the Justice Department and the Criminal Division. For some reason, Pat Moynihan's and John Mitchell's personalities clashed. Pat was passionate in his zeal for social programs and John was—well, John was a bond lawyer. Passion played little part in his portfolio.

Both Moynihan and Kissinger were well educated, articulate intellectuals, but Nixon often found himself more comfortable with men who could express themselves in somewhat earthier terms. He enjoyed the company of self-made men of wealth and power. Certainly there seems to have been an element of hero-worship in Nixon's relations with Lyndon Johnson and John Connally. Perhaps Nixon, an intensely private person, envied the flamboyant extroverted style of the two Texans.

Nixon seems to have been ready enough to accept advice from either man. It was Johnson who told Nixon that tapes of his own presidential business had been invaluable in writing his memoirs. Replacing the old system of Johnson's which had been removed in 1969, Nixon on February 11, 1971, installed a more modern voice-activated taping system in the Oval Office.

Johnson also explained the tax advantages of donating one's vice-presidential papers to the National Archives. Nixon took a $576,000 deduction but soon found himself in trouble with the Internal Revenue Service for fraudulently backdating the deed of gift. That and other irregularities on his taxes ended up costing Nixon money as well as popular support. To some Americans, the president's deliberate backdating of a deed of gift and his evasion of taxes were equally as damning as the Watergate cover-up.

Nixon could conceptualize, but he was not a hands-on executive in running the federal government.

With few exceptions, Nixon was difficult for his staff or anyone else to see. He was content to remain sequestered in his office, dictating memos concerning such things as the contents of the White House wine cellar, the order in which salad should be served at state dinners, the size of the meat entree on the *Sequoia*, or the number of birds who crashed themselves against the Oval Office windows. One memo specified that when he sent out an order "I do not want to see reports of action [except] where orders are not carried out for one reason or another, or are delayed unreasonably." (Oudes, *From: The President,* p. 106) In other words, when Nixon wrote a memo, he expected the task to be as good as done.

He turned down most requests by his Cabinet officers for audiences and directed them to present their problems to him through Haldeman and Ehrlichman. About the only way the president learned about specific problems in a department was when Cabinet officers, the press, or others managed to get the attention of the White House staff.

While Nixon attempted to emulate Eisenhower, he failed to realize that much of the former president's power had come from his proven administrative ability, his vastly greater experience, and his background as a successful military commander—none of which Nixon possessed.

Mercifully, most people have forgotten the unseemly squabble over the fancy uniforms Nixon ordered designed for the White House police and night watchmen. The president probably got the idea from the garb of real palace guards he had observed during his visits to European capitals. The men wore high-collared, double-breasted, cream-colored tunics over their black trousers. Their plastic hats were peaked and visored.

The elaborate costumes were revealed to the public in early February 1970 on the occasion of British Prime Minister Harold Wilson's visit to the White House. The press was quick to point out a striking resemblance to the chorus of a comic opera. The *Chicago Tribune* described the uniforms as a "frank borrowing from decadent European monarchies which is abhorrent to this country's democratic traditions."

Later the uniforms were quietly donated to a high school band.

Nixon personally bought up the hats and saved them to be used as souvenir gifts.

Some critics viewed the president's Sunday White House services as "monarchical"—an effort at an established religion.

Political cartoonists began to characterize Nixon as "King Richard I" and drew him with ermine-trimmed robes, scepter, and crown. Chuck Colson, in his book *Born Again*, recounted an example of Nixon's imperialism. One evening in October 1971, after delivering a national television address on the economy, Nixon decided he wanted to hear a concert by Eugene Ormandy, the director of the Philadelphia Symphony Orchestra. Nixon's daughter Julie had been to the concert at the Kennedy Center a few days before and recommended it to her father. So right after his TV broadcast Nixon called Chuck Colson to arrange it.

After a series of frantic calls, Colson located Ormandy at his home in Philadelphia reading a book. His Washington concerts were over. But Colson discovered that there was a special military band concert for a select group of army officers in progress at the Kennedy Center. Nixon instructed Colson to arrange for him to attend that concert instead. Colson managed to empty the president's box—Gen. Alexander Haig had been using it—to arrange for Secret Service escort, and to have the band play "Hail to the Chief" when Nixon entered the hall near the end of the concert. The president arrived wearing a smoking jacket; he had either forgotten to change or felt he did not need to conform.

In the same book (*Born Again*, p. 54), Colson described Haldeman's irate reaction:

> I agreed it certainly had been stupid, but I asked Bob what I should do if it ever happened in the future.
>
> "Just tell him he can't go, that's all. He rattles his cage all the time. You can't let him out." While I pondered this startling metaphor, the usually stern Haldeman softened. "The President enjoyed himself and it came out well. I guess that's what counts."

But of course Chuck Colson was the quintessential yes-man, and the "cage" was of President Nixon's own making.

CHAPTER 6

The Bond Lawyer and the Watergate Warbler

"I knew then that the costliest mistake John Mitchell ever made was taking the job of Attorney General."
—Leon Jaworski

FOR ME, JOHN AND Martha Mitchell are two of the most tragic figures in Watergate. Their marriage was a time bomb waiting to explode.

Mitchell was a bond lawyer schooled in the highly technical paperwork involved in the issuance of municipal bonds by governmental entities all over the United States. Billions of dollars are paid for bonds on the strength of a respected bond lawyer's legal opinions. He receives as his fee only a small percentage of the bonds issued, but the amounts of money involved are so large that bond lawyers frequently are among the highest-paid members of the bar. Leonard Garment (*Crazy Rhythm*, pp. 117-118) described Mitchell:

> Mitchell was a Fordham Law School graduate who had never run a political campaign, but he had campaigned successfully for legal business and produced billions of dollars of state and municipal financing for a blue-chip list of clients that included governors, mayors, and investment bankers around the country.
>
> His national prominence was based on his knack for devising new ways of raising money through the use of public credit. One of his satisfied customers was New York's governor, Nelson Rockefeller, for whom he invented the "moral obligation" bond—a financial instrument that produced huge amounts of money for Rockefeller's pet projects and even huger headaches

for the future generations of New Yorkers who had to live with the unsecured state debt thereby accumulated.

Mitchell was not an old or lifelong friend of Nixon's. The two men became acquainted following Nixon's relocation from the West Coast in 1963 and the merger of their two law firms.

Defeated in two elections and out of public office for the first time since 1946, Nixon moved from California to New York and joined Mudge, Stern, Baldwin and Todd to practice law—although he realized that such a move inevitably would delay his political career. *(Memoirs,* Vol. 1, p. 248) However, "One advantage of my New York law practice was that it allowed me to travel extensively abroad. . . ." *(Memoirs,* Vol. 1, p. 256) Thus even as he waited for his next opportunity to run for election, he was sharpening his knowledge of foreign diplomacy.

The law firm became Nixon, Mudge, Rose, Guthrie and Alexander. On January 1, 1967, Nixon's firm merged with that of Caldwell Trimble and Mitchell. But "After Watergate, John Mitchell said he believed the merger was the 'one mistake' of his life." (McLendon, *Martha,* p. 59) The relationship between Mitchell and Nixon grew into a warm friendship. Nixon (*Memoirs*, Vol. 1, p. 345) described Mitchell as a "husky, outwardly gruff senior partner. . . . although he had never been involved in a campaign, I felt from our conversation that he had an instinctive talent for politics."

"A sort of Wall Street Gary Cooper" is the way John Ehrlichman (in his *Witness to Power*: *The White House Years*, New York: Simon & Schuster, 1982, p. 75) described Mitchell. He was "smart, tough, energetic and capable. He managed the 1968 campaign effectively, working at a bare desk in a shabby office in the New York Nixon campaign headquarters."

I believe the most accurate description and balanced assessment of Mitchell is given in White's *The Making of a President, 1972* (p. 365):

> More important, he was neither by training, temperament nor traditional code a politician. He was contemptuous of most politicians.
>
> But Mitchell was bound into the President's affections as deeply as [H. R.] Haldeman or [Robert] Finch. During the bitter years of Richard Nixon when, as an exile from politics, he prac-

> ticed law in New York between 1963 and 1967, Mitchell's home in Rye was among those places warmest to him. There, Martha Mitchell played the gracious Southern hostess; there Nixon might join in the singing, as he liked to do, or bang the piano while Leonard Garment, another partner of the law firm, played along on the clarinet.

Nixon found Mitchell to be good company. During those New York years, the two men spent long hours together—Nixon talking about his plans for his political future, Mitchell puffing his pipe and grunting amiably. This is how Nixon (*Memoirs,* Vol. 2, p. 139) remembered Mitchell:

> I am continually amazed whenever I am with John Mitchell about his vast knowledge of people over the country and also in all kinds of fields.
>
> Mitchell has particular knowledge about all kinds of fishing, how the tides operate in various parts of the East Coast, as well as, of course, a wide knowledge of every kind of food and how it is prepared—in addition to having already the deserved reputation for knowing more about more political figures in both parties than perhaps any man in the United States.

When Nixon ran for the presidency in 1968, Mitchell served as his campaign manager, although the public's prevailing belief was that Nixon still ran his own campaign. As a part of his bond practice, Mitchell had a wide experience in dealing with local politicians all over the United States—and possibly had advised them on their re-elections. But he lacked the ingredient of making tough decisions as a candidate, and had little experience in election campaigns. I believe he considered himself to be above politics and politicians.

Elliot Richardson, who eventually would follow Dick Kleindienst as attorney general, later expressed the opinion that Mitchell was not a good working politician. But what Mitchell lacked in campaign experience, he made up for in his excellent network of contacts with state, county, and local governmental officials around the country.

Clearly most of Nixon's initial appointments were drawn from his old campaign crew. These were men on whose loyalty the president could count—people he trusted to take charge of his major projects. Yet they lacked the necessary political administrative experience.

Shortly after the 1968 election, Nixon asked Mitchell to be his attorney general. Mitchell was the president-elect's closest friend and the member of Nixon's inner circle who possessed the most clout.

But Mitchell was torn by the increasing need to care for his emotionally high-strung wife, Martha. The marriage was the second for both, and for a time the couple had seemed happy enough. William Safire *(Before the Fall,* p. 265) wrote that Mitchell was "amused by her, proud of her, defensive about her and obviously attached to her." According to John Ehrlichman (*Witness to Power*, p. 76), when Nixon asked Mitchell to be attorney general "Martha Mitchell was in a sanitorium, drying out, and Mitchell declined Nixon's offer."

I believe that initially John was deeply in love with Martha and, knowing her unstable personality and her growing dependency on alcohol, was hesitant to accept the attorney general's job. Time proved that Mitchell was right in thinking that Martha should not be subjected to the pressures of political life in Washington. How different things might have been for Nixon if John Mitchell had followed his own best judgment, stuck to his determination, and refused the attorney general's job.

Nixon nominated Mitchell anyway.

Mitchell phoned Dick Kleindienst, who had been a campaign manager for Barry Goldwater and was then back home in Arizona. Mitchell asked him to come to Washington as deputy attorney general. Kleindienst said he did not want the job, but Nixon phoned him and made a personal appeal. "Dick, I want Mitchell to be attorney general," Nixon told Kleindienst, "and he says he won't do it unless you're his deputy. So I'm asking you to change your mind." (Strober and Strober, *Nixon, An Oral History*, p. 57)

Nixon also called on Leonard Garment for help. In *Crazy Rhythm* (p. 146), Garment quoted a conversation he had with Nixon during the staff interview period at New York's Pierre Hotel:

> [Nixon] went briskly to his first order of business. . . . "We have the same old problem, Len," he said, "and I need your help. It's Martha. I need John as my attorney general, but he won't do it. He's worried Martha can't handle the Washington pressure. You've got to talk to him and make him understand how important this is. He trusts your judgment on things like this." I said sure, I would give it my best.

Garment was a fan of Mitchell. "I liked Mitchell from beginning to end," he said. "A real study in loyalty, he made a lot of mistakes, got in over his head, and had a lot of problems, but very few people have the almost primitive type of loyalty that he had to Nixon . . . on the one hand, he fought; on the other hand, he did not squeal to hurt Nixon." (Strober and Strober, *Nixon, An Oral History*, p. 26)

John Mitchell repeated on a number of occasions that he had not wanted to be attorney general. Perhaps he had heard what President Eisenhower's former attorney general, William Rogers, had to say: "It's a big job and a bigger headache." Rogers probably came to feel the same way about the job of secretary of state to which Nixon appointed him.

When John and Martha moved to Washington they bought a $140,000 duplex in the plush Watergate East apartment building, a cooperative complex overlooking the Potomac. Martha began an expensive redecorating project.

In spite of her well-to-do life in Rye, New York, as the wife of a successful bond lawyer, Martha retained many of the unsophisticated characteristics of her small-town Arkansas upbringing. In addition she drank more than was good for her, she suffered migraine headaches, popped many different pills, and was full of undisciplined opinions which she expressed without restraint.

Her title as the "Watergate Warbler" came from her Pine Bluff, Arkansas, high school annual. Few school yearbooks have so well characterized what was to become a person's lifelong propensity:

"I love its gentle warble,
I love its gentle flow,
I love to wind my tongue up,
And I love to let it go."

Martha continued amassing piles of newspaper clippings and stacks of fan letters. Some people adored her; some could not stand her. Few were neutral. Martha Mitchell and Vice President Spiro Agnew became the two most visible and audible persons connected with the Nixon Administration. Every word either one said was quoted. Everything they did was news. Everywhere they went they were photographed.

Martha became a media celebrity. She was featured on magazine covers, made guest appearances on television, and distributed signed photos of herself. Like the First Lady, but unlike any previous Cabinet wife that I know of, Martha for a while had her own press secretary.

Martha had been given elocution lessons as a child and was quite comfortable speaking to an audience. But the more engaging—or perhaps outrageous—aspects of Martha's oral delivery may have been due in some part to dyslexia. She had trouble reading, especially reading aloud. Her problem may have contributed to her colorful style of extemporaneous speech, which so endeared her to some audiences and infuriated others.

Her much-publicized long-distance telephone bills may have owed something to her inadvertent tendency to reverse the numbers she dialed and then to feel a courteous Southern obligation to carry on a gracious conversation with whoever answered.

She helped raise money at charity fund affairs by setting up a telephone booth from which she would phone any person anywhere in the world designated by the donor for the cost of the call and a small donation. She was successful both in raising money and in generating publicity for herself.

Martha gave many elaborate, catered parties when she and John lived in Rye. In Washington, she and John entertained the top-ranking Justice officials and their wives with dinner in the elegant formal dining room of the State Department building.

As my wife Marjorie and I arrived at one of those dinners, we stopped for a moment to speak to John and Martha in the receiving line. The band was playing a lively swing tune, and I noticed that Martha's foot had a life of its own, unconsciously tapping in time to the rhythm. I had always enjoyed dancing, ever since my teenage years in Highland Park (Dallas). On an impulse, I held out my arm and Martha glided into my embrace. We moved out on the dance floor.

Martha was an excellent dancer and I soon began making large, twirling turns which showed off her formal gown. Part of the dance floor cleared as the other couples moved to the side to watch us. As soon as the music stopped, we received a round of applause. I returned Martha to a beaming John Mitchell in the receiving line. It was the kind of attention Martha craved.

As long as Mitchell's star was in the ascendancy, he received numerous telephone calls from the White House and enjoyed easy and frequent access to the president. Mitchell was sometimes called "America's prime minister," because his actual role extended far beyond the Justice Department. But the attorney general began to lose some of his credibility with Nixon because of two unsuccessful Supreme Court nominations: Clement Haynsworth and G. Harrold Carswell.

Nixon's instructions to Mitchell had been simple and direct. He wanted a "Nixon Court" composed of conservative, constitutionalist associate justices. He did not want anyone from the Ivy League clique or Eastern elitist establishment; he wanted a Southerner, if possible, or someone from the Midwest.

Mitchell's task went beyond supplying a list of potential candidates who fitted the president's specifications. The attorney general coordinated background checks and often made the initial contacts with the nominee. In the case of Haynsworth, Mitchell personally laid himself on the line as he approached Republican senators in an effort to get confirmation but failed. The Carswell attempt also failed.

During the first year or two of the Nixon Administration, John Mitchell was still very much in the president's favor. But when a reporter asked Mitchell if he wanted to resign, he quipped, "No, but there are times when I would have liked to be fired." He would have preferred to stay in his comfortable New York law practice. As things turned out, I'm sure he came to wish that he had.

For a time, John had easy access to the *Sequoia*. The ninety-nine-foot presidential yacht, which dated back to the early days of the FDR Administration, was manned by a navy crew of fourteen.

Mitchell often invited Justice officials and other top government people to join him and Martha. Marjorie and I found a leisurely evening cruise on the Potomac to be a glamorous escape from the pressures of political life. That's not to say that no government business was ever conducted aboard the yacht; however, as far as I knew, it was usually low-key.

Nixon eventually became less generous. In a memo dated April 7, 1970, Haldeman wrote: "As to the use of the *Sequoia*, in the future [the president] doesn't want to be so free with Cabinet and staff on the use of it. He wants it held for Presidential use." (Oudes, *From: The President*, pp. 113-114)

Deprived of such an elegant perk for entertaining, Martha

soon complained bitterly that John's salary as attorney general ($60,000 at that time) was so much less than they were accustomed to that they were forced to dip into their own savings to maintain their expected Washington lifestyles. John, possibly at Martha's urging, requested the government to pick up part of the tab for their entertaining.

Congressman John J. Rooney (D.–New York), chairman of the House Appropriations Subcommittee, pointed out that members of Congress received salaries of $42,500 as compared to the attorney general's $60,000. Rooney then rejected the request in June 1971, saying "there is not a member of Congress who does not spend far in excess of $2,000 of their own to entertain people who call on them."

In time, Martha's spontaneous and outspoken behavior caused so much embarrassment for the administration that she finally was barred from the *Sequoia,* Camp David, and *Air Force One.*

Martha had always been fiercely protective of John, especially when she felt that "Mister President" was taking advantage of him. The truth of the matter, I believe, is that Martha saw Nixon as a competitor for her husband's attentions. Nixon certainly was demanding of John Mitchell's time.

For whatever reason, Martha kept her husband under a close covert surveillance. She routinely examined the contents of the briefcases he brought home with him each day from the Justice Department. She eavesdropped on private conversations and listened in on his phone calls.

Martha must have believed she knew everything in which John was involved—until Watergate.

Martha had been given a small office in the headquarters of the Committee to Re-elect the President (CRP) in May 1971. At Mitchell's request, Jeb Stuart Magruder was supposed to "give her a hand" and perhaps keep an eye on her. Magruder passed the job to Bart Porter and CRP hired a secretary to help Martha handle her heavy correspondence.

As part of her campaign appearances, Martha was a guest on Rowan and Martin's *Laugh-in,* a popular comedy-variety television program. Martha was paired with actress Lily Tomlin in her trademark role as a sarcastic telephone operator. The skit was a natural for both women's talents.

Martha campaigned tirelessly for Nixon, but relations between the Nixons and the Mitchells had become strained. Once while flying with the Nixon party, Martha slipped away from John and walked into the press section, where she fully expressed her views on the Vietnam War—all contrary to those of the Nixon Administration. Martha was no longer welcome to fly on *Air Force One.*

She spent quite a bit of time and effort trying to bypass the president's gatekeepers and board the president's plane. When she learned that "Mister President" was scheduled to fly somewhere, Martha hastily set up a CRP appearance for herself at the same destination. Then she phoned Jeb Magruder and, with honeyed Southern sweet-talk, tried to get herself on the passenger list.

Since the orders came from Nixon himself, Martha's efforts failed.

When I was at the Justice Department I liked John Mitchell, respected him, and believed that he was determined to do a good job as attorney general. But how well was Mitchell equipped by training, experience, and temperament to be attorney general? Is a lawyer with no litigation experience qualified to be attorney general? Leon Jaworski, a well-known Houston attorney who became the second Watergate special prosecutor, later said that Mitchell's "costliest mistake . . . was taking the job of attorney general. He simply was not qualified for it. He did not have enough experience in politics, or in life, and even his legal training was so narrow as to be useless in terms of that office." (Leon Jaworski with Herskowitz, *Confessions and Avoidance,* New York: Doubleday, 1979, p. 227f)

John Mitchell had been a semi-pro ice hockey player in his youth, but when I first knew him years of enjoying good food and slumping over a desk had taken a toll on his fitness. He almost always had his pipe in his hand. According to Garment (*Crazy Rhythm*, p. 118): "A small neurological injury produced a hand tremor that he concealed by constantly holding, filling, scraping, and tamping down his pipe."

In Washington Mitchell usually walked to work from his nearby Watergate apartment and arrived at his office early. He often ate lunch at his desk and stayed late. Almost invariably he carried his work home with him in his briefcase—which Martha would secretly rifle through every night.

For the first several months of the new administration, newspaper and magazine writers emphasized Mitchell's role as the tough, no-nonsense, law-and-order attorney general that Nixon had promised in his campaign. In addition, as Ehrlichman (in *Witness to Power*, p. 75) later pointed out, "Nixon put [Mitchell] on the National Security Council and gave him extraordinary assignments far beyond the scope of the Department of Justice."

In spite of Mitchell's double burden—and although much of his time as attorney general was absorbed by civil unrest and school desegregation issues—never once while I was at Justice did I ever know John Mitchell to pull back from our Criminal Division's sustained drive against organized crime.

In early July 1970, John and his wife Martha hosted a large party to celebrate the Justice Department's centennial. I think all of us there were proud to be a part of a hundred-year-old tradition of federal law enforcement, but the reputation we honored that day soon was to crumble along with virtually the entire Nixon Administration.

When did Nixon decide to run for re-election? Probably no later than election night 1968. In a memo to Haldeman dated January 8, 1969—before his first-term inauguration—Nixon wrote: "I think it is important now for us to develop a plan for campaign funds for 1972. . . . between now and 1972 we should get substantial contributions in the bank so that we will not have to make a major drive at the beginning of the election year." (Oudes, *From: The President*, pp. 1- 2)

In his last months as attorney general, John Mitchell was much diminished from the confident "strong man" he had been at the beginning of the new administration. He had failed in the important task of selecting an associate justice capable of Senate confirmation. He had lost the confidence of President Nixon and his personal friendship with Richard Nixon. His wife, Martha—once a charming hostess in their Rye, New York, home—had become an object of ridicule throughout the country.

Although the formal announcement of Mitchell's resignation as head of the Justice Department would not be released until February 15, 1972 (effective March 1), Mitchell knew he was being shifted to Nixon's re-election campaign. Now a lame duck, Mitchell was in his office at the Justice Department on January 27, 1972, when he was visited by Jeb Stuart Magruder and John Dean. In tow they had G. Gordon Liddy.

On paper, Liddy's credentials looked good: A law degree from Fordam (Mitchell's alma mater), a career with the FBI, private practice with his father, and a prosecutor with the district attorney's office in Poughkeepsie, New York. His career, to date, was less impressive. He'd been kicked upstairs several times before finally being brought on board the Committee to Re-elect "to satisfy Nixon's demand for a comprehensive political intelligence operation that would get the dirt on Democrats and find out what they had on Nixon." (Garment, *Crazy Rhythm,* p. 246)

Liddy let his imagination run wild in presenting Mitchell with game plans to sabotage the Democratic National Committee. His outrageous scenario for political espionage was "all in code, and involved black bag operations, kidnapping, providing prostitutes to weaken the opposition, bugging, mugging teams," Dean later told the president. *(The Presidential Transcripts*, p. 100)

"Tell me this, did Mitchell go along?" the president asked.

"No, no. Not at all," Dean replied. "He just sat there puffing [his pipe] and laughing." Liddy was told to "go back to the drawing board" and come up with another, less expensive plan. Liddy did as he was told. The Watergate break-in took place six months later.

CHAPTER 7

NIXON VS. KISSINGER

"We are all the President's men."
—Henry Kissinger, 1970

THE EVENTS WHICH CAME to be known as Watergate cannot be understood without an appreciation of the strange and tortured relationship between President Nixon and Dr. Henry Kissinger.

The relationship between Nixon and Kissinger is aptly described as being one of "mutual hostage" in "The Decline and Fall of the Eastern Empire," an article by David Halberstam (*Vanity Fair*, October 1994):

> . . . the bond between Henry Kissinger and the former president, whom he had served as national-security adviser and then secretary of state, had never been warm. Nixon had always been hypersensitive to Kissinger's ambition and his tendency to take credit with journalists for triumphs that Nixon considered his singular territory. . . .
>
> The Nixon-Kissinger relationship, frail and edgy at all times, was particularly fraught at certain junctures: such as the week when *Time* selected *both* as Men of the Year, which enraged Nixon, or the day when Kissinger won what Nixon regarded as *his* Nobel Prize. They survived as colleagues in no small part because they were, for better or worse, bound to each other, essentially each other's hostage.

The fact that Kissinger was the consummate and ultimate courtier to Nixon—while at the same time seeing himself as an independent professional—set up the mutual hostage situation and created the most convoluted loyalty equation of all. It was Kissinger who first used the phrase, "We are all the President's men," from which Bob Woodward and Carl Bernstein later derived the title of their book about the Watergate scandal.

Bruce Mazlish (in his *Kissinger, The European Mind in American Policy*, New York: Basic Books, 1976, p. 98) pictured Kissinger as a man "with great strengths, especially of intellect, memory, hard work, stamina, and commitment. His was also a character of great weaknesses, marred by excessive suspiciousness, deviousness, arrogance, and exaggerated disdain for 'weakness' and respect for power. . . ."

Kissinger was born in 1923 in a Germany still reacting to its defeat in World War I. Young Henry—or Heinz, to use his birth name—quickly learned to avoid anti-Semitic street toughs. His biographer, Walter Isaacson, observed that legacies of Kissinger's experiences growing up in Germany included a deep distrust of people, an unwillingness to reveal personal weaknesses, an admiration of strong, forceful personalities, and a worldview that "was dark, suffused with a sense of tragedy." (Walter Isaacson, *Kissinger: A Biography*, New York: Simon & Schuster, 1992, p. 31)

When the Kissinger family moved to New York in 1938, fifteen-year-old Henry was delighted to discover he no longer had to cross the street to avoid a beating simply for being Jewish. In his new home he worked by day and went to school at night.

In March 1943 at Camp Croft in South Carolina, "Henry Kissinger was made a citizen of the United States . . . the Army routinely naturalized the new recruits who happened to be immigrants." (Isaacson, *Kissinger: A Biography*, p. 39) The army, Kissinger later said, had been an "Americanization" experience for him. He returned to Germany, not as a bullied Jewish boy, but as part of the military occupation of his homeland.

After World War II he completed his education, earning a doctorate and a reputation as a scholar. By the mid-1950s, Kissinger had found a powerful and influential patron, Nelson Rockefeller, who was then President Eisenhower's assistant for foreign affairs. Kissinger remained a consultant to Rockefeller from then until joining Nixon's staff in late 1968. Joan Hoff wrote: "Kissinger may have cinched his appointment in the Nixon administration during the presidential campaign when he leaked information to the Nixon people about Johnson's negotiations with the Vietnamese." (Hoff, *Nixon Reconsidered*, p. 151)

In claiming Kissinger for himself, Nixon felt that in some way he had put one over on Rockefeller and the "Eastern establishment," which he disliked and mistrusted. But Nixon had taken into his inner circle a fierce competitor for publicity.

The unusual thing about Kissinger was not only that he was a Jewish refugee who eventually became secretary of state, but that he was a conservative: "Kissinger became a conservative intellectual, and because of this unusual quality, he was acceptable to the Republican establishment and the military hawks." (Mazlish, *Kissinger*, p. 287)

Nixon and Kissinger "held a shared view about how the United States should deal with the Russians and the Chinese—not as ideological powers but on the basis of a mutual interest with which no middle power should be allowed to interfere." (John Osborne, *The Fifth Year of the Nixon Watch*, New York: Liveright, 1974, p. 36)

Nixon and his foreign affairs adviser were both loners, both secretive, both inclined toward theatrics, both skilled up-stagers. But Nixon was also protective of his presidential prerogatives and Kissinger—a diplomat, after all—was careful to ensure that the president received equal credit for the administration's achievements.

The press, however, found that Kissinger not only made good copy but usually was more available to reporters. And unlike the introverted Nixon, Kissinger enjoyed working a crowd, moving among people with a handshake here, a remembered name there, or a generous compliment voiced in his deep, rich accent.

The inevitable result was an intense rivalry between Kissinger and Secretary of State William Rogers. Nixon's jealousy of Kissinger might not have become so exacerbated had Nixon appointed Kissinger as secretary of state in the first place instead of selecting Rogers.

Nixon later said, "I used Kissinger when I should have been using my secretary of state . . . I didn't even tell Rogers about the China thing until it was a done deal. I regret that because Rogers was smart and a good man." (Crowley, *Nixon in Winter*, p. 293)

Bill Rogers was a New York attorney, one of Nixon's close friends and loyal supporters. The new president had known Rogers since Rogers served as attorney general in the Eisenhower Administration. Nixon saw Rogers as "a strong administrator, [who] would have the formidable job of managing the recalcitrant bureaucracy of the State Department." In that aspect, Rogers was to be a disappointment to the president. Nixon railed at "Rogers always backing up his goddamned bureaucrats." (Ehrlichman, *Witness to Power*, p. 320)

Rogers had not especially wanted the job of secretary of state. Governor Nelson Rockefeller of New York had wanted it very badly.

Rockefeller—he of the Rockefeller-Goldwater contest which had split the Republican party so badly in 1964 and thus inadvertently contributed to Lyndon Johnson's landslide election—had actively supported Nixon in his race against Hubert Humphrey. Rockefeller had a sound knowledge of foreign affairs, and he expected to be appointed secretary of state. He was disappointed. Nixon passed over Rockefeller for appointment to the State Department but chose Rockefeller's protégé, Henry Kissinger, to be assistant to the president as national security adviser.

When Nixon was elected chief executive of the United States, he probably knew more about foreign problems, the State Department, the people in it, and the individuals occupying positions of power in foreign governments than any other modern president. From his experiences as Eisenhower's vice president, it is no wonder that he was at ease in foreign policy and comfortable there. He spent most of his time and mental energy working at it.

And it is no wonder that he was good at it. He had acquired a world vision and could conceptualize it. A volume of his campaign speeches for the 1968 campaign entitled *Nixon Speaks Out (Major Speeches and Statements*, New York: Nixon-Agnew Campaign Committee, 1968) indicates he had by that time planned the end of the cold war, détente with the Soviet Union, and the opening of China.

In his first inaugural speech, Nixon said: "The greatest honor history can bestow is the title of peacemaker." (Nixon, *Memoirs*, Vol. 1, p. 452) His Quaker upbringing, his own experiences in World War II, his service on the Foreign Aid Committee had all left their mark on him. His hope was that generations to come would say of him that "we mastered our moment."

Nixon regarded his choice of a national security adviser as crucial, because he himself planned to direct foreign policy from the White House. In fact, he had been in office little more than a month before he made his first state visits as president to five Western European countries.

The president often regarded his Cabinet officers as competitors. Many of them had been independent administrators and retained the poise of command as a part of their personalities—a trait that none of the bright young men on the White House staff possessed. Except, of course, for Al Haig.

Nixon's efforts to create a centralized executive branch (the Ash Commission)—free and independent of the Cabinet form of government—split the chain of command and set up a climate of secrecy and palace intrigue in the White House that ultimately led to Watergate.

Perhaps Nixon's distrust of the State Department and especially of the permanent federal bureaucracy created the situation. He often complained that only the "Eastern establishment liberals" were attracted to service in the State Department. But for the president to set aside the secretary of state and his advisers and to bring a man like Kissinger into the White House to formulate and carry out foreign policy was an executive blunder of the first magnitude.

Kissinger was one of the few people who had easy access to the president. Although he could flatter and cajole Nixon, he also could be very temperamental and often railed against Secretary Rogers for some imagined slight. In the summer of his first year in office, Nixon formed what Haldeman called the "Henry-Handling Committee," consisting of Haldeman, Ehrlichman, and John Mitchell.

Even though Nixon recognized that Kissinger often required special handling, he also was aware of the growing friction between Kissinger and the titular secretary of state, Bill Rogers. The president was not above playing one man against the other. Recalling a sensitive diplomatic negotiation, Nixon described the scene:

> "Well, what about Bill [Rogers] then," I asked. "If we send the Secretary of State, they'll sure as hell know we're serious." Kissinger rolled his eyes upward. I knew that he would have opposed Rogers on personal grounds regardless, but in this case he had good policy reasons. (Nixon, *Memoirs*, Vol. 2, p. 14-15)

Nixon and Kissinger, while sharing a love of secrecy and a

basic distrust of others, also shared similar views of the United States' role in world affairs and to a large extent made a good team.

Nixon himself described the contrasting combination as "unlikely—the grocer's son from Whittier and the refugee from Hitler's Germany, the politician and the academic. But our differences helped make the partnership work." (Nixon, *Memoirs*, Vol. 1, p. 423) The blend was so complete that some journalists referred to the "Nixinger" foreign policy.

Traditionally the position of national security adviser had not amounted to much. Then, shortly after his election in 1960, John Kennedy said he would like to name McGeorge Bundy as his secretary of state, but Bundy was "too young." So instead Bundy became national security adviser. He soon transformed the office "into the powerful fiefdom it has been ever since." (*Time*, September 30, 1996, p. 34)

Kissinger certainly did not want to divest the position of power; if anything, he wanted to strengthen it. Rather than just advise the president, Kissinger soon began to conduct foreign policy himself. He set out to build his own professional staff, even choosing a number of people known to be liberal Democrats as long as he believed they were well qualified.

At the very beginning, Kissinger made it clear to his staff that he would not tolerate leaks. "If anyone in this administration is going to leak," Kissinger told them, "I will be the one to do it."

In assembling his staff, Kissinger chose two people in what seemed almost to be the intervention of fate itself: Col. Alexander Haig, a professional army aide-de-camp, and Dr. Daniel J. Ellsberg, Kissinger's former research associate from Harvard.

Ellsberg was a Kissinger protégé and a former Defense Department official. He was unusual in that he was a Harvard hawk on the Vietnam War. He had volunteered for service in the U.S. Marines in the 1950s, motivated in part by his high regard for his father-in-law, a career marine officer. Later he went to Vietnam as a sort of civilian observer or apprentice and he saw action in the Mekong Delta. Returning to this country, Ellsberg was a full-fledged "cold war intellectual" who became the Rand Corporation's foremost authority on the Vietnam War.

The Rand report had been commissioned in June 1967 at the request of Robert McNamara, President Johnson's secretary of defense, and dealt almost exclusively with events involving the Vietnam War which occurred during the Johnson Administration. McNamara's instructions to Rand had been clear: "Tell your researchers not to hold back. Let the chips fall where they may."

Some thirty-five years later, McNamara shocked and angered many Americans when he brought out his book, *In Retrospect: The Tragedy and Lessons of Vietnam* (Times Books, 1995). In hindsight the former secretary of defense concluded that the war "was unwinable," and that American troops should have been withdrawn in late 1963, late 1964, or early 1965.

Late in December 1968, Kissinger and Ellsberg met for four days at the Pierre Hotel in New York, where Nixon's new team was being put together. Ellsberg "worked for Henry Kissinger . . . in the White House at the outset of the Nixon administration." (Emery, *Watergate*, p. 42)

By the time the Rand report was completed in June 1969, Nixon had been president and Melvin Laird had been his secretary of defense for six months.

Unfortunately for Nixon and Kissinger, Ellsberg suffered a crisis of conscience about the war and became a born-again dove. He resigned his position with the Rand Corporation but in leaving took with him the top-secret analysis of the Vietnam War.

Ellsberg secretly photocopied the voluminous report and then tried to find someone who would listen to what he had to say. His lawyers pointed out that members of Congress enjoy legislative privilege, and Ellsberg approached at least two senators without success. Over a period of several months, Ellsberg tried to get someone interested in the stolen reports.

Finally, he turned them over to Neil Sheehan of *The New York Times.*

One evening in May 1971, Nixon was aboard the *Sequoia* with Chuck Colson and Henry Kissinger. The president was feeling talkative. He discussed the Soviet Union, Vietnam, and his possible trip to China. Suddenly, his tone and mood changed. "If those liberals on your staff, Henry, don't stop giving everything to the *New York Times*, I won't be going anywhere. . . . The leaks, the leaks. That's what we've got to stop at any cost. Do you hear me, Henry?" (Isaacson, *Kissinger: A Biography*, p. 328)

Kissinger heard loud and clear. He hated leaks and knew their danger. After stories about the May 1969 Cambodian bombings had appeared in newspaper headlines, Kissinger's fury at the leaks led to his insistence on tapping—without their knowledge—most of his staff's personal telephones, those of other possible leakers working in the White House (including Nixon's speechwriter, William Safire, to his great indignation), and several key news reporters. There were seventeen in all, and all taps were conducted as "national security" without judicial warrants. The wiretaps continued in place until February 1971. None of them resulted in actually identifying a leaker.

As the wiretaps gradually were exposed in the unfolding of Watergate, they became a source of embarrassment to Kissinger and Nixon. The taps created staff mistrust and added hostility to attacks by the press.

But at the time of their conversation on the *Sequoia*, neither the president nor his adviser for foreign affairs knew that a team of *New York Times* editors and reporters already were hard at work preparing Ellsberg's stolen papers for publication.

Nixon's eldest daughter, Tricia, and Edward Cox, Jr., a Harvard law student, planned an elaborate White House wedding for Saturday, June 12, 1971. As president, Nixon was able to do what many fathers of the bride have often wanted to do: he ducked out on some of the last-minute preparations. Thursday evening he gathered up some companions—Treasury Secretary John Connally, Secretary of State Bill Rogers, Nixon's political and economic adviser Peter Flanigan, along with Haldeman and Ehrlichman—and took another cruise on the *Sequoia*. The trip was not the serene getaway the president might have hoped for, since Rogers took the opportunity to air some complaints.

As Tricia's wedding approached, the special day seemed to threaten rain. Nixon worried about possibly moving the ceremony indoors. In an uncharacteristic gesture, he walked to the press tent and visited one-on-one with the journalists gathered there. The weather cleared and the First Family went ahead with the wedding in the Rose Garden.

The president tended to view everything from the standpoint of public relations. He must have been pleased when Chuck Colson was able to report: "The total ratings for the wedding shows last weekend equal 59 million viewers. 15 million additionally viewed the CBS Friday night preview."

Ordinarily, Nixon depended on his staff to prepare brief daily summaries of the news. But on Sunday morning Nixon looked at the front page of *The New York Times*—and yes, there was a two-column, full-length photograph of the president standing beside his radiant daughter. The accompanying article reported that Tricia's had been the first outdoor wedding at the White House in its 117-year history.

Opposite the wedding story and photograph were two articles, one by Neil Sheehan and one by Hedrick Smith, explaining that the *Times* had "obtained" the Rand Report, "History of U.S. Decision-Making Process on Vietnam Policy, 1945-1967," which "will be described and presented in a series of articles beginning today."

The *Times* had known about both stories—the White House wedding and the purloined report—for months. Their juxtaposition on the front page may not have been entirely coincidental.

The articles were presented in a low-key format; there were no bold "screamer" headlines to attract attention. If Nixon read all three inside pages of the documents, initially he could see no danger in them. John Mitchell read them without reaction. Bob Mardian, chief of the Justice Department's Internal Security Division, was in California and did not learn about the *Times* stories until he returned to Washington.

Two men who were apprehensive about the threat were Kissinger and his aide, Al Haig. "Haig called to tell me about it before I had seen the *Times*," Haldeman noted. "Apparently we didn't know that the papers had been taken out and *The New York Times* has all of them except one volume. . . . [Haig] feels that it will cause terrible problems with the South Vietnamese government." (*The Haldeman Diaries*, p. 299)

Nixon described the incident in his *Memoirs* (Vol. 1, p. 629) and said, "The defense and intelligence agencies raced to obtain copies of the study. . . ." but that all came later.

The documents quickly became known as the Pentagon Papers. On Monday morning the next installment appeared in the *Times*. Predictably, the day in the White House began with hastily called staff meetings and a flurry of memos. Nixon was somewhat concerned about the foreign relations aspects, but he could not see how documents from the Kennedy-Johnson years and before could possibly hurt his administration. He was, however, greatly concerned with the identity of the unknown leaker.

"We need someone to handle this whole situation on an overall basis," Nixon said in an ACTION PAPER dated June 15, 1971. "We need to get across the feeling of disloyalty on the part of those that publish these [Pentagon] papers." (Oudes, *From: The President,* p. 271)

Attorney General Mitchell sent a telegram to the *Times* asking them to cease publication of the Pentagon Papers and to return all documents to the Department of Defense. He cited "irreparable injury to the defense interests," but the stories continued to appear in each day's edition.

Failing to get voluntary cooperation from the *Times*, Mitchell moved for an injunction. The U.S. District Court in New York ordered a halt for four days, thereby "restraining a newspaper in advance from publishing specific articles for the first time in the history of the republic." (Ben Bradlee, *A Good Life: Newspapering and Other Adventures*, New York: Simon & Schuster, 1995, p. 312)

A syndicated cartoon by Pat Oliphant showed the attorney general, pipe firmly in place, garbed in armor, holding a sword labeled CENSORSHIP in his hand, and run through by a pen. The caption read: "Mightier than the sword."

On Tuesday Nixon sent a memo to Haldeman that "under *no circumstances* is anyone connected with the White House to give an interview to a member of the staff of the *New York Times* without my express permission. I want you to enforce this without, of course, showing them this memorandum." (Oudes, *From: The President,* p. 270) Haldeman met with senior staff members and made sure everyone understood they were not to talk to reporters.

The Washington Post had been scrambling to catch up with *The New York Times* on the story—and there was no injunction against the *Post*. Wednesday one of the *Post*'s editors flew to Boston and flew back Thursday morning with some 4,000 pages of the Papers. After consulting with the Post Corporation's legal counsel and getting a go-ahead from the publisher, Katharine Graham, the *Post*'s editors ran the story in Friday's edition.

About 3:00 on Friday afternoon, Assistant Attorney General William H. Rehnquist at the Justice Department phoned Ben Bradlee, the *Post*'s managing editor, and read a prepared statement. Rehnquist cited the Espionage Law, Title 18, U.S. Code, Section 793. The *Post* suspended further publication of the Pentagon Papers. "For the next eight days—until just after 1:00 P.M. on Saturday, June 26, in the Supreme Court of the United States—[the *Post*'s counsel] were almost full time in the U.S. District Court for the District of Columbia, the U.S. Court of Appeals for the District of Columbia, the District Court again, the Court of Appeals again . . . or in various legal offices, researching and writing affidavits and legal briefs." (Bradlee, *A Good Life*, p. 318)

Dean Erwin N. Griswold, as solicitor general, had the responsibility of taking the government's case to the Supreme Court—with about three hours' notice. Always a stickler for decorum, Dean Griswold felt that the business suit he happened to be wearing was not entirely appropriate. He phoned his wife and arranged for a dark suit and conservative necktie to be delivered to him. Wednesday, June 30, the Supreme Court ruled 6-3 for *The New York Times* and *The Washington Post*. Both newspapers resumed publication of the Papers, and others around the country quickly joined in.

Failing of the Court's support, President Nixon called Attorney General Mitchell, Secretary of Defense Laird, and Henry Kissinger in for a meeting. Why not, Laird suggested, simply declassify and release the Papers? But Kissinger was adamant that government security be uncompromised.

The Pentagon Papers had not touched upon Nixon's or Kissinger's roles in Vietnam. Kissinger later commented rather mildly that "the sudden release of over 7,000 pages of secret documents came as a profound shock to the Administration. The documents, of course, were in no way damaging to the Nixon Presidency." (Kissinger, *White House Years*, p. 729)

But at the time, Kissinger was widely reported to be furious. He hated leaks under any circumstances, and he immediately believed that the leaker could be no one but his former protégé, Daniel Ellsberg.

Ellsberg, it would appear, had never intended to remain anonymous after he succeeded in getting out his message about the Vietnam War. On June 28 he had surrendered himself to a U.S. marshal in Boston. On that same Monday, while the administration was still seeking to suppress the Pentagon documents, a Los Angeles grand jury indicted Daniel Ellsberg on two counts: unauthorized possession of national defense information, and theft of government property.

Haldeman believed that what really bothered Kissinger was the fact that Ellsberg had been one of Kissinger's own people. He felt personally betrayed. "In the four and a half years in the White House I listened . . . to many Kissinger rages, but the Pentagon Papers . . . was Kissinger's premier performance," Haldeman wrote. (*The Ends of Power*, New York: Times Books, 1978, pp. 110-111) "As I remember, it ended with charges against Ellsberg by Kissinger that in my opinion go beyond belief. . . . By the end of this meeting Nixon was as angry as his foreign affairs chief."

Whether Kissinger's charges of Ellsberg's corrupt and dissolute personal behavior were true or not, Kissinger must have known they would inflame Nixon's strict sense of personal morals. Kissinger insisted that Ellsberg "must be stopped at all costs"—but surely he did not foresee that the efforts to stop Ellsberg would be the first in a chain of events that would lead to Watergate and the destruction of the Nixon Administration.

"Kissinger's connection to Watergate was indirect," wrote Isaacson. "He was not involved in the break-in or even the cover-up, but he had acquiesced in—even contributed to—the mind-set that had bred the scandal." (Isaacson, *Kissinger: A Biography*, p. 600)

"Leaks will eat you up," Johnson had warned Nixon. He should have added: "But there's not much you can do about them." I believe President Nixon made a great mistake in allowing himself to become so obsessed with stopping leaks. He should have concentrated on more important matters.

Instead, Nixon's efforts to stop the leaks did far more damage than any of the leakers—with the possible exception of the anonymous Deep Throat informant.

Kissinger's insistence that the president do something to punish Daniel Ellsberg and stop the leaks led Nixon to set up a White House Special Investigations Unit. In a taped conversation with Haldeman and Kissinger (Stanley J. Kutler, *Abuse of Power*, New York: Free Press, 1997, p. 7) Nixon referred to his own Hiss investigation and said the job of the unit would require eighteen-hour days. "It takes devotion and dedication and loyalty and diligence such as you've never seen," Nixon said. He assigned the task to his domestic affairs adviser, John Ehrlichman. Ehrlichman put a former member of his law firm, thirty-two-year-old Bud Krogh, in charge of stopping leaks.

Krogh was a young man "of immaculate personality and character," White observed (White, *Breach of Faith*, pp. 148-149), and completely loyal to Ehrlichman and Nixon, but he had neither the mindset nor the experience required for political espionage. He did, however, have the authority to recruit a staff. Krogh himself chose Gordon Liddy, whom he had known from Liddy's stint at Treasury. Kissinger's offices sent over David Young. Chuck Colson recommended E. Howard Hunt, a former CIA officer.

As an aside, Hunt had an earlier contact with Nixon. In November 1952 Nixon visited Mexico City to attend the inauguration of the new Mexican president. Among the young embassy aides, one was particularly admiring and slipped a calling card into the pocket of the vice president-elect as he stood in the receiving line. "My wife and I want to thank you for the magnificent job you're doing for our country," said the handwriting on the back of the card. The other side announced "E. Howard Hunt, Jr., Attaché." (Roger Morris, *Haig, The General's Progress*, New York: Playboy Press, 1982, p. 865)

Soon there was a simple sign on the door of Room 16 in the basement of the Executive Office Building: PLUMBERS. The name—an apt one for men whose job it was to stop leaks—stuck.

They had a four-room office. "We were in it [Room 16]," Liddy later observed, "before the paint was dry." (G. Gordon Liddy, *Will: The Autobiography of G. Gordon Liddy*, New York: St. Martin's, 1980, p. 146) The men had a secretary, an alarm system, a combination safe, and three phones lines that did not go through the White House switchboard. With only the foggiest of melodramatic ideas of how to conduct political espionage, the Plumbers Investigating Unit was in business.

> The Plumbers had barely time to settle down . . . when on July 23 another major newspaper leak convulsed the administration. . . . This time the scoop was nothing less than the U.S. "fallback" position in the SALT negotiations with the Soviet Union. Kissinger was again beside himself and Nixon responded by ordering Krogh to give lie-detector tests to practically everyone in the bureaucracy, immediately. Dealing for the first time face-to-face with the president, Krogh was given to understand that he must stop at nothing. (Emery, *Watergate*, p. 58)

The Plumbers' attention again focused on Ellsberg.

The Ellsberg prosecution was well under way in Los Angeles before Judge William Matthew Byrne, Jr., U.S. District Court for the Central District of California, as an orthodox trial being handled in a conventional manner by J. Fred Buzhardt, Jr., general counsel of Department of Defense, along with the Justice Department and FBI. The government had an open and shut case; there was little reason for the prosecutors to expect anything but a conviction.

In spite of all that, the Ellsberg case was the Plumbers' first - assignment.

If Ellsberg could be proved to have Communist leanings or to have been involved in espionage with the Soviet Union, that would suit the administration just fine. But there was nothing in Ellsberg's conduct to indicate espionage—far from it.

Publishing the material was the exact opposite of espionage. Before anyone knew the classified Pentagon Papers were missing, Ellsberg had them in his possession. If he had been bent upon espionage, he easily could have transferred the documents quietly and directly to the Soviet Union. Instead he delivered the material to *The New York Times* for publication as a part of his personal protest against the Vietnam War.

"I think I've done a good job as a citizen," Ellsberg told the press.

In a country being torn apart by protesters against the Vietnam War, Nixon and Kissinger believed it was crucial that Ellsberg not be seen as a national hero. If he were not guilty of espionage, could he be discredited in some other manner?

Emery wrote that "certainly the emerging Colson-Hunt conspiracy to smear Ellsberg in press articles and congressional hearings was at the verge of obstructing justice. Still, had the Plumbers held back from the next step, they, and Nixon, might have gotten away with it." (Emery, *Watergate*, p. 59)

Far from holding back, Liddy and the Plumbers raced ahead.

Without consulting anyone else directly involved in Ellsberg's prosecution, Liddy and Hunt devised plans to obtain a possibly damaging psychological profile of Ellsberg by breaking into the offices of his psychiatrist and looking at Ellsberg's files.

"We knew," Liddy wrote (in *Will*, pp. 157-158), "that Ellsberg used to phone his psychiatrist, Dr. Lewis Fielding in Beverly Hills, at all hours to tell him the most trivial details of his life. . . . he might well have told Fielding . . . who, if anyone, were his accomplices and to what extent he was involved, if at all, with Soviet intelligence."

The scheme was both outside the law and useless as far as the government's prosecution of Ellsberg was concerned.

Liddy sold Bud Krogh on his irresponsible idea. Krogh turned to Chuck Colson, special counsel to the president, for approval. Colson, a lawyer, should have known that in the absence of a search warrant such an act was illegal. Colson, in turn, submitted Liddy's plan to Nixon's adviser for domestic affairs, John Ehrlichman. Ehrlichman, himself a lawyer, certainly should have known that "evidence" obtained from an illegal raid on the psychiatrist's files was tainted and could not be used in a court of law. Furthermore, such a raid—if discovered—could be used by Ellsberg's defense counsel to obtain a final dismissal. And that is exactly what would happen later in the Watergate disclosures.

Ehrlichman's first reaction should have been to fire Liddy for suggesting the illegal, hazardous, and needless raid. Instead he approved Liddy's plan as a "covert operation" with the naive proviso that it be "done under your assurance that it is not traceable" back to the White House. (White, *Breach of Faith*, p. 150) Ehrlichman apparently did not realize that it is physically impossible to conduct an illegal entry and theft which cannot be traced—even if the job is done by professional burglars. Certainly not if done by the rank amateurs who were going to attempt the raid. His response was an effort to create official "deniability"—a fad then in style among the upper echelon in Washington.

To have gone a legal route and obtained a search warrant would have taken the whole affair away from Liddy, Krogh, and Colson and would have placed it in the hands of the lawyers prosecuting the case in Los Angeles. But that was not what the inexperienced people working in the White House wanted. So they handled the matter illegally and began the destruction of the Nixon Administration. Their actions support the thesis that the appointment of White House staff is among the most critical and dangerous appointments a president makes.

Later, in his testimony before the Senate Committee, Ehrlichman explained his role in approving the Fielding break-in: "You get into these conflicting duty situations. . . ."

Hunt flew to Miami and recruited three men for the job, and Liddy concocted an elaborate plan to break into the psychiatrist's Los Angeles office. No Ellsberg files were found.

In the whole Plumbers' chain of command, Liddy was out of control and Colson, Ehrlichman, and Krogh were all amateurs at law enforcement. They were seemingly unaware of the risks involved in such a raid and equally unable to recognize Liddy for the dangerous James Bond sort of man he was.

Therefore, because of the dramatic covert nature of Liddy's plan, Ellsberg ultimately would go scot-free and—again because of Liddy's bad judgment—Liddy, Krogh, Colson, and Ehrlichman each had taken a giant step toward indictment, conviction, and prison time.

CHAPTER 8

My Brother's Keeper

"And the Lord said unto Cain, Where is Abel thy brother? And he said, I know not. Am I my brother's keeper?"
—Genesis 4:9

AS HEAD OF NIXON'S Committee to Re-elect the President, John Mitchell's salary was the same as he had earned as attorney general—$60,000 a year.

But the salary did not matter. "John Mitchell viewed his second campaign as the broad highway back to a lucrative and honored private life, and accepted it thinking that the 1972 campaign would be like 1968 all over again, only easier." (Safire, *Before the Fall,* p. 634)

Mitchell's happy illusion was enhanced by the location.

Committee headquarters were conveniently located at 1701 Pennsylvania Avenue—a block away from and described by some as "an extension of" the Nixon White House. The offices accommodated "125 [employees] at last count and growing in number by the day," wrote John Osborne. (*The Fourth Year of the Nixon Watch*, New York: Liveright, 1973, p. 56) The Washington offices of Nixon's old law firm were in the same building. Mitchell had two offices: one for his law practice and one for his campaign duties. Garment found the proximity "troublesome" and warned against "ethical vulnerabilities."

Mitchell stepped into a committee that had been in operation for almost a year, with Jeb Stuart Magruder as chief of staff. "As the number two man," Magruder wrote, "I was responsible for working out the details of the campaign." (*From Power to Peace*, Waco: Word Books, 1978, p. 27)

At thirty-one, Jeb Magruder was altogether too young and inexperienced for the job of chief of staff in charge of the Committee to Re-elect. As it turned out, Magruder was not strong enough to deal with the pressures to "do something" about political intelligence coming from two loose cannons—Gordon Liddy and Chuck Colson, special counsel to the president.

With Mitchell's steady hand gone from the Justice Department, Nixon wrote that he found himself turning more toward Chuck Colson as his "political point man. . . . When I complained to Colson I felt confident that something would be done, and I was rarely disappointed." (Nixon, *Memoirs*, Vol. 1, p. 615)

When Nixon called, Colson came running, the pin already pulled from the figurative grenade in his hand, ready to take on the machine-gun nest of the president's enemies (and there were many targets of opportunity). Nixon's former law partner (Garment, *Crazy Rhythm*, p. 199) described Nixon as an "equal opportunity hater." As Nixon's chief political hatchet man, Colson had already made himself useful with efforts to discredit Daniel Ellsberg with a wild plot to firebomb the Brookings Institute, and dangerous plans to break into the office of Ellsberg's psychiatrist, Dr. Fielding. The staff said Colson was in sync with the darker side of Nixon's character.

Mitchell had been in his campaign office two weeks when he received a memo from Liddy, dated March 15 and respectfully addressed to "The Honorable John N. Mitchell." The subject of the memo was "Democratic National Convention Finance Investigation." The report was direct and businesslike. Nothing in it to set off alarms. But Mitchell should have remembered the crazy covert activities Liddy had suggested in the January 27 meeting in the attorney general's office. After that, no one in the Committee to Reelect—least of all the former attorney general—should have allowed Liddy to act without supervision.

Nevertheless, Liddy did act.

He asked Chuck Colson to "get a decision on GEMSTONE." (Emery, *Watergate*, pp. 99-100) Operation GEMSTONE was the code name for one of Liddy's intelligence plans. Colson phoned Magruder and said: "Let's go on it."

Magruder and Mitchell "discussed it for some twenty minutes and then Mitchell [Magruder said] approved it, providing for an initial entry into the Democratic National Committee offices at

Watergate." (Emery, *Watergate*, p. 103) "Mitchell has always been adamant that he said no such thing."

While Mitchell had been attorney general he became accustomed to court-approved burglaries and wiretappings conducted by the FBI. Certainly he knew—as I did while I was at the Justice Department—that internal security (foreign espionage) wiretaps were installed without warrant under supervision of the Internal Security Division of the Justice Department. Mitchell also may have heard the same story Dick Kleindienst had told me—that in the Rockefeller vs. Goldwater campaign for the Republican nomination in 1964, both candidates had mobile trailers parked near the entrance to San Francisco's Cow Palace, and used them as campaign headquarters. Each candidate had the other's trailer bugged and tapped.

Those and other experiences may have led Mitchell to believe covert intelligence gathering was the common and necessary practice in political campaigns. For whatever reasons, during the early stages of CRP Mitchell clearly did not pay serious enough attention to the incredible schemes burgeoning in Liddy's fertile imagination. With his plan approved, Liddy went forward, unsupervised, on his own initiative, to search and wiretap Democratic headquarters.

On May 28 Liddy's men secretly entered the offices of the Democratic National Committee and succeeded in placing bugs on the telephones.

Liddy brought transcripts of the DNC phone tap and photographs from the first break-in to Magruder and Mitchell in early June. "This stuff isn't worth the paper it's written on," Mitchell told Liddy. Did Liddy interpret Mitchell's words as an implicit authorization for a second raid?

Liddy dashed out, Magruder observed,

> and Mitchell and I returned to other business. In retrospect, that would have been a fine time to abort the Liddy plan, but I don't think that occurred to anyone. His mission had acquired a certain amount of bureaucratic momentum—the concept had been approved, the money expended, operations begun, and the first results obtained. True, there was a small problem, but Liddy, the professional, would take care of that. (Jeb Stuart Magruder, *An American Life*, New York: Atheneum, 1974, p. 210)

Someone must have believed "Liddy, the professional" deserved encouragement—a quid pro quo, as it were. On June 6, a few days after the first break-in, John Ehrlichman wrote a letter recommending Liddy for admission to the Bar in Washington, D.C.: "He was a very effective member of the staff [in 1970] and undertook numerous difficult assignments with great skill. He possesses a keen legal mind and is certainly highly qualified for the practice of the law. He has approached all problems, even the most sensitive, with the greatest sense of integrity." (Oudes, *From: The President*, p. xl)

In *The Making of the President, 1972* (pp. 360-361), Theodore White wrote that the Committee to Re-elect

> was born of legitimate purpose, but was entrusted not only to men ignorant of American politics, but *to amateurs who were among the most stupid and criminal operators in electoral history*. . . . [Emphasis added]
>
> And why should such an enterprise have been carried on at the end of May, when—with the elimination of George Wallace from the campaign, the successful gamble of the President in Vietnam, a blaze of triumph sure to arise from his trip to Russia—victory was assured? Why, at this moment, should so much have been risked in so squalid an adventure?

And why—one must ask—place the "squalid adventure" in the hands of such inexperienced men?

Nixon's communications director, Herbert Klein, described the situation (White, *Breach of Faith*, p. 145): "What they wanted at the White House was a game plan for public relations . . . with items to fill TV programs on talk shows, which people on which newspapers to be contacted. . . . There were these young people who'd drop the name of the President as if they ate, drank and golfed with him, and I'd get memos from Jeb [Magruder] saying, 'The President wants this' or 'The President wants that.' "

Magruder soon must have suspected Liddy was uncontrollable, but he gave in to Liddy's steady pressure for money and allocated $500,000 for an intelligence unit. Liddy's abrasive personality rapidly made sharing an office with him unbearable for Magruder. When he could no longer tolerate Liddy's eccentricities, in another kicking upstairs Magruder transferred Liddy to the Finance Committee under Maurice Stans.

Stans had resigned his post as secretary of commerce in order to supervise Nixon's war chest. He was busy raising money, an absorbing job made more difficult by changing campaign finance legislation. Haldeman told the president that Stans "just got on his horse and rode, and he really worked on it, and he just sucked that money in as fast as he could suck it in." (Stanley Kutler, *Abuse of Power: The New Nixon Tapes,* New York: Free Press, 1997, p. 42) Stans was a skilled fundraiser, but he lacked knowledge of clandestine investigations and had no interest in exercising effective supervision over Liddy. The end result was that the nutty Liddy was set free with a half-million-dollar budget and no one to rein in his bad judgment.

Disaster inevitably followed from Nixon's own bad judgment.

President Nixon prepared to submit the nomination of Richard Kleindienst to replace Mitchell as attorney general—Mitchell had insisted on that—and of L. Patrick Gray to replace Kleindienst as deputy. Dick and I had been close friends, and I also had known and liked Pat Gray during my years in the Justice Department.

Kleindienst survived a long and stormy confirmation hearing. Finally, he was sworn in on Monday, June 12, 1972.

Just four nights later—on Friday, June 16—the second Watergate break-in occurred.

John and Martha Mitchell, the Mardians, the Magruders, and several other CRP members were in Los Angeles on Friday, June 16, helping to raise funds for the Republican party. Henry Kissinger had been scheduled to attend, but at the last moment the First Lady went in his place. Martha enjoyed mingling with the glamorous headliner entertainers but was annoyed that Mrs. Nixon had snubbed her; Mitchell had also witnessed the incident.

Jeb Magruder was at breakfast in California the following Saturday morning, June 17, when he received a long-distance telephone call from Liddy telling him that the burglars arrested in the Watergate break-in were agents of the CRP. After consultation with his companions in California, Magruder told Liddy that the new attorney general was playing golf at the Burning Tree Golf and Country Club in Maryland. Magruder instructed Liddy to go there, seek out Kleindienst, and ask him to get the men out of jail.

Liddy and Powell Moore, the deputy press spokesman for the Committee to Re-elect, went to Burning Tree, found Kleindienst in the dining room, and told him their mission. The quick-tempered Kleindienst was furious. In his memoirs, titled *Justice* (Ottawa, Illinois: Jameson Books, 1985, p. 146), Kleindienst stated that he told Liddy and Moore to leave immediately and not to contact him again. He phoned Henry Petersen, chief of the Criminal Division, and instructed him to treat the prisoners as any other prisoners would be treated and to proceed with the prosecution. To distance himself from the whole mess, Kleindienst issued a public statement, saying: "Let the chips fall where they may."

His statement was both unnecessary and imprudent. Some mighty big chips were to fall—including himself, John Mitchell, and ultimately Richard Nixon.

According to author Fred Emery (in *Watergate*, pp. 146-147), Kleindienst did sit down with Liddy that Saturday morning at Burning Tree and did find out the facts. In any event he soon found out Mitchell was deeply involved. No matter which version you accept, it is safe to say that Kleindienst reacted with anger. As to springing the burglars, Liddy quoted Kleindienst: "What happens to the *President* if I try a fool thing like that?" (Emery, *Watergate*, p. 147)

Kleindienst blew it. The first fundamental rule for any criminal litigator—whether prosecutor or defense lawyer—in approaching a criminal case is: First get the facts—*all* the facts—before doing anything. As soon as Nixon was back in Washington, Attorney General Kleindienst should have insisted on an immediate conference with the president and outlined the facts.

A second fundamental rule for a litigator is that he or she must not let the opponent be the first to inform the jury of anything really damaging against the client. The litigator should bring out the bad facts himself—the sooner, the better.

What Kleindienst should have done was to drop everything else and take Liddy in tow to Henry Petersen for a debriefing of the entire Watergate affair that very morning.

But the illegal DNC entry was only the latest in a series of illegal and unethical events—among them the break-in of Dr. Fielding's office, the laundered campaign money, and CRP member Donald Segretti's dirty tricks against political opponents—which Mitchell had labeled "The White House Horrors." Magruder was told by John Dean and others: "It's not just Watergate, Jeb, there's more that we can't let come out." (Magruder, *An American Life*, p. 238) This should all have been put in the Watergate package.

At that point, the men involved in the break-in probably were hoping nothing would go beyond a relatively simple night court procedure. Except for James McCord, nothing led from the jail back to the White House.

Except for McCord . . .

As soon as the news broke, the party atmosphere in California quickly vanished. Nixon's people were anxious to return to Washington as fast as possible. Martha Mitchell sensed that something had gone terribly wrong.

John Mitchell suggested that the exhausted Martha might enjoy staying on for a few days of luxurious rest in the California sunshine. She would not be entirely alone, her husband promised. He would ask his secretary, Lea Jablonsky (who had been Martha's first secretary at CRP, after Martha had adopted her role as part of the re-election team) to remain behind with her, along with a security guard, Steve King.

King was "no pug; he was a bright, efficient, good-natured man in his early thirties whom we all enjoyed dealing with," according to Jeb Magruder. (Magruder, *An American Life*, p. 224)

John Dean had been in the Philippines at the time of the DNC break-in on Friday night, June 16. Sunday morning when he landed in San Francisco he telephoned his deputy, Fred Fielding.

"You'd better get back here fast," Fielding told Dean. (Emery, *Watergate*, p. 159)

The story of the Watergate break-in had hit the Sunday morning newspapers. Garment—on his way back to Washington after a junket in the Far East—read the news. His immediate thought was: "It had to be Colson and his army of screwballs." (Garment, *Crazy Rhythm*, p. 248)

Dean and Fielding met briefly in Washington that night, and Dean learned more of the particulars. He too guessed that Colson had been somehow responsible for the Watergate break-in. Dean later recalled his first thought had been: "My God, one of Colson's crazy schemes has finally backfired."

President Nixon had been in Key Biscayne, resting from his trip to the Soviet Union. In his *Memoirs* (Vol. 2, p. 109) Nixon wrote: "When I got to my house I smelled coffee brewing, and I went to the kitchen to get a cup. There was a *Miami Herald* on the counter, and I glanced over the front page. . . . There was a small story in the middle of the page, on the left-hand side, under the headline: 'Miamians Held in D.C. Try to Bug Demo Headquarters.'" The president wrote that he scanned the story and "dismissed it as some sort of prank." He did, however, telephone Haldeman at the Key Biscayne Hotel, although his *Memoirs* do not suggest that the break-in was mentioned.

Marjorie and I were in our Austin home, enjoying a leisurely Sunday breakfast. I opened the *Austin American-Statesman,* and a "teaser" on the front page caught my attention: "Five Nailed at Democratic Offices, page A14."

I immediately turned to the inside page. My eyes raced through the two-column story and I re-read certain portions. The burglars' names—later proved to be false—meant nothing to me. According to the article, all had been involved in anti-Castro activities and all were believed to have some connection with the Central Intelligence Agency. Apparently, they acted without a warrant to search or wiretap.

When the men were arrested in the sixth-floor Watergate offices of the Democratic National Committee, they were wearing rubber surgical gloves. Their equipment included two 35-millimeter cameras, rolls of unexposed film, lockpicks, bugging devices, and walkie-talkie radios. They had large amounts of cash, much of it in $100 bills.

That certainly sounded less like a burglary and more like an intelligence-gathering operation, but a campaign office usually would be a particularly barren place to look for political intelligence. Still, I asked myself, who but Republicans could want information from the Democratic headquarters? On the other hand, why would *anyone* want to tap a campaign office? The DNC offices were unlikely to contain intelligence of sufficient importance to justify such a senseless and illegal exercise. Anyone who has ever worked in a campaign knows that telephone taps in a campaign office would be dull listening indeed. Most of the calls involve assignment details, committee meetings, job seekers, salesmen soliciting advertising, and others trying to extract money from the campaign.

Theodore White described the Democratic National Committee headquarters as open and welcoming. There was no need for a covert operation—a good clipping service would have provided the Committee to Re-elect with more information than any number of wiretaps. "Nonetheless, in the enlarged imaginations of Hunt, Liddy and their amateur superiors, the bugging of the Democratic

National Committee seemed a glistening target." (White, *The Making of the President, 1972*, p. 390)

Nixon returned from Florida to Washington on the following Monday night. "On the way back, I got the disturbing news from Bob Haldeman that the break-in of the Democratic National Committee involved someone who is on the payroll of the Committee to Re-elect the President. Mitchell had told Bob [Haldeman] on the phone enigmatically not to get involved in it, and I told Bob I simply hoped none of our people were involved." (Nixon, *Memoirs*, Vol. 2, pp. 111-112)

An interesting item: One of the burglars, "Edwin Martin," later identified himself as James W. McCord, Jr., a former CIA agent. McCord, who appeared to be calling the plays at the time of the break-in, was a security adviser for the Committee to Re-elect the President.

When John Mitchell returned to Washington from California after the Watergate burglars were arrested, he faced a situation with which he was ill-equipped to deal. He quickly understood the enormous consequences of the illegal break-in, but—as director of the Committee and the man who had given his okay to Liddy's Operation GEMSTONE—he was hardly in a position to speak out publicly.

The president apparently viewed his own position to be as vulnerable as Mitchell's. Nixon had campaigned as the "law and order" president and brought his close friend into the cabinet as attorney general. Could he, the chief executive, admit to breaking the law? Did he owe a debt of loyalty and aid to men who resorted to illegal acts in behalf of the president's re-election? Did he have a responsibility to protect the integrity of the office of the presidency? Or was his chief concern to preserve the place of Richard Nixon in history?

All of these, to one degree or another. But "In trying to prove himself innocent of the break-in and cover-up of Watergate, Nixon ultimately proved his own willingness to put image ahead of reality, his personal interest ahead of the nation's interest." (Safire, *Before the Fall*, p. 131)

Nixon said: "This incident was so clumsily handled that it probably doesn't deserve the criminal penalty that such incidents would ordinarily bring." (Stephen Ambrose, *Nixon: The Triumph of a Politician, 1962–1972*, New York: Simon & Schuster, 1989, p.

575) He hoped Watergate "was just a Washington story" and of no interest to the rest of the country.

In this, Nixon was mistaken. An essayist, Mary McCarthy, was traveling across the United States when the Watergate story broke. In a piece written for the (London) *Observer,* dated June 17, 1973, McCarthy said: "In every city I arrived at, the local papers were full of Watergate; regardless of their politics and of pressure, if any, from their advertisers, they were keeping the readers in touch with the most minor episodes in the fantastic crime serial." (Mary McCarthy, *The Mask of State: Watergate Portraits,* New York: Harcourt Brace, 1974, p. 3)

The media's attention to the break-in kept the matter alive. In one conversation with Ehrlichman, Nixon again cited the Alger Hiss case and said: "You know, I'd like to see this thing work out, but I've been through these. The worst thing a guy can do, the worst thing—there are two things and each is bad. One is to lie and the other one is to cover up . . . If you cover up, you're going to get caught. . . . and if you lie you're going to be guilty of perjury. Now, basically that was the whole story of the Hiss case." (Kutler, *Abuse of Power,* p. 93)

Had Nixon been in the position to issue a frank statement and to handle the matter in a proper legal fashion, he undoubtedly would have faced a firestorm of unfavorable publicity—but in my opinion the entire matter of Watergate would have been swallowed up in the forthcoming campaign. Instead, he vacillated—discussing and rejecting various scenarios with his palace guard.

While Nixon moved farther behind a Chinese wall, Liddy took immediate measures to separate the administration from himself and the certain consequences of the bungled burglary. He quickly began shredding any incriminating documents, and he put in a call to his former law associate, Peter Maroulis.

The men Liddy had recruited for the Watergate break-in may not have been competent burglars, but they were passionate anti-Castro Cuban revolutionaries, loyal to the anti-Communist cause and to the president. They believed they were working for the president. They expected him to take care of them.

Liddy reminded Bob Mardian and Fred LaRue that "certain commitments had been made" to the burglars regarding bail, legal expenses, and support for their families. "They won't talk," Liddy assured Dean. "But I think it's imperative we get them bailed out . . . and they expect it. They were promised that kind of support." Mardian tried to see if the CIA "might provide the men's bail and salaries." (J. Anthony Lukas, *Nightmare*, p. 249) The idea was rejected.

In my judgment the Committee to Re-elect the President owed the burglars support and reciprocal loyalty. Such was in accordance with traditional espionage.

But President Nixon did nothing and allowed the burglars to stay in jail. Like Kleindienst, he directed his efforts at putting distance between himself and the burglars. He issued a statement to the press that disassociated himself from the men caught in the Watergate break-in. The president followed Kleindienst in the press as saying: "Let the chips fall where they may."

Two thousand miles away, in Austin, I read the president's "let the chips fall" statement. "The president can't do that!" I said to Marjorie. "Those were the president's men. Whatever they did, they were doing for him. He can't throw them to the wolves. This will destroy him!"

And so it did.

Within a day or two after the DNC break-in, Martha Mitchell heard or read enough in California to realize that James McCord was one of the men under arrest for the Watergate break-in. McCord had driven for the Mitchell family; Martha liked and trusted him. She grabbed a telephone and called Magruder, now back in Washington.

"Why are you throwing McCord to the wolves?" she demanded. Magruder tried to explain that McCord could not be kept on the campaign payroll after he had been arrested. (Magruder, *An American Life*, p. 224) Of the immediate circle around Nixon, Martha Mitchell demonstrated the truest political instincts. Nixon could *not* throw McCord to the wolves and hope to survive.

A conversation between Nixon and Haldeman took place about noon on June 20, 1972. That eighteen-and-a-half-minute segment of the tape subsequently was erased—perhaps by Nixon's loyal secretary, Rose Mary Woods—and no known transcript of the conversation exists.

The gap remains a perplexing mystery. As recently as January 2000, the National Archives considered whether modern methods of technology might recover parts of the original conversation. ("Audio experts to try again to decode Watergate tape," Associated Press, January 16, 2000)

Haldeman's entry (*The Haldeman Diaries*, p. 473) for the June 20 date mentions meetings with Ehrlichman, Mitchell, and Dean.

The transcript of Nixon's late afternoon meeting with Haldeman in the Executive Office Building—the earliest known recorded Nixon post-Watergate conversation—was not released to the public until 1993. (Kutler, *Abuse of Power*, p. 48) The tape begins with Nixon asking Haldeman: "Have you gotten anything further on that Mitchell operation?" (Kutler, *Abuse of Power*, p. 47) Emery pointed out that "This question . . . suggests that Nixon had already decided, with some accuracy, whose responsibility Watergate was." (Emery, *Watergate*, p. 176)

Haldeman told the president that the Democratic National Committee had filed a civil suit against the Committee to Re-elect the President and the Republican Committee for $1 million. From both a political and a legal standpoint, such a suit was a good move on the part of the DNC in that it promised to keep the break-in in the news and also held the door open for a continuing investigation by means of the legal discovery process.

They made a mistake, however, in filing the suit "in the name of all Democrats." Such wording automatically included all Democratic judges—or rather, excluded them. Democratic judges were automatically forced to recuse themselves. The suit went to U.S. District Court Judge Charles R. Richey, a Republican, and "allegedly a friend of the Nixon administration, [who] ruled that nothing further should be made public in the proceedings until after polling day." (Emery, *Watergate*, p. 217)

The DNC would "want to get depositions," Haldeman told Nixon.

"I don't know what the law says," Nixon replied. "I mean, I don't know how long it takes." Haldeman relayed Dean's opinion that Nixon could "stall it for a couple of months." (Kutler, p. 47f)

Bob Mardian and Fred LaRue met with Liddy that afternoon. Mardian said he was "now CRP's in-house attorney and whatever Liddy said was protected by attorney-client privilege." Liddy spoke freely but "asked them to leave a radio playing" in case the room was tapped. Mardian and LaRue learned the extent of Liddy's covert activities from the September 1971 raids on Dr. Fielding's Los Angeles office—which had not yet become public knowledge—to the Watergate break-in. In his later testimony, Mardian said he was "shocked and half-disbelieving" and that Liddy said in the second Watergate break-in the men were "operating under a budget approved by Mitchell and the White House." (Emery, *Watergate*, pp. 179-180)

Mardian, LaRue, Magruder, and Dean rushed to Mitchell's Watergate apartment and briefed him. When Magruder asked what he should do with certain sensitive documents, Mitchell suggested it might be a good idea if Magruder had a fire at his house.

Mitchell had devoted himself to Nixon since the 1968 campaign. As attorney general he had fought hard to carry out the president's domestic programs. I think it is reasonable to assume that as soon as he heard about the DNC break-in and realized the extent of involvement, he began at once trying to minimize the damage to Nixon personally and to the prestige of the office of president. Mitchell and the president's other loyal men got caught up in a giant snowball that gathered momentum and—picking up dirt along the way—turned into an avalanche as it plunged on its downhill path. After that, Nixon lost all ability to control it.

The president, in a Wednesday morning meeting with Haldeman and Colson, asked, "What's the dope on the Watergate incident?" (Lukas, *Nightmare*, pp. 50-51) Haldeman told the president that Mitchell had "laid out the scenario" that Liddy should take the entire blame.

"You mean you'd have Liddy confess and say he did it unauthorized?" Nixon asked. "Unauthorized," Haldeman agreed. Nixon's ruminations reveal his concern for Colson. Colson was known to be directly associated with the White House. To a lesser degree, so was Howard Hunt.

If the investigation got beyond McCord, Liddy, Hunt, and Colson, the president faced a thorny problem: What about his friend and confidant, John Mitchell? Mitchell—as chairman of the Committee to Re-elect—was the person with ultimate responsibility. If Mitchell's role came to light, an indictment was sure to follow. But an indictment of a former attorney general was unthinkable.

President Nixon made one of the worst decisions of his presidency. He decided to make John Dean responsible for a containment of all the Watergate events. Dean's main job was to keep Watergate out of the news through the election the following November. Henry Petersen, in charge of the Justice Department Criminal Division, was told to keep Dean posted on all developments coming from the FBI investigation and the United States Attorney's office in Washington, D.C. Thereafter Dean was privy to everything that happened in Watergate. He was present when the FBI interviewed witnesses.

Dean worked hard at the containment and was largely successful at keeping Watergate out of the news. As a young and inexperienced lawyer who knew practically nothing about criminal procedures, he did not consult an experienced criminal lawyer or anyone in the Criminal Division. He shot from the hip, without supervision. To keep the burglars quiet he paid them hush money. An experienced criminal lawyer could have told him that hush money would soon turn into blackmail, and that is what happened. Dean coached the Nixon staff members about their testimony before the grand jury and soon was knee-deep in perjury. Apparently unversed on the obstruction of justice statute, he violated it frequently. All of this became known as the "cover-up."

In California, Martha Mitchell called her good friend, Helen Thomas of United Press International, on Thursday, June 22. Martha said she had given her husband an ultimatum: *Get out of politics!* At that point "Steve King rushed into the room, threw her across the bed, and ripped the telephone out of the wall." (McLendon, *Martha*, p. 11) Martha was whisked off under guard.

There soon followed Martha's almost incoherent accounts of having been manhandled, sedated against her will, and held prisoner. Martha again phoned Thomas. "I'm not going to stand for all these dirty things that go on," she told the newswoman. "If you could see me, you wouldn't believe it. I'm black and blue."

Nixon could have pardoned his friend and former attorney general for his role in Watergate. The trouble was that President Nixon was heading into a campaign for re-election in the fall of 1972—and Mitchell's involvement certainly suggested White House involvement.

"In the early days of the cover-up," Magruder wrote, "there had been a sense of camaraderie among Haldeman, Dean, Mardian,

Mitchell, Strachan, LaRue and me. Our first reaction to Liddy's bungled break-in had been: 'How did we ever turn a nut like that loose?' Then we moved on to asking, 'How can we get this thing under wraps?' It became a game. Would the FBI get us or could we outwit the FBI? When Liddy, Hunt, McCord and the others agreed to take the blame, we were pretty confident of the outcome." (Magruder, *From Power to Peace*, p. 36)

"We're back in the problem area [on the DNC break-in]," Haldeman told the president on Friday morning, June 23, "because the FBI is not under control [of then acting FBI director Patrick Gray] because Gray doesn't exactly know how to control them. . . . Mitchell came up with yesterday, and John Dean analyzed very carefully last night and concurs now with Mitchell's recommendation that the only way to solve this. . . ." Haldeman trailed off, discussed network coverage of the break-in, and then apparently returned to Mitchell's suggestion: "That the way to handle this now is for us to have [CIA Deputy Director General Vernon] Walters call Pat Gray and just say, 'Stay the hell out of this . . . we don't want you to go any further on it.' " (Oudes, *From: The President*, p. 502)

"Um huh," was the president's noncommittal taped reply.

Nixon asked several questions and then said, "This involves the Cubans, Hunt and a lot of hanky-panky we have nothing to do with ourselves. What the hell, did Mitchell know about this thing to any much degree?"

"I think so," Haldeman replied. (Oudes, *From: The President*, pp. 503-504; Kutler, *Abuse of Power*, p. 68) "I don't think he knew the details but I think he knew."

Mitchell "definitely learned some things in those ten days after Watergate," wrote Ben Bradlee, quoting a conversation with Bob Woodward. "He was just sick, and everyone was saying he was ruined because of what his people did." (Bradlee, *A Good Life*, New York: Simon & Schuster, 1995, p. 333)

To Mitchell it was obvious he must resign from the Committee to Re-elect. "The longer you wait, the more risk each hour brings," Haldeman pointed out. Martha had created the perfect cover when her ultimatum—to choose between politics and his wife —appeared in the newspapers on June 25. Haldeman suggested that the president could use news items about Martha to explain

Mitchell's resignation from CRP. "And we would leak out the fact that she was not well," the president replied. (Lukas, *Nightmare*, p. 75) "[I]t's a beautiful opportunity. He'll gain great sympathy," Haldeman said, comparing Mitchell's resignation to "the Duke of Windsor giving up his throne" for the woman he loved. (Emery, *Watergate*, p. 203)

Haldeman suggested the contents of a news release: "John Mitchell announced today he's resigned as campaign director for the Committee to Re-Elect the President in order to devote more time to his wife and family. He will continue in an advisory capacity." (Kutler, *Abuse of Power*, p. 81)

"Right, that's excellent," Nixon said.

In his letter of resignation, Mitchell did cite Martha's health as his reason for leaving the president's campaign team. Fred Emery (*Watergate*, p. 202) wrote: "The real reason, as has become even clearer from recently released tapes, was that Nixon and Haldeman realized Mitchell would most likely become the target of both the investigation and the media. Mitchell was too close to Nixon for comfort."

On the other hand, it was important that the White House not appear to be "throwing [Magruder] or Mitchell overboard, it might have discouraged Hunt and Liddy, and everything depended on their keeping silent." (Magruder, *An American Life*, p. 238)

Haldeman's strategy worked perfectly. The Associated Press article appeared on the front pages of almost every newspaper in America. *The Dallas Morning News,* July 2, 1972, bannered the story:

MARTHA WINS; JOHN QUITS
MITCHELL RESIGNS POST IN NIXON RE-ELECTION CAMPAIGN

In accepting Mitchell's resignation, the president said: "I have often noted that the greater sacrifice is usually the wife's, since she must not only share the disappointments and the brickbats but must accept the frequent absence of a husband and father. . . . I am most appreciative of the sacrifice Martha and you have both made in the service of the country."

There was not a single reference to the Watergate break-in—a marvelous illustration of Nixon's skill in accomplishing a cover-up.

The time would come, however, when the American press would lose it naiveté. Investigative reporting by Bob Woodward and Carl Bernstein would create an adversarial relationship between the White House and the press corps.

Inexplicably—from Martha's viewpoint—one of the last things Mitchell did before he resigned from the committee on July 1 was to arrange for the promotion of Steve King to replace James McCord in charge of CRP security, and Lea Jablonsky to head CRP's Young Voters for the President. (McLendon, *Martha*, p. 186) Later, when Martha's biographer asked John Mitchell if Martha's account of physical abuse at their hands was accurate, Mitchell admitted that it was "essentially true" but explained that "These kids [King and Jablonsky] were scared to death. . . . They thought they were protecting me." (McLendon, *Martha*, p. 222)

Mitchell's place on the committee was filled by Clark MacGregor, a former Minnesota congressman who had been on the White House staff since early 1971. "We got into the Mitchell thing at lunch today," Haldeman recorded on Friday, June 30. "The [president] met at 5:00 with MacGregor and told him he wanted him to take on the campaign manager job. We went on to some of the details with him and think we have the whole thing set." (*The Haldeman Diaries*, pp. 478-479)

"I don't need to know anything about the past," MacGregor told Nixon, "but I need to, I guess, to know something about the future." MacGregor went on to assure Nixon that he believed "the Committee to Re-elect the President and the White House had absolutely nothing to do with this . . . incident."

"[T]hat's the line you should take," Nixon responded. (Kutler, *Abuse of Power*, p. 81) The president added that "as far as Mitchell is concerned, he of course had nothing to do with it."

A memo from Haldeman noted that the president did not want MacGregor "to be tied to the office running details . . . he should concentrate on the big plays." Fred Malek was brought in as deputy director to handle field operations. Jeb Magruder was told the White House wanted him to stay on; he was bumped up from chief of staff to deputy director of the CRP. Magruder later wondered: Had he become so dangerous the White House wanted to keep an eye on him? (Magruder, *An American Life*, p. 238)

"There's some new problems on the Watergate caper," wrote

Haldeman on the same date, June 30, "leading us to the probable decision that the way to deal with this now is to put all of them together, tie it all into Liddy's lap and let him take the heat for it, which is actually where it belongs anyway." (*The Haldeman Diaries*, pp. 478-479)

The Mitchells did not leave Washington immediately. John moved to the Washington offices of his law firm. Although he now had no formal campaign title, Mitchell kept working with Nixon's other men in an attempt to contain the Watergate affair and win the president's re-election. Even though he held neither elective nor appointive office, anything he said or did was picked up by the press.

"For the next few weeks Mitchell, Magruder and LaRue—sometimes joined by Mardian and Dean—met regularly in Mitchell's office to work out the story." (Lukas, *Nightmare*, p. 238)

Mitchell also reassured Magruder, who quickly had come into the direct line of fire. Mitchell suggested a lawyer would be a good idea and promised the CRP would pay Jeb's legal costs. Mitchell even recommended a lawyer—James Bierbower. As Magruder recalled, Mitchell added: "But don't tell your lawyer the truth. Tell him the cover-up story." (Magruder, *From Power to Peace*, p. 47)

Magruder's first appearance before the Watergate grand jury was July 5. Two days before, Mitchell went over Magruder's testimony with him; Dean took his turn with the witness the following day. "All this preparation left Magruder in good shape to handle the prosecutor's questions. . . . Magruder left the jury room feeling he had given a 'successful performance.'" (Lukas, *Nightmare*, p. 244)

Mitchell, as a lawyer and as a former attorney general, certainly knew that perjury before a grand jury is a serious felony, as is subornation of perjury. If—instead of Dean—an experienced criminal lawyer had been in charge of the whole thing, Magruder's appearance before the grand jury legally could have been postponed until after the fall election and there would have been no political need for Magruder to perjure himself.

On July 19, about two weeks after Magruder's appearance, Nixon and Ehrlichman discussed the Watergate affair in the Oval Office in a midday meeting. Ehrlichman reported (Kutler, *Abuse of Power*, p. 93) "that this little scenario that they had dreamed up that was going to preserve Magruder is not going to work and Magruder is probably going to have to take the slide. . . . [H]e'll just have to take whatever lumps come, have to take responsibility for the thing. They're not going to be able to contrive a story that indicates that he didn't know what was going on."

"Did [Magruder] know?" the president asked.

"Oh, yes. Oh Lord yes," Ehrlichman replied. "He's in it with both feet."

Magruder's second appearance was scheduled for August 18. Although grand jury proceedings are supposed to be secret, Henry Petersen kept Dean filled in.

Deep in his Oval Office bunker, Nixon must have felt himself besieged on all fronts. He continued to fret about what Lawrence O'Brien, chairman of the Democratic National Committee, knew and what he would do with that knowledge. Even after the Chappaquiddick tragedy in 1969, could O'Brien somehow revive the Kennedy clout? And was there some connection between O'Brien and the reclusive millionaire Howard Hughes?

Nixon ordered an IRS audit. O'Brien needed time to gather his records and asked for an extension until after the election. "He's got a nerve, to say to put it off until after the election," Nixon huffed. (Kutler, *Abuse of Power*, p. 132)

Mitchell was also called by the grand jury. Martha fought valiantly for her husband as events turned against him. "He's being used and he doesn't even know it," she told reporters. She refused to let John take the full blame for Watergate and be Nixon's scapegoat. "They tried to make my husband the fall guy," she wailed. "And who do you think he was protecting? Mister President!"

For some reason Martha was especially bitter toward John Connally, perhaps because Connally largely had replaced her husband in the president's favor. Connally had said "everyone will be exonerated" and "not to worry about Watergate since it had all been done by the Democrats so damn many times," Martha reported. (McLendon, *Martha,* p. 89) Of course, that was poor advice on Connally's part (Connally had practically no experience in criminal trial work).

Efforts continued to discredit Martha by spreading the word that she was sick. Martha unintentionally helped these rumors along. She began drinking more and hiding it less. She grew careless of her appearance. She became destructive.

As Martha elaborated to the press on her mistreatment at the hands of King and Jablonsky, she was invited to stay away from the Republican National Convention in Miami Beach which began on August 21, 1972. The convention "was more a coronation than a political gathering." (Ambrose, *Nixon: The Triumph of a Politician, 1962-1972*, pp. 599-600) Nixon was nominated by a vote of 347-1. The candidate's political handlers had been wise to minimize his campaign appearances. When Nixon arrived at the convention to give his acceptance speech, he seemed rested and vigorous as the entire audience stood and broke into cheers of "Four more years!"

Even after the nomination, Nixon continued to ponder actions to minimize the dangers of Watergate. On September 13 Nixon, Haldeman, and Colson discussed a possible Warren Commission—but Chief Justice Earl Warren was known not to be amenable to such a suggestion. Haldeman suggested former Justice Abe Fortas "whom the Nixon Administration forced from the bench for ethical improprieties."

"Fortas is a Johnson man," the president observed.

"He was the biggest supporter, advisor, Lyndon Johnson had," Colson said. "That's turning it over to a guy who has every reason to embarrass you. . . . You are going to the extreme." (Kutler, *Abuse of Power*, pp. 140-141)

On the same day Nixon showed that he still viewed his problems as a matter of public relations. Haldeman wrote (*The Haldeman Diaries*, p. 503) that in a meeting with Colson, the president wondered about "getting F. Lee Bailey in as associate counsel to try to stir up some publicity. Wants to get American flags on all of our people . . . get the flags out to wear on lapels."

Mitchell must have believed he had done all he could to serve the president. Finally it was time to leave Washington. John and Martha found a Fifth Avenue apartment close to their daughter's school in New York. Martha moved some of the couple's household goods on September 13.

At noon that day Mitchell, Magruder, and Dean met once more in Mitchell's law office to coach Magruder through his third appearance before the grand jury. That evening "[The president] had Mitchell, MacGregor, and Connally up for dinner and a political planning. Spent quite a little time on the Watergate. He agreed that the commission idea was no good, we'll just go with the press conference by [Henry] Petersen of Justice with a follow up by [Clark] MacGregor." (*The Haldeman Diaries*, p. 503)

Two days later, September 15, when the grand jury handed down indictments of the five burglars plus Hunt and Liddy, the cover-up crew were ready to relax their efforts—at least for a while.

Mitchell rejoined his law firm in New York. The partners moved out the lawyer who had occupied Mitchell's old office and returned it to him. He had never wanted to leave the bond practice, and now he was back.

A couple of weeks after the fall presidential election, Nixon and the First Lady went to New York for a bit of a holiday. Nixon paid a visit to the New York offices of his old law firm, where Mitchell was then a senior partner. Little things had begun to grate on Mitchell. While someone else had used Mitchell's office, *Nixon's* former office—with his name still on the door—was exactly as he had left it. The partners made sure clients saw the name and were suitably impressed. And although the older partners were courteous to Mitchell, he believed that the younger lawyers snubbed him. Mitchell received several other job offers—including one from wealthy Texas Republican Ross Perot—and may have considered them.

A late night phone call from *Washington Post* reporter Carl Bernstein on September 29 apparently caught Mitchell off guard. Instead of simply saying "no comment," Mitchell angrily made a rude remark about Katharine Graham, publisher of *The Washington Post.*

As more and more information seemed to point to John Mitchell's involvement with Watergate, *Post* reporter Bob Woodward decided to interview Martha. Of course, Martha knew Woodward, as she did many other Washington reporters. She had talked to him so often and so freely that a *Washington Star* columnist speculated that "Martha was part of the composite Deep Throat." (McLendon, *Martha*, p. 126) Woodward's secret informant, Deep Throat, had told the reporter that Martha didn't know anything "but that won't keep her from talking."

Woodward flew to New York to interview her. When he managed to gain entry to Room 710 of the Marriott, where John and Martha were staying, Martha apologized for her lack of makeup. During their fifteen-minute chat, Martha dodged direct questions with indirect answers. Anything she knew, she told Woodward, she was saving for the book she planned to write.

On January 8, 1973, Mitchell's name was back on the door. "All I ever wanted," he told reporters, "was to be a fat, happy Wall Street bond lawyer." Twelve days later Nixon's second inauguration —with Jeb Magruder in charge of planning—came and went. Mitchell must have breathed a sigh and believed that the worst was behind him. But he also must have been a man waiting for the other shoe to drop—and it soon did.

Mitchell, Maurice Stans (former secretary of commerce and principal Nixon fundraiser), and Robert Vesco were indicted on May 10, 1973, by a New York federal grand jury for conspiring to arrange a secret $200,000 contribution from Vesco to Nixon's 1972 campaign fund. The indictment charged that Mitchell and Stans had conspired to obstruct an investigation by the Securities and Exchange Commission into Vesco's financial dealings.

Nixon was incensed. In a telephone conversation with William Rogers (Kutler, *Abuse of Power*, pp. 450-451) the president said: "Good God, when they today indict that poor damn Maury Stans and John Mitchell for the most utter stupidity. . . . it's awful." The president added: ". . . in this case they should have told me at least. . . . But they didn't." It is unthinkable that a president's attorney general and best friend—along with his national fundraiser—could be indicted in the Federal United States Attorney's Office without the sitting president being aware that it was happening. This vividly illustrates the fact that the administration was crumbling fast and that Nixon had lost communication with the U.S. Attorney's Office in New York.

A bond lawyer's greatest asset is his reputation, and John Mitchell's was now seriously compromised. The day after the indictment was returned, the law firm ordered Mitchell's name removed from his office door and announced he was taking "a leave of absence." Mitchell hired as counsel William G. Hunley, a friend and golf partner.

"Mitchell and I managed to conceal our tension from each other," Stans wrote. "He is a sturdy man and despite continuing family problems with his wife, Martha, and his other mounting legal problems, [he] was stolid and emotionless throughout." (Stans, *The Terrors of Justice*, New York: Everest House, 1978, p. 329)

Mitchell testified ahead of Stans, who recalled: "He was terse, direct and positive, and I felt sure that his sincerity got through to the jury." (Stans, *The Terrors of Justice*, pp. 329-330) When it came Stans' turn to take the stand, a writer described him as a "Magic fund-raiser [who gave a] demonstration of the athletics of evasion." (McCarthy, *The Mask of State*, p. 7) Mitchell and Stans were acquitted on all counts on April 28, 1974. When the press interviewed one of the jurors, she said, "We felt these men were just doing their jobs. As for Mitchell, we felt he answered all the questions truthfully." The verdict was made even sweeter by the implication that John Dean, whose testimony had been crucial to the prosecution's case, had been lying. (Stephen Ambrose, *Ruin and Recovery, 1973–1990*, New York: Simon & Schuster, 1991, p. 331)

But even so, it was a flawed victory for Mitchell. The month before, March 1, 1974—just two years from the day he officially took the helm at CRP—Mitchell had been indicted for his role in the Watergate cover-up along with six other former Nixon aides: Haldeman, Ehrlichman, Colson, Mardian, Kenneth W. Parkinson, and Gordon Strachan.

The former attorney general was indicted on charges of conspiracy to impede the Watergate investigation, obstruction of justice, making false declarations, perjury, and lying to the FBI.

The entire episode was an awful thing to happen to John Mitchell. A Washington lawyer who represented another defendant on that same case later told me that when Mitchell's Washington lawyer told Mitchell he was to be indicted, the attorney general went into the bathroom and vomited.

President Richard M. Nixon–a popular campaign photo.

President Nixon's 1970 Justice Department in gymnasium class. Heads of divisions in the department, including the author, are (back row, beginning at second from left) William Rehnquist, Jerris Leonard, Johnnie M. Walters, Will R. Wilson;. (front row) Shiro Kashiwa, Robert Mardian, Richard Kleindienst, Pat Gray, and Leo M. Pellerzi.

—Author's Collection

J. Edgar Hoover with author, preparing to board President Nixon's yacht, circa 1970.
—Author's Collection

Justice Department Assistant Attorney Generals, none of whom had any federal law enforcement experience: (back row, from left) Pat Gray, Will R. Wilson, Johnnie M. Walters, Richard M. McLaren, William H. Rehnquist, Jerris Leonard, Robert Mardian; (front row, from left) Leo Pellerzi, Richard Kleindienst, John Mitchell, Erwin Griswold, Shiro Kashiwa.
—Author's Collection

John Mitchell and J. Edgar Hoover observe as President Nixon signs several Congressional bills.

Texas Congressman Jake Pickle (left) and author dressed as French police at a costume party in Wilson's home.
—Author's collection

Martha Mitchell, wife of Attorney General John Mitchell, with Everett Hutchison at a costume party given by the Wilsons.
—Author's collection

Meeting of the chiefs of the Organized Crime Strike Force. From left standing: William Lynch (chief), Will Wilson, Attorney General John Mitchell, and Henry Petersen, the author's deputy.

Three members of President Nixon's Justice Department at a meeting in the 1970s. From left: William Lynch, Will R. Wilson, Henry Petersen.

—Author's collection

The author, Will R. Wilson, in his office in the Criminal Division of the Justice Department during the Nixon administration.

—Author's collection; courtesy Consolidated News Pictures

Will Wilson and his wife, Marjorie.

—Author's collection

CHAPTER 9

Free Fall Toward Impeachment

"I just can't function with half an attorney general."
— President Nixon to Richard Kleindienst

THAT FATEFUL WEEK after the break-in, President Nixon's return from Key Biscayne was delayed by Hurricane Agnes, but in Washington he faced a "political hurricane." (Emery, *Watergate,* p. 161)

On his first day back—Tuesday, June 20, 1972—Nixon should have demanded an immediate conference with Attorney General Kleindienst and learned the facts of the Saturday night break-in for himself. Since he apparently did not summon his attorney general, it is incredible to me that Kleindienst did not insist on an audience with the president. Not only Kleindienst's official position as attorney general but his many years of political association with Nixon made direct contact both logical and feasible.

Instead of taking direct action, the president ensconced himself in his Oval Office and left his men scrambling to deal with a rapidly escalating publicity crisis. The president's daily press summary showed that all three major television networks of the day—ABC, NBC, CBS—were keeping the story alive. (Oudes, *From: The President,* p. 497) The morning's *Washington Post* banner proclaimed: "White House Consultant Tied to Bugging Figure."

Almost as soon as Haldeman reached his desk, he received a telephone summons to Ehrlichman's office, where Ehrlichman, Haldeman, and Mitchell "had a long meeting." (*The Haldeman*

Diaries, p. 473) The three men asked John Dean to join them. Dean described the meeting in detail. *(Blind Ambition: The White House Years,* New York: Simon & Schuster, 1978, p. 108ff)

Dean said he found Ehrlichman, Haldeman, and Mitchell seated around Ehrlichman's coffee table. It was the first time Dean had ever seen the three of them together in one room.

"Well, if it isn't our traveling counsel," said Haldeman with a laugh. This group, Dean thought, was in surprisingly fine spirits. The meeting "seems to have been a falsely cheerful session," Emery wrote, "with the president's top men circling each other warily." (*Watergate,* p. 171)

Ehrlichman leaned over toward Mitchell, smiling. "We thought we should have our lawyer [Dean] here while the Attorney General of the United States [Kleindienst] cools his heels in the west reception room." Ehrlichman wanted the president's appointment as attorney general but had missed out twice. Dean observed that Ehrlichman loved "to stick it to Mitchell and Kleindienst."

Mitchell said nothing.

Ehrlichman told Mitchell that the White House would steer all Watergate press inquiries to the Re-election Committee. Mitchell nodded—not happy, not objecting.

The men added Kleindienst to the meeting from 9:55 to 10:30 A.M., "according to Ehrlichman's office log records for the date." (Emery, *Watergate,* p. 51, n19) "Kleindienst's reported presence," Emery noted (p. 171), "indicates clearly their need to get on top of the criminal investigation of the break-in." The attorney general later wrote (*Justice,* p. 148): "I never attended such a meeting. . . . I talked to John Mitchell [who] said, he too had never attended a White House meeting at which Ehrlichman, Haldeman, and Dean were all present at once."

Kleindienst was in an awkward position. As attorney general he had both a duty and a professional obligation to fight for the truth. And he might have done so—except for the early and obvious involvement of his friend and mentor, John Mitchell.

Ehrlichman asked Kleindienst about the Watergate leaks. Kleindienst said the problem would soon be solved, since the FBI was assuming jurisdiction over the investigation. Kleindienst's press statement said hundreds of FBI agents were being assigned to the investigation, which would be the most thorough and complete investigation since the Kennedy assassination.

In his diary entry for the day, Haldeman wrote, "The conclusion [of the discussion] was that we've got to hope the FBI doesn't go beyond what's necessary in developing evidence and that we can keep the lid on that, as well as keeping all the characters involved from getting carried away with any unnecessary testimony." (*The Haldeman Diaries*, p. 473)

After the meeting in Ehrlichman's office, Haldeman met from 11:26 A.M. to 12:45 P.M. with President Nixon in the Executive Office Building (Kutler, *Abuse of Power*, p. 47) It was the tape of this meeting that included the infamous gap of eighteen and a half minutes.

Nixon gives his own account of what took place during the missing minutes of tape: "According [to Haldeman's notes] one of my first reactions to the Watergate break-in was to instruct that my EOB office be checked regularly to be sure that I was not being bugged by anyone. They also indicate a concern about the political ramifications. . . ." (*Memoirs*, Vol. 2, p. 117)

The president, Haldeman noted, "was concerned about what our counterattack is, our [public relations] offensive to top this."

The president was always concerned about public relations—and that, White pointed out, was another legacy of California politics. "PR—public relations—was the name of the game in California. To master PR required ever larger sums of money. . . . The cost of politics was going up to its 1972 peak. And perhaps it should be noted that the fund-raising scandals of the national election of 1972, organized by Californians, may eventually bring an end to the PR era that began there—by the restrictive new campaign laws the 1972 scandals have produced." (White, *Breach of Faith*, p. 55)

White was right to hope but wrong in his expectation. As we saw in the 1996 and 2000 presidential campaigns, large sums of money are still raised and spent. PR is still the name of the game.

While Haldeman reported to the president, Kleindienst and Dean left the White House together and went to the Justice Department to meet with Henry Petersen. After Petersen gave a brief status report, he turned to Dean and said, "John, I don't know who I am talking about but whoever is responsible for this is a damned idiot."

We now know that John Dean and Gordon Liddy shared the

"damned idiot" honors—inasmuch as Dean was far too young, too inexperienced to be counselor to the president, and Liddy's penchant for James Bond-type espionage adventures made him too reckless to operate without close supervision.

"There is only one thing the president of the United States can do," Petersen continued, "and that is cut his losses. The way he should do that is to instruct the attorney general publicly to run an all-out investigation and *let the devil take the hindmost.* And that ought to be done immediately." (Emphasis added) (Kleindienst, *Justice,* p. 146f)

The trouble with "devil take the hindmost" is that it is not team-building. Rather, it is team-shattering. Petersen's advice was straightforward law enforcement, but harsh indeed. It did not take into consideration that such a tactic might open other vulnerabilities, nor did it satisfy the immediate political situation.

Kleindienst left the meeting. Dean and Petersen continued their conversation as reported by Dean in *Blind Ambition* (p. 112). Kleindienst returned, sighed, and said he needed a drink. Lighting another of his habitual cigarettes, Petersen joined him. The three men talked for a few minutes and Dean left for his office. Reviewing the meeting, Dean believed White House vulnerability had just diminished.

The president met with Haldeman again late that afternoon of June 20, as related on page 101, and they discussed what Nixon termed "that Mitchell operation."

On Tuesday following the break-in, Kleindienst met with Petersen and Dean. Kleindienst told Dean: "The president should understand . . . that if anyone associated with the White House in any way had any connection with the break-in it will be a matter of grave concern for the presidency and for the country." (*Justice,* pp. 146-147)

Dean offered to communicate the advice to the president. Kleindienst wrote (*Justice,* p. 147) that he and Petersen waited to hear from the president, but no word came. "As it turned out, it was my mistake to ask Dean to carry a message of such importance to the president. . . . Time after time, in the following months, Petersen would remind me of the Dean meeting and deplore the fact that nothing ever came of it."

Dean had more at stake than any of the staff. He almost certainly knew that the case could not legally be contained. He must have realized that he himself would be a certain target once the investigation got beyond the Committee to Re-elect.

If only the investigators could be kept from stumbling into other areas, Dean reasoned—areas which in his mind ran from campaign contributions to the Ellsberg break-in—things might not be as bad as they looked.

When Nixon and Haldeman met in the Oval Office on the morning of June 21, 1972 (Kutler, *Abuse of Power*, pp. 54-60) they discussed Gordon Liddy.

"John [Mitchell] laid out a scenario . . . would involve this guy Liddy at the committee confessing and taking, moving the thing up to that level, saying: 'Yeah, I did it, I did it.'" Haldeman reported to the president.

"Is Liddy willing?" Nixon asked.

"He says he is," Haldeman replied.

According to Haldeman, "the beauty of the Liddy scenario is that as far as anybody under him is concerned, he's where it came from. . . . So even if we can't count on the guys [burglars], if we admit—if Liddy admits guilt, then those guys can think any way they want and it won't matter." Haldeman added that Liddy "is a little bit nutty, and obviously we'll have to get rid of him, we made a mistake in having him in there and that's too bad."

Colson joined the men. Nixon asked if "we ought to put Liddy up there and tell him to take the rap . . . See, it's the PR aspect."

"Well, I'd like to cut our losses and get out," Colson replied. Did he remember his EYES ONLY (Oudes, *From: The President,* pp. 299-300) less than a year earlier (July 22, 1971) to John Ehrlichman? "RE: Further on the Pentagon Papers," Colson noted: "At the moment I think Bud [Egil Krogh] has a good investigative mechanism although he thinks he will need the full services of Jack Caulfield. . . . Leddy [sic] is an excellent man. Hunt can be very useful."

Liddy, the "excellent man" carried on the rolls of Maurice Stans' Finance Committee, was fired within the week.

The following day, June 22, Haldeman was able to tell the president: "Today's news is all good. In the first place, we got [U.S. District Court Judge Charles R.] Richey for the civil case." (Kutler, *Abuse of Power,* p. 63) Richey, a Republican, and "allegedly a friend of the Nixon administration, ruled that nothing further should be made public in the proceedings until after polling day." (Emery, *Watergate*, p. 217)

Indictments against the burglars were returned on September 15, 1972.

The taped conversation of that day's "fateful meeting" in the Oval Office of the president with Dean and Haldeman "gives the lie to Nixon's later claims that he never met John Dean until late February 1973." (Kutler, *Abuse of Power*, pp. 146-152) Nixon appeared to be in a good mood. He greeted Dean. "Well, you had quite a day today, didn't you? You got Watergate on the way, huh?"

Dean replied, "Quite a three months." This statement clearly refers to a cover-up attempt from the beginning.

"How did it all end up?" Haldeman asked. "Whitewash?"

No, Dean answered. The five indicted burglars plus "two White House aides" [Hunt and Liddy] took the edge off any charges of whitewash. Dean did not mention he had arranged for perjured testimony to be presented to the grand jury. Dean reviewed the first three months of the Watergate investigation and assured the president that "fifty-four days from now (election day) not a thing will come crashing down to our surprise." (*The Presidential Transcripts*, p. 36)

President Nixon complimented John Dean on his accomplishment in keeping Watergate out of the newspapers during the campaign.

"We are all in it together," Nixon said midway into the meeting. "This is a war. We take a few shots and it will be over. We will give them a few shots and it will be over. Don't worry. I wouldn't want to be on the other side right now, would you?"

The men apparently felt their own situation was safe enough that they could once again go on the offensive. Dean used the opportunity to tell the president that he had been taking names "of people who are emerging as less than our friends." Edward Bennett Williams, the lawyer for the Democrats and *The Washington Post*, almost certainly was on the "less than our friends" list.

"The Bureau [FBI] ought to go into Edward Bennett Williams and. . . . Keep him tied up for a couple of weeks," Haldeman suggested. Nixon added, "I wouldn't want to be in Edward Bennett Williams' position after this election."

In an earlier (June 21, 1972) taped conversation with Colson,

Nixon showed partial good judgment when he said, "I just hope we get a good lawyer. . . . Somebody to take on Bennett Williams." (Kutler, *Abuse of Power,* p. 57) But hope—or luck or chance—was not enough. The president should have had an experienced counsel already in place in the White House. Failing that, he should have acted immediately to fill the void. Once more, he failed to take executive action.

The break-in cases were routinely set for trial in January 1972. Thus the entire matter was passed over until after the November election.

This election had been President Nixon's first concern at the time the DNC break-in occurred. He was afraid of the effect the incident might have on his campaign against the Democratic candidate, George McGovern.

"Nixon's ideas about how his nation worked and what its groups sought, matched against George McGovern's ideas," Theodore White wrote, "would have won, Watergate or no Watergate, organization or no organization, in 1972." (*The Making of the President, 1972*, p. 441)

A third-party candidate, George C. Wallace of Alabama, might have damaged Nixon by drawing off votes. But an attempted assassination removed Wallace as a serious candidate.

During the campaign, Nixon stuck to his intention to run as an incumbent rather than as the candidate of his party. I believe we can look back and regard conducting a presidential campaign divorced or estranged from the political party as partially responsible for the withering away of the strength and importance of traditional parties in America.

The technique for running such a campaign, wrote White (*Breach of Faith*, p. 53), "would probably have been invented by *someone*. . . . Its apotheosis was to be reached in 1972 in Richard Nixon's CREEP—Committee for the Re-election of the President."

Without Nixon's insistence on running apart from the Republican National Committee, Ervin wrote (*The Whole Truth,* p. vii), "[T]here would have been no Watergate. Its members would have known that the activities of Watergate were outside the political pale."

Late in October 1972, articles about Watergate resurfaced in newspapers, especially in *The Washington Post.*

The newspaper stories seem to have done Nixon no harm in

voters' minds. Even if the full extent of Nixon's character flaws had been revealed, I do not believe the voters would have denied Nixon his second term. Historically, character flaws seldom seem to have been determining factors in American presidential elections—although they may determine the length of a president's stay in the White House.

For the last six weeks of the campaign, Nixon was running virtually unopposed. When he realized his own re-election was not in jeopardy, he easily could have diverted his campaign funds—some of the $55 million that Maurice Stans and Herbert Kalmbach had raised—along with his team's energy in an all-out effort to elect the Republican candidates running for the House and the Senate.

On election day Bob Haldeman noted in his diary: "[The president] was concerned about how we would answer the question of losing the House and the Senate. . . ." (*The Haldeman Diaries*, p. 531)

Nixon's lack of loyalty to his party would prove to be one more factor in his ultimate downfall. For although Nixon won four more years in the White House by a margin of sixty percent, the Democrats held on to both houses of the 93rd Congress.

The time would soon come when the president would need all the congressional support he could muster, but he would find few friends on either side of the aisle.

In his effort to "contain" the Watergate break-in, Dean had been paying large sums of hush money to the burglars. Their insatiable demands for more money accelerated and became—well, ugly. Dean soon exhausted all the loose money left over from the campaign. He approached Nixon's original fundraiser, Herbert Kalmbach. When Dean broke the unhappy news that between fifty and one hundred thousand dollars were needed, Kalmbach explained the problem to Maurice Stans, and Stans came up with over $75,000.

Dean and Frederick C. LaRue dispatched Powell Moore "to visit Mitchell in New York to see about raising more. Mitchell's reply, considering the stakes, was surprising. 'Tell them to get lost!' was the message he gave Moore for Ehrlichman and Haldeman." (Emery, *Watergate*, p. 241)

Dean became desperate and went directly to Nixon.

By discussing the hush money and blackmail with President

Nixon and seeking his help, John Dean brought the president into the obstruction of justice case as a co-conspirator. Their discussion on March 21, 1973, about paying blackmail—the so-called "cancer on the presidency" tape—along with the earlier "smoking gun" tape of June 23, 1972, would seal Nixon's fate. Once these two tapes were heard by the Senate Select Committee, the president lost the last vestiges of support even among his own party. But that was still in the future.

Federal District Judge John J. Sirica, in whose court the burglary cases were pending, was indignant about what he viewed as an obvious containment of the investigation. Working with the local prosecutors, the judge imposed "provisional" maximum sentences on the burglars and—except for Liddy—broke their wills. They turned, became hostile to Nixon and the White House staff, and testified for the government—including their sketchy knowledge of who authorized the burglary.

One of the "few shots" Nixon had predicted earlier was about to be fired. McCord had turned over a letter, dated March 19, 1973, to Judge Sirica. On Friday, March 22, the judge read McCord's letter aloud in a crowded courtroom. (Ervin, *The Whole Truth,* p. 60) The effect was more than a shot; it was a bombshell. It blew the containment into bits.

Mitchell flew to Washington for a series of meetings about Watergate. The March 22 meeting was among those taped (*The Presidential Transcripts*, pp. 152-177), so we have an idea of the content. Nixon, Haldeman, Ehrlichman, Dean, and Mitchell met in the Executive Office Building for almost two hours.

The president faced the problem of deciding which of his aides should go before the Senate Select Committee. In the course of the conversation, Nixon asked, "What about Colson—does he go or not?"

"Everybody goes—including Ehrlichman and me," Haldeman said. "Everybody except John Dean, who doesn't go because he's got the lawyer is privilege." (Ervin, *The Whole Truth,* p. 55)

Nixon had, on March 15, taken measures to keep Dean from having to testify to the Judiciary Committee considering Patrick Gray's nomination as FBI director. Nixon asserted that Dean had "a double privilege, the lawyer-client relationship, as well as the Presidential privilege." (Ervin, *The Whole Truth,* p. 39)

The president asked, "What is your position on having Dean testify? We would have to draw a line there, wouldn't we, John?"

Mitchell agreed with the president. "To have your counsel testify would be a mistake." Mitchell's advice became moot when John Dean turned. The meeting broke up about 3:45 so Mitchell could catch his plane back to New York.

Late in March 1973 Nixon asked Ehrlichman to look into the whole matter and submit a written report. Ehrlichman insisted on a signed memo from Nixon, thus hoping to establish an attorney-client privilege, before undertaking an investigation. Ehrlichman concluded that John Mitchell was criminally responsible for the burglary.

Ehrlichman passed his conclusions to the president. Nixon instructed Ehrlichman to tell Mitchell he "should not remain silent out of loyalty to the president." A double message indeed. That would make John Mitchell the president's fall guy—just as Martha had predicted.

John Dean concluded that *some* Nixon insider was going to be the fall guy. He decided that the way things were shaping up, he himself was the most likely candidate. The only thing to do was what the president should have done: Dean hired a personal lawyer, Charles N. Shaffer.

Shaffer had started his professional career as one of Attorney General Bobby Kennedy's assistants in the "get Hoffa squad."

On March 30 Dean and his lawyer spent several private hours together. As Emery described the situation (*Watergate*, p. 292), that was when Dean began living "a double life: by day still the president's counsel, by night the ultimate stool pigeon."

Shaffer wanted to begin negotiations with the prosecutors for a plea bargain in which Dean would become the principal witness against the Nixon Administration in exchange for a grant of immunity for all criminal acts on Dean's part. Shaffer began offering the prosecutors, Earl Silbert and Seymour Glanzer, all the information about Watergate—and anything else Dean had except his conversations with the president—in his client's desperate attempt to gain immunity.

But this was not some petty street crook turning against an organized crime boss. This was an attorney—Dean—turning against his client, the president of the United States. From the standpoint of legal ethics, the very idea of the president's lawyer negotiating to save his own skin by providing testimony against the president on a legal matter he had been handling for the president is outrageous. However, as Ervin (*The Whole Truth*, p. 75) pointed out, Nixon's apparently believed that "the attorney-client privilege constitutes an absolute cloak of secrecy, it can be invoked only if the disclosure of a communication . . . is for a lawful purpose or in furtherance of a lawful end."

Colson sent word through Haldeman (Kutler, *Abuse of Power*, pp. 272-273) that "the President needs one independent person to advise him who is a good, skilled trial lawyer. . . . because none of us can render good advice to the President." Had Nixon followed Colson's suggestion, he might have saved his presidency. Instead Nixon allowed himself to listen to Haldeman—who was not a lawyer. Haldeman said "to hunker down" and do nothing. That was scarcely the sound, legal advice the president so badly needed.

I do not understand why Dean did not go directly to the president, lay the whole problem of his own vulnerability in the president's lap, and offer his resignation to be accompanied by a full pardon. Had Dean done that, and had Nixon been counseled by a knowledgeable defense lawyer instead of by federal prosecutor Henry Petersen (who was intent upon turning Dean to make obstruction cases), Nixon might have averted the awful fate that was to overtake him by reason of John Dean's testimony.

The following conversation on March 28, 1973 (Kutler, *Abuse of Power*, pp. 281-282) between Nixon and Haldeman shows Haldeman's lawyering in advising Nixon about court strategy and Nixon's confusion about the case being developed by Henry Petersen against the president and his administration. Nixon did not recognize the dangers presented by John Dean.

"I really feel that Dean's—Dean is a damn good thing here," Nixon told Haldeman. "I mean, I personally would stand back of him on it, that the White House counsel simply can't talk. You know?"

"Well, he's got to talk on his own charge," Haldeman pointed out. "I mean, if he's charged directly, unless he takes the Fifth, and then you've got to fire him."

Early in April, Nixon summoned Haldeman and Ehrlichman. The president, Haldeman noted (*The Haldeman Diaries*, p. 623), wanted to make two points about the Watergate situation that he thought were very important.

First, Nixon wanted everyone to understand that he was busy with other problems and "can't talk to the people that are concerned, that is Dean, Mitchell, Moore, Colson. . . ." Ehrlichman must deal with them.

Second, "there must be no falling out amongst our people. Having all of them going off in all directions. We can't have a situation of every man for himself. They're all on the team. No one's going to flush anybody and they must understand that." But loyalty does not flow on edicts. It is a contract. It must be mutual. This Nixon did not understand.

Nixon added that he felt "we've crossed the bridge on Dean and [the president] is not going to permit Dean to go up and testify."

The final meeting between John Dean and John Mitchell was emotional, dramatic, and loaded with tragedy. The two talked on April 10 in Mitchell's Washington law office. According to Emery (*Watergate*, p. 301) "the prosecutors urged Dean to go wired, but he says he indignantly refused."

How does a young man tell his benefactor, his mentor, and his father figure that he is turning state's evidence to save his own skin?

Well, here's how John Dean said he did it. (Dean, *Blind Ambition*, pp. 244 ff) Entering and taking a seat, Dean launched into it directly.

"John, the idea of having to testify against you is not a pleasant thought for me," Dean said. "You have to know that. But it may come to that if I'm called."

Dean explained that the cover-up had to end—it was ruining lives and endangering the president. Dean said he had tried to stop "this thing" in the first place. But now "Everybody's protecting themselves, and I think I've got to do the same thing. That's why I hired a lawyer. I don't want to be the scapegoat on all this."

"Don't get the impression, John, that I think you should take the rap for others," Mitchell said. "But I think your testimony could cause a terrible problem for the president."

Dean thought Mitchell was reaching for his "loyalty button."

"I know that, John," Dean replied, "and I don't want to do that. But I think we've already caused problems for the president, and they're going to be there no matter how I testify."

Mitchell nodded unhappily but said nothing. There was not much left to say. At least Dean gave notice to Mitchell what was coming, which is more than he did for Nixon. (Emery, *Watergate*, p. 302)

"The Mitchell thing is goddamn painful," Nixon said.

Mitchell returned to Washington on April 14 and made his last visit to the White House. Mister President had asked him to come, Martha said, but then did not meet with him. Instead of facing Mitchell himself, Nixon assigned Ehrlichman the task of getting Mitchell to take the rap for everybody. (McLendon, *Martha*, pp. 208-209)

Of course, Nixon never willingly gave anyone bad news. But the fact that Nixon did not participate in a face-to-face confrontation with his old and loyal friend is another example of the president's weaknesses.

Ehrlichman drew the assignment because he was a lawyer; Haldeman was not. The choice was unfortunate because of the deep animosity that existed between Ehrlichman and Mitchell.

Mitchell told Ehrlichman he knew nothing about the burglary and had nothing to offer. "There's certainly no possibility," Mitchell said, "that I would ever turn around and say, 'Yes, I was part and parcel of this.'" From Mitchell's standpoint, the whole scheme had been hatched by a group of White House aides whom he distrusted and some of whom he disliked, but he had not acted to quash Liddy's plan.

Ehrlichman reported their conversation to the president and offered the conclusion that Mitchell was not willing to be the fall guy. Mitchell was not Nixon's greatest danger. Dean was.

From the prosecution's standpoint, John Dean was the only person besides Haldeman and Ehrlichman who could testify to direct conversation with Nixon on the payment of hush money and blackmail. As things stood, without Dean's testimony the prosecutors had no case against Nixon himself. Now was the time for the president and his aides to conciliate Dean if they were ever going to do it. A good criminal defense lawyer—had Nixon had one at this point—almost certainly would have brought up the necessity of doing so.

At this juncture, President Nixon still could have legally pardoned Dean, Mitchell, Haldeman, Ehrlichman, Magruder, Liddy, and the burglars while accepting their resignations.

When the president found out that Dean was not going to produce the report he'd been asked for—but instead was negotiating a plea bargain for himself with prosecutors—one might have expected a presidential explosion of ire and indignation. The truth was that President Nixon was so vulnerable to Dean's testimony he dared not risk antagonizing Dean. The president assured Dean that he would be treated just as fairly as anybody else—that chilling pledge alone should have given Dean pause—and maintained a cordial relationship with Dean.

How does a young lawyer tell his client—the president of the United States—that to save his own skin he's going to turn state's evidence and testify against the client? Well, here's how John Dean says he did it (Dean, *Blind Ambition,* p. 258):

Dean dreaded this meeting with the president. He was embarrassed because he believed the president knew he had turned to the prosecutors. Dean wanted to tell Nixon before he heard the news from someone else, but he was afraid it was too late.

"Mr. President," Dean began, "I don't know if you've been told, but I have talked to the prosecutors. . . ."

"Yes," Nixon replied. "Kleindienst and Petersen were here to see me today."

Dean assured the president he had not acted out of disloyalty. "I hope someday you'll know I was being loyal to you when I did this." Dean said he felt it was the only way to end the cover-up, "and now I think you're in a position where you can step out in front of it."

The president nodded affirmatively and seemed quite friendly. "I understand, John," he said. "I want you to know I understand."

Then Nixon said, "John, let me ask you this. Have you talked to the prosecutors at all about your conversations with the president?" (Nixon often referred to himself by his title.)

"No, sir, Mr. President," Dean replied immediately. The John Dean I knew at the Justice Department was always properly deferential. "I haven't even talked to my lawyer about anything in that area. Those are privileged areas, as far as I'm concerned."

Dean thanked the president for his time and left. As he walked out, he felt relieved that the president had not exploded and called him a Judas.

Nixon believed from this interchange that John Dean was going to turn on Haldeman and Ehrlichman but was not going to testify against the president himself.

Apparently, Dean's first plan was to obtain immunity for himself in exchange for testifying against Haldeman and Ehrlichman. Dean maintained that both men were guilty of the cover-up along with him in arranging the flow of hush money and blackmail. But as the pressure mounted, Dean would not be able to protect the president.

He remained the president's nominal legal counsel, although he no longer came to his White House office nor did he perform any legal work for the president. Nixon phoned Dean from Key Biscayne on Easter Sunday, April 22, inviting Dean to "stop by the Oval Office at any time" and adding: "Remember, you're still the president's counsel." Another double message.

Soon Dean began sounding the president out on the question of immunity for himself. Nixon clearly saw a danger to himself in Dean's bid. At this stage of Watergate it must have appeared to the president that giving immunity to any of his staff was risky.

A grant of immunity—or a pardon—would have deprived John Dean of his right to invoke the Fifth Amendment against self-incrimination. Immunity might not have made much difference in the eventual outcome of the Democratic headquarters break-in case—the burglary and wiretapping cases were going to open up with or without John Dean. But it would have made a big difference in the obstruction cases. Even if Dean and Nixon had acted together to assert an attorney-client privilege (although we now know that communications between a government official and a government lawyer are *not* privileged), Dean would still have been compelled to testify to his conversations with Nixon because of the criminal nature of the conversations. But Dean might not have cooperated as fully and enthusiastically with the prosecution as actually happened.

Instead the president began negotiating with him as to the timing and conditions of the termination of his services. The president's apparent weakness emboldened Dean to demand the simultaneous resignations of Haldeman and Ehrlichman. Nixon became convinced that was the only way he could safely rid himself of Dean. Once Nixon made the decision to cut his men loose, he threw Kleindienst into the mix.

Kleindienst had recused himself—removed himself "entirely from the Watergate investigation." (Kleindienst, *Justice,* p. 164) But perhaps that wasn't enough. Perhaps he should offer to resign. "How can one be half an attorney general?" he asked himself. "Particularly when the bigger half is Watergate." (*Justice,* p. 166)

Nixon went to Camp David—and not, as he told Henry Petersen in a phone call, "to look at Easter lilies." He had to make his final decision. Should he grant leaves of absence to his men? Or should he ask them to resign? Ironically, this time Nixon had no one whom he could use as a sounding board.

Sunday, April 29, Kleindienst received instructions to take a White House helicopter to Camp David. The attorney general later wrote that he was shocked when he saw the "tired man" with "the weight of the world on his shoulders."

"I just can't continue on and I'm deeply sorry," Kleindienst said.

"[T]hat is why I asked you to come up here. . . . I want you to resign. I just can't function with half an attorney general," Nixon said.

"Then," Kleindienst later wrote, "came the blockbuster." Nixon intended to announce all the resignations—John Dean, John Ehrlichman, Bob Haldeman, and Attorney General Richard Kleindienst—at the same time. (Kleindienst, *Justice,* pp. 168-170)

The president already had an idea for Kleindienst's replacement. In a telephone call from Camp David (Kutler, *Abuse of Power,* p. 370), Nixon told Ehrlichman, "I have another name, John. . . . It occurred to me last night. . . . if I get an affirmative on it, I'll call you back and let you know."

Word of the possible shake-up in Nixon's top men leaked to the press. Henry Petersen told the president he had had a call from a newsman who said "they had a report out of the White House that—let me use his words—that two or three people in the White House were going to be *thrown to the wolves.*" (Emphasis added.)

Were the president's men thrown to the wolves? Indeed they were. Nixon's ultimate sacrifice did not divert the wolf pack. By that time the forest of Washington was full of hungry wolves in full cry. The wolves brought down the horses. President Nixon was left in the sleigh isolated and alone. The sleigh did not make it to the safety of the next village.

At nine o'clock in the evening of April 30, 1973, President Nixon went on national television to announce the "resignations" —a Washington euphemism for firing. In his talk, Nixon played on the sympathies of the American people with the same virtuosity he had displayed in 1952 in his "Checkers" speech—demonstrating that he still was more concerned with his public image than with his own vulnerability to possible criminal charges.

Nixon described Haldeman and Ehrlichman as "two of the finest public servants it has been my pleasure to know." Nixon said Kleindienst, "a distinguished public servant, my personal friend for twenty years," was resigning because of his "close personal and professional" association with people involved in Watergate. Then Nixon lifted one corner of the carpet and neatly swept John Dean under it. "The counsel to the president, John Dean, has also resigned."

He went on to say that "In any organization, the man at the top must bear the responsibility," and that he had "personally assumed the responsibility for coordinating intensive new inquiries into the [Watergate] matter." Perhaps the president hoped he was giving the nation the impression that he had cleaned out the Oval Office and that there would be no more surprises.

After his address, Nixon kept anxious tally over his personal telephone calls of congratulations. The loyal Haldeman was the first caller. Nixon fretted that the members of his cabinet had not called him. Like any actor, when Nixon put on a performance, he wanted critical acclaim.

Any chance Nixon had of surviving as president had been almost extinguished by the "resignations." In sacrificing his two gatekeepers and his attorney general, Nixon had increased his own vulnerability. Contrasted to a sixty-eight percent approval rating in January 1973, nationwide polls after April 30 indicated that forty-five percent of the public did not believe the president was telling the truth.

Nixon was in free fall toward impeachment. He had failed to realize that "The men and women who attach themselves to potential presidential candidates, whose glib TV images increasingly take precedence over substance—campaign managers, pollsters, advertising professionals, and speech writers—often exhibit the same rootless, non-ideological brand of loyalty that is frequently as ephemeral as that of the public at large. (Hoff, *Nixon Reconsidered*, p. 11)

Nixon made the fatal mistake of bringing his campaign aides into his administration as unsupervised people making independent, executive-level decisions. He compounded this mistake by failing to have an experienced criminal defense litigator as his own personal lawyer.

Nixon observed in his *Memoirs* (Vol. 2, p. 347): ". . . when everything began to fall apart, all that was left to me was to try to get myself into a position to be able to claim that I had cracked the case, trying to garner some credit for *leadership that I had failed to exert.*" (Emphasis added.)

"It took me a long time," Nixon told Monica Crowley *(Nixon in Winter*, p. 287) "to accept the fact that what happened [in Watergate] was my fault."

If the president understood this, it was a lesson tragically too late in the learning.

President Nixon did not crack the case. The case cracked due to the turned witnesses among Nixon's own men and to the persistent efforts of the U.S. attorneys, the courts, and Henry Petersen.

CHAPTER 10

Pressure Points

"*. . . it was the spring of hope, it was the winter of despair. . . .*"
—Charles Dickens

EVEN BEFORE NIXON BEGAN making strategic Watergate decisions, he was under terrific pressure from other aspects of his presidency. If he did not realize this at the time, he did so in retrospect: "Imagine the kind of pressure we were under!" (Crowley, *Nixon Off the Record*, p. 193) "We had the [Vietnam] war, hundreds of thousands of demonstrators, the press kicking us every night. And this was well before Watergate!"

"Without Vietnam," Haldeman said, "there would have been no Watergate."

The most immediate problem Nixon had to face in his first term was America's involvement in the Vietnam War, which the president inherited from his predecessors in the White House. Early in 1969, Nixon ordered secret bombings in neutral Cambodia.

The Vietnam War was costly in both lives and money and was extremely unpopular with large segments of the population, especially with college students. Frequent anti-war demonstrations resulted.

The president intended Veterans Day—November 11, formerly known as Armistice Day—to be part of a big National Unity Week effort. Instead, the war protesters decided to use the occasion to shut down the government with a gigantic anti-Vietnam protest demonstration in Washington. Their plan called for thousands of college students to descend on Washington, camp in the streets, block traffic, and shut down the capital. How shocked Nixon would have been if he had known that someone on the White House team later wrote: "My nephew [and] a dozen friends from Princeton, came down for the demonstration. . . . I [gave] them a ride to the White House . . . where they would demonstrate outside while I worked inside, and it gave me a good feeling." (Safire, *Before The Fall*, p. 427)

The government moved in 9,000 troops on November 12 and stationed them around Washington to help the metropolitan police and federal park police maintain order.

On the same day Mitchell's predecessor at the Justice Department, Ramsey Clark, announced he had recruited two hundred lawyers and seventy-five clergymen to help monitor the demonstration. Clark had a strong record in the area of individual and civil rights. As attorney general, he had helped draft the 1968 Civil Rights Act under President Johnson.

At first the November demonstration was comparatively orderly. Friday night, November 14, marchers held candlelight parades and gathered in front of the Vietnamese embassy.

The following day the demonstrations turned really ugly. Some 350,000 students and other protesters jammed the street, halting traffic. They tore down the American flag and ran up the Viet Cong banner. The Washington metropolitan police had assigned extra-duty policemen, and they handled the situation very well. The protesters did not succeed in shutting down the government, but in the afternoon the mob—which is exactly what it had become by that time—attacked the Justice Building. The police responded with tear gas.

Mitchell said he could smell tear gas in his offices for days. The press quoted him as comparing the demonstrators to "Hitler's Brownshirts." Trust Mitchell's wife Martha to be more colorful. She phoned one of her reporter friends and said when John looked down from his Justice Department window he thought it looked like the Russian revolution.

Nixon expressed what he called "cool contempt" by letting it be known he was watching a college football game on television while the protest was going on. He wanted to make it perfectly clear that demonstrations such as these would have no effect on the administration.

I was out of town during the November 1969 demonstration but I was directly involved in the big May Day demonstration in

1971. This particular civil disobedience demonstration began in late April with a five-day encampment of thousands in West Potomac Park for a rock concert. The anti-war people recruited the concert-goers to join the protest. The May Day demonstrators marched on the Pentagon, jamming traffic.

Again the stated purpose of these demonstrations was to shut down the government simply by making it impossible for government workers to reach their offices. They chose Monday morning, May 3, to block as many streets and bridges as possible to prevent people from getting back into the city to go to work. The plan failed because federal workers came back into town late Sunday night or before dawn Monday. The barricades created much commotion and frustration, but the demonstrators did not accomplish their mission.

In addition to some 5,000 Washington police, 2,000 District of Columbia National Guardsmen and 10,000 soldiers and U.S. Marines had been called in, along with helicopters for observation.

The Washington police canceled the demonstrators' permit and arrested between 7,000 and 12,000 anti-war protesters, the number depending upon who gave the accounting. Most of them were young people. Of course, no municipal jail is built to house that many people, so at first demonstrators were detained outdoors in a football field. The Washington spring weather was cool, and I seem to remember it was somewhat rainy. The detainees were moved to the enclosed Uline Arena.

Dick Kleindienst called me late that afternoon and asked me if I would help out. I was assigned to Uline Arena and was the senior Justice official on the scene. A number of young lawyers from the department were on hand as well as some high-ranking metropolitan police officers.

The sports arena had been used for horse shows, dog shows, and many other types of entertainment. Large ranks of powerful lights hung overhead along with colorful banners from some previous event. A railing extended around the floor of the building, with tiers of spectators' seats above the railing.

The protesters were transported by busloads. Police began by processing the detainees—that is, taking fingerprints and photographs or mug shots and checking the person's identity against outstanding warrants—as each got off the bus. This slow procedure created a bottleneck, so at the time that the protesters were moved to the arena, the police set up tables inside the building, did their processing, including mug shots, and released each person as the routine was completed.

In addition to the Washington police, a battalion of National Guard had been assigned to help us and were deployed in the spectators' seats. As the protesters were brought in, they remained on the floor level of the stadium. The police and the Guardsmen issued blankets and passed out bologna sandwiches. I suspect the sandwiches were prepared by trustees in the jail kitchen and sent over to us. They were not much—just two slices of bread and a slice of meat—but it was all any of us had to eat that night.

I set up a command post of sorts in the tiered seats. Every twenty or thirty minutes some of the police checked with me on points of law—most questions hinged on whether the person was to be charged and face prosecution or released without bond.

Luckily the police set up urns of hot black coffee for us. We needed the caffeine to keep us going all night. Most of the college students were keyed up on natural adrenaline—some possibly on drugs—and they were having a high old time. They apparently believed the attention they were getting was somehow helping to advance their cause. They were clapping, chanting, and singing.

In the middle of the night I watched a tall, rather dark and hairy young man get up and start a striptease chain dance. Although his action was spontaneous, I judged him to be a trained professional dancer. The others quickly formed in a long queue and followed him. Soon many were dancing along behind him and others were clapping in unison. The leader took off his shirt and tossed it in the air. Some behind him removed their shirts. He kept taking off his clothes one item at a time. Eventually he got rid of everything until he was stark naked. (This was two or three years before "streaking" became a national fad.) The other young people continued to dance but did not remove all their clothes.

As I watched their light-hearted shenanigans I could not keep from observing the obvious contrast between these idealistic youngsters and the organized crime figures who were the targets of the strike forces.

I believe it was not until about 3:30 in the morning that things subsided. Most of the demonstrators wrapped themselves up in their government-issue blankets and went to sleep. When they were all bedded down, I looked below me to the floor of the large sports arena to see a mosaic of closely packed olive-drab cocoons. The scene was almost pastoral.

We stayed there all night. Those protesters who remained—processed or not—were released around daylight. The police captain in charge wanted to stop and turn the rest of them loose in the middle of the night. I insisted that he keep going until daylight. I hoped we would catch Abbie Hoffman or the rest of the Chicago Seven, but that did not happen.

That morning Mitchell, Kleindienst, and I, with other Justice people, looked out of our office windows. *The New York Times* ran a photo of us watching yet another demonstration, this one much more peaceful. One of the leaders used a bullhorn to yell at the protesters, "Keep cool, man!"

What became known as the May Day conspiracy got national press coverage. Washington Police Chief Jerry V. Wilson (no relation) was given credit for the way he handled the situation. Jerry had served as an under-aged sailor on a navy minesweeper in World War II and later as a U.S. Marine Corps military policeman. He joined the police force in 1949 and worked his way up to chief in 1969. The law-and-order advocates could not have asked for a stronger ally.

Walter E. Washington's name appeared in many of the news stories. President Johnson had appointed him as chief commissioner of Washington, D.C. in 1967. (Congress had taken control of the city in 1874 with the president being given the responsibility for making appointments. Not for one hundred years, until May 1974, were the residents given the right to vote for their city officials.) Lyndon always called Washington "mayor" rather than commissioner. Dubbed the "walking mayor" by the press, Walter Washington was the first black mayor of any major American city.

None of us was especially surprised at the statements protesters gave to reporters. One protester said: "We were herded about like sheep by the cops."

As an outgrowth of the demonstrations, on May 13 the protesters filed a gigantic class action damage suit for $30 million in the United States District Court against Mitchell, Kleindienst, Chief of Police Wilson, Mayor Washington, and me. The suit alleged the May 3 mass arrests were "false and unreasonable," the charges were "malicious and wholly unsupported," and confinement was under "inhumane conditions."

Within the week the American Civil Liberties Union placed a full-page ad in *The Washington Post* asking anyone who had been arrested on May 3 to come forward and give affidavits. Thomas A. "Tom" Kennelly, formerly with the Criminal Division's Special Crimes Section, represented me in the class-action suit.

The case dragged along for nearly ten years after I left Washington, during which time I had to footnote the pending case in my financial statements. Eventually the action was dismissed.

Despite the turmoil resulting from continual protests, Nixon strengthened his determination to be re-elected in 1972. He scored a landslide victory over Democratic candidate George McGovern.

The years 1972, 1973, and 1974 should have been the best of his years. Instead they were the worst. On August 14, 1973, Congress ordered an immediate halt to the bombing of Cambodia. In the rapid changes of international alignments, the Egyptians—thinking that the American presidency would be paralyzed—commenced the Yom Kippur War on October 6, 1973, with surprise attacks on Israel. With the Soviet Union supporting Egypt and the United States continuing its support of Israel, the Yom Kippur War easily could have erupted into a global crisis. Nixon "reveled in crisis management [and ordered] the Pentagon to accelerate the airlift to Israel." (Emery, *Watergate*, p. 387)

On October 17 the Arab nations—members of OPEC (Organization of Oil Exporting Countries)—chose this troubled time when the presidency and the country were paralyzed to cut off oil shipments to the United States. OPEC nationalized U.S. oil holdings around the Persian Gulf.

Discover magazine (June 1999, p. 81ff) described the result of this:

> . . . When Arab nations cut off oil shipments to the United States during the 1973 war in the Middle East, prices abruptly rose 40 percent and panic ensued. Motorists idled in long lines at gas stations, where creeping tensions led to fights and even occasional shootings. Automakers scrambled to retool their assembly lines to manufacture miserly compacts rather than gas guzzling behemoths. Entrepreneurs poured millions into upstart solar-energy and wind-power companies.

Although North Vietnam had signed a cease fire, there was in fact no cease fire. The North continued a steady build-up of troops, roads, and war supplies, while both the government and economy of South Vietnam steadily degenerated. Throughout the year 1974, the North watched the development of Watergate closely. North Vietnamese generals concluded that because of Watergate, the United States would no longer defend South Vietnam. Soon after Nixon resigned, the North struck a decisive blow. Lacking support of the United States, the government of South Vietnam was destined to be crushed.

But Nixon's efforts on the international stage did nothing to protect his administration from internal problems. In the month of October 1973, President Nixon received Spiro Agnew's resignation as vice president, fired Archibald Cox (the Watergate special counsel), failed in his attempt to screen the White House tapes through Senator John Stennis, and gave up his fight against releasing the White House tapes as ordered by Judge John Sirica.

The press had seldom treated Nixon with total journalistic objectivity. When it was discovered that Nixon had lied about the secret Cambodia bombings, the suspicion arose that a president who could lie about that might be lying about other matters as well. Thus the press and the president became deadly adversaries.

Bob Woodward and Carl Bernstein of *The Washington Post* were young, charged-up investigative reporters who covered the Watergate break-in almost from the first day and just kept digging. Once their journalists' instincts were aroused, they would not let the story die. They wrote a series of articles which won a Pulitzer Prize for the *Post* and resulted in a best-selling book, *All the President's Men*, and later a popular motion picture.

As Ben Bradlee, executive editor of the *Post,* said: "Woodward and Bernstein . . . didn't have a back burner." (Bradlee, *A Good Life*, p. 331)

Early in their investigation, the two reporters became convinced that the Watergate break-in was only one of an astonishing number of illegal acts, including bugging, releasing false press leaks, faking a letter and altering documents, interfering with the Democratic party's campaigns, hiring dirty tricks, and planting spies and provocateurs among the Democrats. So the two reporters were motivated not only by a desire to be first with their stories but also by a determination not to let Nixon get away with a cover-up.

What they needed to keep their story alive was material to meet the journalistic demand for a new headline every few days. Woodward and Bernstein built a series of articles based on tips from an inside secret source in the White House they called Deep Throat.

Did Deep Throat really exist? Or was he a journalistic invention to dramatize and give credibility and unity to bits and pieces of information picked up from different sources?

Many people believed that Deep Throat simply appeared out of the woodwork—or, rather, out of a dark parking garage—only after the scandal of Watergate began unfolding. But Woodward said the two men had been friends for some time. "[Woodward's] friendship with Deep Throat was genuine, not cultivated. Long before Watergate, they had spent many evenings talking about Washington, the government, power." (Bernstein and Woodward, *All the President's Men*, New York: Simon & Schuster, 1974, p. 130)

At first Woodward said his informant talked to him on the telephone. Then Woodward said Deep Throat became uneasy and insisted on a set of prearranged signals. Woodward would leave a red flag in a flower pot on the balcony of his apartment. Deep Throat would mark a page of Woodward's *New York Times* with a drawing of a clock, indicating a time to meet.

Woodward said he never did know how Deep Throat got to his morning newspaper to mark it.

Woodward said that the two men—Woodward and the informant—met covertly. Deep Throat fed Woodward tantalizingly small bits of information at a time, probably to protect his own secret identity. "If he told me everything he knew all at once, a good Plumber might be able to find the leak. By making reporters go elsewhere to fill out his information, he minimized his risk." (*All the President's Men*, p. 243)

From Nixon's point of view, Deep Throat was a mole—a highly placed insider who spies for the enemy.

Some suspect that Woodward created his own mole—Deep Throat—and used him to lend authenticity to his Watergate stories and also as a divisive psychological weapon in his effort to expose the Nixon cover-up. The constant references to a successful mole operating inside the top level in the Nixon Administration helped create an atmosphere of frustration, confusion, and mutual suspicion. This probably gave Woodward and Bernstein more leaks. It also undermined the morale and confidence of people working in the White House and of Richard Nixon.

Complying with newspaper tradition, and the journalistic code of ethics, Woodward at first refused to identify his source—even to his editor, Ben Bradlee, or to the *Post* publisher, Katherine Graham. Later, he told them both.

Woodward did say Deep Throat talked as "an act of conscience—a result of his own disillusionment." The reporter repeatedly insisted that Deep Throat was a real person, not a composite, and that his co-author Carl Bernstein knew Deep Throat's real identity.

In the extensive literature about Watergate, there are a number of suggestions as to Deep Throat's true identity.

The first is from Ehrlichman's *Witness to Power* (p. 394): "As we crossed the prairies our car radio couldn't pick up all of Kleindienst's testimony, and we missed most of Henry Petersen, too; but I heard enough. Petersen was a bureaucrat with a cause; I suspect his objective was always Richard Nixon's ruin. If I were required to make a nomination for 'Deep Throat,' Henry Petersen would be mine."

Petersen well may have been leaking to Woodward—and almost surely was—but I do not think that he himself was Deep Throat. Prior to his April 15 meeting with the president, Petersen had no access to inside White House information except through FBI reports. I think it unlikely that Petersen could have known about the eighteen-and-a-half-minute gap on the June 20 tape, which Deep Throat reported at a time when the gap was known only to a very few people working in the White House. Many of Nixon's and Petersen's conversations were recorded on tape and have since been published. I found nothing to indicate that anyone told Petersen about the gap. I feel quite sure Petersen had never been to the offices of the Committee to Re-elect and would not have known anyone working there.

A second suggestion for the identity of Deep Throat is contained in the book *Silent Coup: The Removal of Richard Nixon* (New York: St. Martin's, 1991), by Len Colodny and Robert Gettlin. Their candidate is Gen. Alexander Haig, whom they say had contacts with Woodward while Woodward was a young naval officer assigned to the Joint Chiefs of the General Staff as a briefing officer. After Haldeman's resignation, General Haig became White House chief of staff for a brief period and guided Nixon toward resignation.

Colodny and Gettlin believed that even if Haig had not been Woodward's source for Bernstein and Woodward's *All the President's Men*, he may well have been the source for *The Final Days* (Bob Woodward and Carl Bernstein, *The Final Days,* New York: Simon & Schuster, 1978). They said (*Silent Coup*, p. 89), "Articles and reviews in 1976 and since that time have wondered whether Haig was a key source for that book, because on page after page the authors reconstructed what was said in White House meetings and conversations of the most intimate and sensitive kind, many of which involved Haig . . . some passages include private scenes between Nixon and his chief of staff, Haig, in which the thoughts and feelings of both men are described."

Asked if he believed Haig had been Deep Throat, Nixon said, "No, they are wrong about that. . . . Haig was not the source. He was damn loyal." (Crowley, *Nixon in Winter,* p. 298)

Haig was not unaware of rumors linking him to Deep Throat. When Haig became a candidate for the Republican party's nomination for president in 1988, he begged *The Washington Post* to print a story stating that he was not Deep Throat. Woodward finally made a public statement to that effect.

A third suggestion as to the identity of Deep Throat is contained in George V. Higgins's *The Friends of Richard Nixon* (New York: Little, Brown, 1975, p. 126). Higgins said that "Mark Felt [then associate director of the FBI] knows more reporters than most reporters do and there are those who think that he had a *Washington Post* alias borrowed from a dirty movie."

When Bob Haldeman suggested that Felt and Deep Throat were one and the same, Felt snapped back: "This is not the first time Haldeman has been wrong."

The public's curiosity about Deep Throat's true identity continues—or at least, recurs. Twenty-five years later, David Daley of the *Hartford* (Connecticut) *Courant* (July 31, 1999) again raised the question of Mark Felt. Felt certainly had access to the FBI reports on the Watergate investigations. However, as far as I know he would have had no knowledge of the activities inside the Committee to Re-elect the President headquarters, nor of the events taking place in the internal turmoil of the Nixon White House.

According to Bob Woodward, Deep Throat was a patriotic federal official who secretly met with Woodward "trying to protect the office [of the presidency], to effect a change of conduct before all was lost."

If you are seeking a detective to track down Deep Throat, you could not do better than to employ John Dean. After his release from prison, Dean set himself the task of identifying Deep Throat with the assistance of a source he dubbed "Deep Thought."

The last chapter of Dean's second book, *Lost Honor* (Los Angeles: Stratford Press, 1982), is devoted to marshaling all the clues to Deep Throat's identity. He concluded that Al Haig was Deep Throat. If Dean guessed correctly, Al Haig would emerge as a sinister figure—one who, while ostensibly giving Nixon support and encouragement as his chief of staff, steadily and unrelentingly worked toward the president's resignation.

The secret informant's identity remained an especially vexing puzzle for Bob Haldeman. Deep Throat surely must have been someone Haldeman knew and worked with on a frequent basis. In *The Ends of Power* (New York: Time Books, 1978, p. 135), Haldeman cites a CIA memo that Robert Bennett "is feeding information to Bob Woodward." Bennett was president of a public relations firm and represented the interests of Howard Hughes in Washington. Could Deep Throat have been one of Hughes's "interests in Washington"?

But Haldeman rejected Bennett and proposed Fred Fielding, John Dean's staff assistant. Haldeman argued that Fielding would have been well placed to know much of what was leaked to the *Post*. On the other hand, Haldeman said, Fielding did not know everything; his attempts to guess or to fill in with his imagination may have accounted for any misleading information Woodward received from Deep Throat.

Why has continued anonymity been necessary for Deep Throat? Jim Hougan (*Secret Agenda: Watergate, Deep Throat, and the CIA*, p. 281, New York: Random House, 1984) has an interesting hypothesis. "Clearly, Deep Throat's anonymity has nothing to do with job security. . . . [he] remains anonymous because if he is identified our perception of him and of the *Post*'s Watergate reportage would change."

Hougan concluded that Al Haig matched a large number of the "clues" revealed by Woodward and Bernstein. If not the well-known Haig, then perhaps an unknown member of the intelligence community—to whom the flag-in-the-flowerpot routine would have seemed like standard operating procedure.

Speculation also focused for a time on Diane Sawyer, television journalist and co-host on CBS's *60 Minutes*. In late June 1995, she denied a claim that she had been the source of Woodward's information.

Woodward and Bernstein operated in an atmosphere of running warfare and hostility between journalists and public officials. This team was more responsible for the exposure of Watergate than any other journalists, and *The Washington Post* clearly took the lead among newspapers in bringing about Nixon's downfall.

Bob Woodward, in *Shadow*: *Five Presidents and the Legacy of Watergate* (New York: Simon & Schuster, 1999), traces the influences and effects of Watergate through the presidencies of Gerald Ford, Jimmy Carter, Ronald Reagan, George Bush, and Bill Clinton.

Even if Deep Throat was pure fiction, such a journalistic device might be justified as furnishing cover for those White House insiders who were leaking to Woodward and Bernstein.

Woodward's book would seem to be his wrap-up of Watergate. He does not reveal the identity of Deep Throat. Woodward stated that he sought permission to reveal Deep Throat's identity, but the informant held Woodward to his promise—Deep Throat will remain anonymous until after his death.

CHAPTER 11

The President and Henry Petersen

"[Petersen is] all I've got, Bob."
—President Nixon to Haldeman

AT A CRUCIAL TURNING point in Watergate, President Nixon—at the suggestion of Attorney General Richard Kleindienst —turned to Henry Petersen for legal advice and guidance. Petersen, in direct command of the prosecutors, was busy supervising the making of criminal cases against Nixon's key staff members who were still in place in their jobs.

Did Nixon choose the right lawyer to advise him?

Legal ethics are much like natural laws. They are as much a formula that is certain to work as they are rules of conduct. This new assignment presented Petersen with two ethical questions. The first involved his directive limiting the original investigation to the men already arrested for the break-in. Did this violate his duty as a Justice Department official? The second was his designation by Kleindienst as counsel to the president. Did this create a "client" conflict between his duties as chief prosecutor and his loyalty to the president?

From his widespread sources of information—built up over a number of years as a career Civil Service person—Petersen had been the first Justice Department official to learn of the Watergate break-in.

People like Henry Petersen, scattered throughout the federal government, make its cumbersome bureaucracy work well in spite of the constitutional divisions into executive, legislative, and judicial branches. Petersen could communicate quickly by telephone across departmental boundaries with second- and third-level people in other departments whom he knew on a first-name basis from old cases and past crises. Petersen knew those connections were his advantage vis-à-vis the political appointee occupying the top spot who came and went with each new presidential administration.

He maintained, as well, close personal contacts in the key big-city U.S. attorneys' offices, so it was within standard operating procedure for Harold Titus, U.S. attorney for the District of Columbia, to phone Petersen the minute he learned that the five burglars arrested in the Watergate break-in had connections to the federal government.

Petersen had been my deputy during the almost three years I headed the Criminal Division. Henry and I had worked closely together in the Criminal Division. I knew him well and liked him.

Like so many of us at the time, Henry was a veteran, having served in the U.S. Marine Corps during World War II. His first job was in the FBI as a messenger and tour guide while working his way through Georgetown University, the country's oldest Jesuit university, and then as a night student at Catholic University Law School. He was brittle, caustic, and rather blunt. He saw issues in clear-cut black or white, rarely allowing his quick judgments to be clouded by shades of gray. He perfectly mirrored his Jesuitical training.

He was also smart and effective and completely loyal to the Justice Department, where he had spent his entire professional career. He was totally dedicated to his work, much of which had been against organized crime—a field of endeavor often involving political risk.

As a Civil Service career man, Petersen spent most of his time in a comparatively comfortable position. The political appointees were out in the glare of publicity, taking the responsibility and the credit or heat for the wisdom or error of departmental decisions.

When I resigned from the Justice Department in late 1971, Attorney General Mitchell recommended that Petersen be moved up to my slot. Then Petersen—as the assistant attorney general, Criminal Division—was himself in the position of a political appointee. The press made a point of describing Petersen as the first career Justice person to be appointed as assistant attorney general.

Traditionally such positions have been patronage appointments to supporters from the president's political party. In a conflict of loyalties, this distinction could make a big difference.

Petersen did not get his job by being a loyal Nixon Republican. He always kept his politics separate from his profession, but he was in fact a registered Democrat and this truly reflected his blue-collar origins.

Even more significant from Nixon's viewpoint, Petersen had been closely associated with Robert Kennedy. By chance, Petersen's and Kennedy's first jobs were as lawyers in the Justice Department at the same time. Later, when Kennedy became attorney general, Petersen was a member of his Organized Crime section and a vital part of the Band of Brothers. Furthermore, Petersen regularly played golf with William Hundley, former special assistant to Attorney General Kennedy, reflecting his grounding as a Kennedy insider.

From my observations of Henry's conduct and a careful study of the presidential transcripts, I believe his personal loyalty to the Kennedys was never a factor in the Watergate investigation. I see nothing arising from Petersen's former association with Bobby Kennedy to indicate shaping of his degree of loyalty to the Nixon Administration. Henry was a professional.

When Attorney General Kleindienst and John Dean met on June 20, 1972—that first Tuesday after the weekend Watergate break-in—Kleindienst already was aware from his Burning Tree golf course encounter with Gordon Liddy that Watergate might go to the top. "If Mitchell is involved," Kleindienst told Dean, "I'll resign before I prosecute him." (Emery, *Watergate*, p. 172)

Henry Petersen was called in to join that first meeting. From the start Petersen knew what Kleindienst knew. In his later testimony before the Senate Watergate Committee, Petersen said he had wanted to urge the president to "run an all-out investigation and let the devil take the hindmost"—to which Dean had replied: "I don't think the White House can stand an all-out investigation." (Emery, *Watergate*, p. 172)

Kleindienst said he cautioned Dean that a Justice Department investigation was like a river. "Once it starts flowing . . . it must take its inevitable course. The president should understand this." According to Emery (*Watergate*, pp. 171-172), "It sounded great, but it didn't happen." Emery suggested that "Kleindienst's version [Kleindienst, *Justice*, p. 146] of this meeting is totally self-exculpatory."

Kleindienst, Petersen, and Dean agreed that there should not be an investigation of the White House during an election year. Petersen assured Dean that the assistant U.S. attorney, Earl Silbert, had been instructed to limit his investigation to the break-in itself and not to use the case as an excuse to investigate White House activities. That was just what Dean wanted to hear, but not what happened. Both Silbert's staff and the FBI ignored this and continued to follow their leads.

I would defend Petersen in those first instructions, which resulted from his having worked some twenty years in the Justice Department. Petersen was a cautious man. I suppose that in any large organization it would be very dangerous to investigate your superiors. In this fallible world, Petersen was quite right in assuming control of the case himself, in attempting to place boundaries around it, and in treading carefully in investigating White House staff members. But he should not have attempted to limit the investigatory agencies following their leads. It was this very area that later got Nixon involved in an obstruction charge when he suggested using the CIA to stop the FBI investigation of the laundering in Mexico of money paid to the burglars.

It is true that the mark of a good investigation is the ability to focus on the main event and not chase rabbits on side trails which take the investigator off the main target. But the main target here was the discovery of the author of the break-in—the person who planned it, employed the burglars, and funded the operation. The first man in the chain was Gordon Liddy.

If Petersen's instructions to the prosecutors to confine the case to the men arrested had been followed, the investigation would have missed Liddy. Silbert and Glanzer ignored Petersen and went right ahead developing a case against Liddy, who was indicted along with the others.

Dean told the president that some people might go to jail—Dean himself, for one.

"You go to jail?" The president clearly was surprised. "Oh, hell no! I can't see how you can. . . . What would you go to jail for?"

"The obstruction of justice," Dean explained. "That is the only one that bothers me."

"I feel it could be cut off at the pass, maybe—the obstruction of justice," the president told Dean. (*The Presidential Transcripts*, pp. 116-117)

Nixon had never been a prosecutor. It is obvious to me that he knew very little about the dynamic of an expanding criminal investigation.

In the transcripts of the same meeting, Nixon asked, "Why did Petersen play so straight with us?" The very fact that the president could ask such a question indicates that he did not consider Petersen to be a part of the Nixon inner circle.

"Because Petersen is a soldier," Dean replied. "He kept me informed. He told me when we had problems, where we had problems. . . . He believes in you and he believes in this administration. This administration has made him. I don't think he has done anything improper but he did make sure that the investigation was narrowed down to the very, very fine criminal thing which was a break for us."

The "us" Dean had in mind were the two cover-up conspirators, Nixon and himself. Much of the conversation among Nixon, Bob Haldeman, and Dean on that tape involved the men's plans to use Petersen, to take advantage of his honesty and integrity.

"Henry Petersen is the only man I know," said Dean, "[who is] bright enough and knowledgeable enough in the criminal laws and the process that could really tell us how this could be put together so that it did the maximum to carve it away with a minimum damage to individuals involved." This statement should be emphasized. Dean did not know any criminal defense lawyers.

Referring to the cover-up, the president asked: "Petersen doesn't know, does he?"

"That's right. No. I know he doesn't know," Dean replied. "I know he doesn't know. I'm talking about somebody who I have over the years grown to have enough faith in. . . . It would have to put him in a very difficult situation as the head of the Criminal Division of the United States Department of Justice, and the oath of office. . . ."

But his job also put John Dean in a very difficult position.

Later in the same conversation, the president proposed a special prosecutor. "We could use Petersen, or use another one."

"I would like to have Petersen on our side, if I do this [grand jury] thing," Dean responded. The grand jury "thing" to which Dean referred was the use of perjured testimony.

"Well, Petersen is honest. There isn't anybody about to question him, is there?" Nixon asked.

"No," Dean said, "but he will get a barrage when these Watergate hearings start."

Nixon, Dean, and Haldeman discussed the various investigations they faced. Dean returned to the subject of Petersen. "I will tell you the person that I feel we could use as counsel on this, because he understands the criminal process better than anybody over here does." Dean admitted Petersen's position would make it "awkward" for him. "We almost need him out of there [Justice Department] to take his counsel. . . ." That was a very shrewd observation on Dean's part. They did badly need someone outside of the Justice Department to counsel and guide them.

Nixon had a remedy. "Why couldn't the President call him in as Special Counsel to the White House for the purpose of conducting an investigation?" Nixon did not act on this at once, but events yet to come gave the president an opening to take advantage of Petersen's expertise.

Soon Petersen was placed in the position of serving two masters.

"Petersen won't know what happens at the grand jury until late in the day, but we can probably find out from him," Haldeman wrote in his first reference to Petersen in *The Haldeman Diaries* (March 27, 1973, p. 612). From then on Petersen kept Dean, in his ostensible role as the president's legal counsel, informed about the progress of the government's case, even to the extent of providing summaries of grand jury testimony—right up until John Dean cracked and turned.

Kleindienst received a rather lengthy phone call from John Ehrlichman on March 28, 1973, and the call happened to be one which was taped and later transcribed. (*The Presidential Transcripts*, pp. 216-220) Kleindienst mentioned his Sunday, March 25, television appearance during which he repeatedly said: "The President wants this investigated, let the chips fall where they may." Ehrlichman responded that "the best information [the president] has is that neither Dean nor Haldeman nor Colson nor I nor anybody in the White House had any prior knowledge of this burglary." And that may have been true.

Ehrlichman's statement did not extend to John Dean's cover-up. In light of Dean's previous "cancer on the presidency" conversation, obviously Ehrlichman was not yet considering the cover-up as a separate obstruction of justice offense.

"[The president is] concerned about Mitchell," Ehrlichman continued, and Kleindienst replied, "So am I." Ehrlichman said the president would expect a "private communication" from Kleindienst if any information developed "with regard to John [Mitchell]."

Kleindienst clearly perceived the potential problem. "When you talk about Mitchell and me that really creates the highest conflict of interest," he said. He again used the opportunity to suggest a special prosecutor—although he added "by doing that you in effect say publicly, well, okay, the Department of Justice and the attorney general, the U.S. attorney and the FBI are all corrupt."

Although John Ehrlichman himself was a lawyer with some seventeen years of experience, he was not familiar with criminal law. Ehrlichman asked Kleindienst who had authority to appoint a special prosecutor and how it could be done.

"Well, I don't know," Kleindienst replied. "I think the president could appoint somebody as a special prosecutor to direct the FBI to cooperate with him, giving them an opportunity to hire some attorneys, you know, on his staff and then just have complete authority to have his own investigation and if there's evidence that comes out that there were acts of criminal behavior have them presented to a grand jury then proceed with it."

There's an interesting comment by Haldeman (*The Haldeman Diaries*, p. 623) that Richard Moore, a longtime friend of Nixon's, "had lunch with Kleindienst and [they] got into the special prosecutor thing, and John [Ehrlichman] feels that's simply a device on Kleindienst's part to avoid Kleindienst having to do in Mitchell."

Ehrlichman questioned Kleindienst closely about immunity—how it was granted and to what purpose. "And this business of the grant of immunity to witnesses before the grand jury," Ehrlichman asked. "Is that peculiarly in the province of the court?"

Ehrlichman, at least, seems to have been considering immunity for someone.

The president had taken no immediate action to bring Petersen into the White House. I do not believe there was any way that a tough, experienced, and outspoken criminal lawyer like Petersen could have been brought that close without becoming a serious danger to the conspirators and without learning of Nixon's vulnerability. To have invited Petersen into the White House would have been tantamount to calling in the cat to guard the mice.

And yet, that is exactly what Nixon did do when he chose Petersen as his legal counsel for the critical and pivotal weeks leading up to the firing of Haldeman and Ehrlichman and the resignation of Kleindienst.

For Nixon and his administration, everything began to fall apart in April 1973. One by one the last standing dominoes began to topple until no one would be left but the president and his prosecutors—who were, as it turned out, locked in a death embrace.

While Dean was talking to the federal prosecutors, Acting Director Pat Gray was suffering through his Senate confirmation hearing upon his nomination to become permanent director of the FBI. When it became obvious Gray could not be confirmed, he withdrew his nomination. The president asked the Environmental Protection Agency director, William Ruckelshaus, to step in and hold the FBI together until a new permanent director could be nominated.

While the president and his aides were watching to see how Mitchell and Dean were standing up to pressure, Jeb Magruder became the first White House insider to turn and accept a plea bargain in exchange for his full testimony.

Anyway you look at it, Magruder's turning was dreadful news for the other Nixon men and for Nixon himself. If Nixon had had the advice of a good criminal defense lawyer, his counsel could have analyzed the situation in advance and should have advised the president to make his peace with Magruder long before he was turned by the prosecutors.

Magruder submitted to the advice of his attorneys, James Bierbower and James Sharp, and "got a deal they couldn't refuse—a one-count felony indictment . . . in exchange for Magruder's full cooperation. Magruder, the former deputy director of the President's re-election campaign, grabbed it." (Lukas, *Nightmare*, p. 308) Magruder's testimony took the prosecutors beyond Liddy to Dean, Haldeman, and Ehrlichman and gave the trial prosecutors a giant step forward in increasing the voltage of the case.

Although the turning of Magruder became a critical factor in the fall of President Nixon, the negotiations between Silbert and

Glanzer and Magruder's lawyers were handled as a local prosecution and were not submitted to the president. The fact that the prosecutors working in the district court could turn Magruder without Nixon knowing about it in advance indicates that Nixon was exercising no command authority over the prosecutors. It is likely that the prosecutors used information from their conversation with John Dean to turn Magruder and information from their conversations with Magruder to turn Dean. This is the way they usually worked.

We do not know how much if anything Petersen knew about the negotiations with Magruder's attorneys before his turning. But someone would have had to approve the diminution of sentence for Magruder, and that was probably the U.S. attorney. He may not have submitted the question to Petersen. Again it is strange that Nixon did not have enough personal contact with his own U.S. attorney in Washington, D.C., Harold Titus, to learn beforehand about the turning of his own deputy campaign manager. This is a testimony to the tightness of the barriers erected by Haldeman around Nixon. I can't imagine something as serious as this slipping up on Lyndon Johnson.

Kissinger told the president that the time had come "to take some brutal measures." Nixon replied, "There's no more brutal measures . . . than [sacrificing] John Mitchell and Magruder . . . Mitchell's a decent man. Magruder's a decent man. (Kutler, *Abuse of Power,* p. 314f)

That same afternoon, Silbert and Glanzer met with Petersen in his Justice Department office and spread out the whole case for him—everything they had learned so far from negotiations with Dean, now apparently substantiated by Magruder. Putting together all the information, the federal prosecutors now saw a massive obstruction of justice case against Mitchell, Dean, Mardian, LaRue, Magruder, Haldeman, and Ehrlichman—but not necessarily reaching Nixon himself.

Petersen's "world had fallen in," as Emery put it. "Mitchell had been his boss, given him his chance and his unprecedented promotion . . . [Petersen] had trusted Dean, but [Dean] and Mitchell had duped him." (Emery, *Watergate*, p. 319)

Later that Saturday evening, Kleindienst struggled with his white tie, getting ready to attend the annual dinner of the White

House press corps. Nixon also attended the White House Correspondents' Dinner. He noted in his diary: "It's rather ironic that the winners of the awards are from the *Washington Post.*" (Nixon, *Memoirs,* Vol. 2, p. 350)

The following account is based on Kleindienst's *Justice,* pp. 158-160.

Ehrlichman phoned Kleindienst and broke the news that Jeb Magruder had decided to "come clean" and "implicated everybody . . . in the Committee to Re-elect." Ehrlichman did not tell Kleindienst where he had gotten his information.

"No kidding," Kleindienst replied. "Magruder?"

"Yep. Cold turkey."

Kleindienst and Ehrlichman continued their conversation, discussing possible acts of perjury and conspiracy which may have been committed. "Be very careful what you do," Kleindienst warned Ehrlichman. "Yours is a very goddamn delicate line as to what you do to get information to give to the President and what you can do in giving information to the Department of Justice."

Ehrlichman closed the conversation with the unwelcome news that Magruder had also implicated two of Kleindienst's friends, Bob Mardian and Fred LaRue, both Nixon insiders.

Shortly after midnight, a very agitated Petersen phoned Kleindienst, saying, "I have to see you at once." He arrived at the attorney general's McLean, Virginia, home with Harold Titus and Earl Silbert in tow.

"What about the president?" Kleindienst asked when he had heard their account of Magruder's story. Neither Magruder nor Dean implicated the president, the prosecutors said. Haldeman and Ehrlichman had "erected a shield in front of the president," Kleindienst was told. Apparently, Dean was keeping to his plan to turn on Haldeman and Ehrlichman but not on Nixon.

The prosecutors gathered at Kleindienst's house and talked until the early hours of Sunday, April 15. Later that morning, Kleindienst phoned the White House and requested a meeting with the president. An interesting sidelight: at the press corps dinner the night before, Kleindienst had agreed to a meeting at his home with "Woodstein" (Woodward and/or Bernstein) for Sunday. Mrs. Kleindienst had to make Dick's apologies.

Kleindienst had to wait until Palm Sunday services were concluded at the White House. Nixon met with him at about 1:12 in the afternoon in the president's office in the Executive Office Building.

"You . . . would, you'd believe John Mitchell, I suppose, wouldn't you?" (*White House Transcripts*, p. 450) Later in the conversation, the president suggests to Kleindienst: "You step aside, say that the Deputy Attorney General of the United States will be in charge of the matter." (*Transcripts*, p. 455)

The president concludes: "Dean doesn't know personally anything about criminal law." Once again, Kleindienst argues for a special prosecutor.

Kleindienst plunged right in, telling the president the gist of Petersen's report. Nixon interrupted him to offer coffee or a soft drink, but Kleindienst kept to the subject.

"I [am] wondering whether Magruder is telling the whole truth on John Mitchell . . . have you talked to Mitchell?" Nixon asked.

"No, and I'm not going to," Kleindienst answered. "I don't think that I can talk to him."

It is strange that Nixon was not talking to John Mitchell almost daily. During the time I knew him, Mitchell had constant contact with the president. It is strange that after John Mitchell advised Magruder to get an attorney, Mitchell seems to have had no further contact with Magruder. Magruder must have felt isolated and completely abandoned by Nixon and his staff.

Nixon questioned the attorney general closely: Just exactly what constituted obstruction of justice? Kleindienst took him through the point of law step by step. Clearly, Nixon was just learning about the obstruction of justice statute after most of the cover-up had already been done.

While I was in the Justice Department, I do not remember using the obstruction of justice statute in any but organized crime cases. I must say that it is not unusual for lawyers who have not been federal prosecutors nor practiced criminal law to be unfamiliar with the federal obstruction of justice statute—as Nixon, Ehrlichman, and Dean all were obviously unfamiliar with it at the beginning of Watergate. I have concluded that in June 1972, when Nixon first assigned John Dean the job of containing the Watergate break-in until after the presidential campaign, Nixon was not even aware of the obstruction of justice statute. I will go further and add that I believe any person assuming the presidency should have a complete and thorough briefing on the obstruction of justice statute before taking the oath of office.

Nixon and Kleindienst discussed the pros and cons of appointing a special prosecutor. Nixon said, "See, my point is [if] you call in a special prosecutor, he's got to learn the whole damn thing." (*The Presidential Transcripts*, p. 387) Kleindienst explained that a special prosecutor would not try the case; Silbert, as the U.S. attorney, would do that. I do not know where Kleindienst got this idea.

Late in the conversation the president asked, "What is Petersen's reasoning?"

Kleindienst replied, "Petersen's reasoning is that I should recuse myself now that it looks like Mitchell. . . ." Kleindienst was having difficulty facing up to destroying John Mitchell. He explained his withdrawal would not be made public but rather would be "internal—administrative."

Kleindienst suggested that an independent lawyer—someone with no connection to the Justice Department—should be brought on board to develop the government's case in the Watergate break-in. Nixon rejected the scheme, calling it "too much of a reflection on our system of justice." Kleindienst then suggested Henry Petersen for the job.

We know from the March 21 tapes that Nixon had already received good job references for Petersen.

"Petersen is the fellow to approach?" the president asked.

"Yes, he is," Kleindienst affirmed.

"I didn't—he was—he is a career man—I didn't appoint him in the first place," Nixon mused as he evaluated Kleindienst's recommendation. (*The Presidential Transcripts*, p. 401)

Kleindienst returned to his office and phoned Petersen to join him.

Petersen had been spending his Sunday afternoon working on his boat. When the attorney general summoned him, Henry was wearing a smudged T-shirt, jeans, and tennis shoes. He lighted another of his inevitable cigarettes and listened tensely as Kleindienst explained that the entire responsibility for the Watergate prosecution now devolved upon him.

While Kleindienst and Petersen were talking, the president phoned and asked Kleindienst to return. Kleindienst requested permission to bring Petersen along. For Kleindienst to ask Petersen to accompany him as a technical adviser on criminal law matters was proper. In my opinion, however, Kleindienst should not have delegated responsibility to Petersen to advise the president. At this juncture Kleindienst—as attorney general and with his president in high danger—should have assumed personal command of the situation. Also he should have insisted on the president's having his own personal counsel, and he should have urged the president to employ the best criminal defense lawyer he could find.

Kleindienst, sick with worry about Mitchell's situation, allowed this to confuse his obligations as attorney general to the president. But with Kleindienst's withdrawal, Petersen became both the president's de facto attorney general for Watergate and his personal legal adviser.

Petersen worked hourly and daily with a president who was caught between his own conflicting loyalties—his duty as president to enforce the law on the one hand and on the other his loyalty to himself, his continuity in office, his men, and the Republican party.

In judging Henry Petersen's ethical conduct during the next two weeks, one must first ask the same questions which were asked so often about President Nixon by an Ervin Committee member, Senator Howard Baker: What did he know and when did he know it? How much did Petersen know about the president's vulnerability that Sunday afternoon when he went with Kleindienst to meet with the president?

Petersen knew soon after the Watergate break-in that the burglars were employees of the Committee to Re-elect. He knew that in the beginning the supervision of the Watergate problem had been assigned not to the Justice Department but to John Dean, the president's legal counsel. (As an aside, this is an example of Nixon's distrust of the federal bureaucracy and of his use of a Nixon loyalist to circumvent the bureaucracy.)

Petersen was not yet certain of Dean's exact role, but he did know that in the beginning the FBI—at the president's request—had allowed Dean to sit in on their interviews with White House personnel. He was aware of a shifting of emphasis, and of the great opportunity opening to the prosecutors signaled by the ongoing attempts to turn John Dean and obtain his testimony. He was aware of Dean's eager bargaining for immunity and of the prosecution's refusal to grant it—and why. He was aware that Magruder had turned.

Also, he was aware that John Dean, counsel to the president, had very little legal experience and practically no criminal law experience. And he knew the awesome power of the federal trial prosecutors in a situation of this sort. Once a witness starts talking, that witness usually will be unable to hold back anything. Petersen realized the entire command of the situation rested with the president—who might himself be the number-one target.

On the other hand, Petersen was not yet aware of Dean's very incriminating March 21, 1973, "cancer on the presidency" conversation with President Nixon. He was not aware of John Dean's coaching of Magruder to commit perjury before the grand jury and of John Dean's payment of hush money to the burglars. But he had reported to John Dean the substance of Magruder's grand jury testimony that Magruder had not implicated the president. He was not aware of Nixon's efforts to use the CIA to block the FBI from tracing the route of some $89,000 in campaign-donation checks through Mexico. He was not aware of a taping system within the White House.

And he was not yet aware of the Fielding break-in—though he soon would learn—nor was he aware of the real reason for Nixon's overriding desire to keep the Fielding break-in from becoming public.

That fateful Sunday afternoon of April 15—and with this degree of knowledge—Petersen accompanied his boss to the White House.

Although Petersen had seen the president at certain official or ceremonial functions, that was the first time Nixon had met Petersen. Nixon later wrote in his *Memoirs* (pp. 357-358) that he liked the man at once. Petersen courteously apologized to the president for the way he was dressed, but the Henry Petersen I knew would have been too poised and self-confident to let his informal attire place him at any disadvantage.

Upon opening the conversation, Petersen did not give President Nixon the prosecutor's Miranda warning. This is a face-to-face notice to a possible defendant that he does not have to talk to the prosecution and that if he does talk, what he says can be used against him in a trial. Knowing as Petersen did that the trail led right up to Nixon's front door, and being in charge of the prosecution, I think Petersen should have given Nixon a Miranda warning before talking to him. His failure to do so undermined his position as chief prosecutor in charge of the case. And being chief prosecutor of the case was his first and highest duty. Since there was no arrest involved, the failure to give a warning may seem trivial, but this grave caution would have impressed upon the president the danger of his own vulnerability and clearly would have fixed Petersen's position —not as defense counsel but as prosecutor.

Admittedly, giving such a warning to the president of the United States would have taken a good deal of courage.

When I started at the Justice Department, I believed that the Miranda warning obstructed swift law enforcement. I am now reconciled to it. The warning gives status and dignity to the police and the prosecutor and formally sets the relationship between law enforcers on the one hand and the target of their investigation on the other. Any sense of camaraderie between the two sides is shattered. Examining the whole Watergate situation has strengthened my belief in this institutional procedure. It would have been a statement to Nixon that no man is above the law.

During his hour-long conversation with Nixon and Petersen, Kleindienst expressed his belief that "it's going to take four or five years for Mitchell to run the full legal course on trials and so forth." (*The Haldeman Diaries*, pp. 636-637) Kleindienst suggested that perhaps recusing himself was not enough. Perhaps he should resign. Petersen was quick to scotch that idea. He argued that Kleindienst's resignation at that point would reflect badly both on the attorney general personally and on the Justice Department institutionally.

It is clear to me with the wonderful benefit of hindsight that Kleindienst should have stuck to his position—either appoint a special prosecutor or he would resign. Or he could have taken command of the situation and worked to save the presidency. It is clear to me also that what Petersen should have done was to give Nixon the Miranda warning and to insist that Nixon bring in an outside lawyer to guide him through Watergate. Both Kleindienst and Petersen could have done their duty to the offices they occupied, and both could have walked away clean. Petersen then could have discovered the whole situation. But I suspect Nixon would not have gone forward with further conversation with Petersen. At this juncture, the presidency was not lost and might have been saved had Nixon had the right lawyer counseling him.

Petersen did suggest, however, that Haldeman and Ehrlichman should resign. "The question isn't whether or not there is a criminal case that can be made against them that will stand up in court, Mr. President," Petersen said. "What you have to realize is that these two men have not served you well."

Petersen's advice was based on the fact that he knew that John Dean's turning would result in an indictment of Haldeman and Ehrlichman.

Petersen's advice to fire Haldeman was squarely contrary to the advice of their lawyer, John J. Wilson, that both men be retained until and unless they were indicted. On hindsight, Petersen's advice was neither good nor wise advice for President Nixon. By this time Nixon and Haldeman had grown together and seemed to function as one person. Haldeman was now more than a gatekeeper. He had become Nixon's alter ego. Nixon furnished the vision and the long view. He made the big decisions. Haldeman was the real executive of the two. He was the "get it done" man. Losing Haldeman would be a terrible blow to Nixon. In addition, the firing of Haldeman would serve notice that Nixon was not going to back up his subordinates. This was a breach of loyalty. It had been Nixon's idea to turn Watergate over to John Dean. The firing of Haldeman was a team-shattering event for the Nixon Administration.

Apparently the subject of trying to reverse Dean's and Magruder's decisions to bargain for immunity did not come up that Sunday afternoon. How awkward that would have been! The prosecutors regarded Dean's and Magruder's decision to turn state's evidence as a great breakthrough for them—and it certainly was, even though they decided not to pay for it by granting Dean immunity.

The prosecutors passed on to Petersen the information obtained from John Dean's bargaining, which Petersen then told Kleindienst and also told Nixon. This seems a major breach of confidence which Dean might have used in an attempt to squelch his indictment. But with the explosive information John Dean was delivering in his bargaining, it would have been very difficult to keep it confidential to the trial procedure. In any event, no effort was made to keep it that way and it quickly made its way up the chain of command to the president. But it is interesting that at this juncture John Dean had not given anything that directly implicated the president, which must have strengthened Petersen's belief that the president was not vulnerable. And it must have strengthened Nixon's belief that he could stonewall Watergate himself and let his subordinates take the fall.

Without the testimony of Dean and Magruder, there probably would have been no Watergate cases against the White House staff and perhaps no presidential impeachment. John Dean's decision to make peace with the law was difficult for all concerned.

Had Nixon pardoned Dean, or had the Justice Department granted him immunity, Dean would no longer have been able to invoke the protection of the Fifth Amendment against self-incrimination so he could have been forced to tell all under cross-examination. A pardon or grant of immunity would have left Dean subject to being compelled to testify.

The prosecutors decided to try Dean in court and win a conviction. They knew they could depend upon Judge John Sirica to impose a heavy penalty. After that, an offer to reduce the sentence could be used as leverage to force Dean to open up and tell the whole truth. Nixon's short conversation with Petersen in *The Presidential Transcripts* (pp. 675-676) illustrates this:

> President: . . . But my point is, you have got to—ah—I don't know what you prosecutors think, but if your prosecutors believe that they have got to give Dean immunity, in whole or in part, in order to get the damned case, do it. I'm not—I'm not telling you what to do but—you understand? Your decision.

You must stop to ask yourself: What in the world was the president thinking of in authorizing the turning of John Dean—the man who could bring down his entire administration?

Dean was the witness needed to connect Nixon to the cover-up. Here Nixon badly needed expert criminal law advice. Instead he may have been relying on a Faustian bargain with Dean that Dean would send Nixon's subordinates to the penitentiary but not Nixon himself. But what does this say of Nixon's loyalty to Haldeman and Ehrlichman?

Continuing the above conversation, Nixon said:

> President: Now, in Dean's case, I do not want the impression left that—I have gone over with you before, that by saying "Don't

grant immunity to a major person," that in so doing I am trying to block Dean giving evidence against Haldeman and Ehrlichman.

Petersen: I understand that. (*The Presidential Transcripts*, p. 675)

It is obvious that Petersen did not believe that Dean could testify to criminal conversations with Nixon which would convict Nixon. Again continuing the conversation:

President: Now have you talked to the prosecutor about this situation?

Petersen: They vacillated. In the first instance they, I think, felt quite strongly that Dean should be immunized, and I was resisting. And the last time we discussed it, why they had made other—

President: Why? Maybe because of what I said? See? I don't want—I don't want them—

Petersen: No. I don't [think] so, because, one, they are in a position to simply make the recommendation and let me shoulder the heavy burden.

President: Why do you think that they had turned around?

Petersen: Well, I think they see the question of credibility. They have come to the recognition if they are going to put him on the stand and [if] he's going to have any credibility at all, he'll have most credibility if he goes in and pleads and testifies as a codefendant against Ehrlichman and Haldeman as opposed to someone who has been given immunity and is testifying against them.

President: Even an old man like Wilson [John Wilson, Haldeman's attorney] will tear hell out of him.

Petersen: Well, John Wilson may be old, but he's one hell of a lawyer. (*The Presidential Transcripts*, pp. 675-676)

Of course, in using a conviction with a harsh sentence and then a reduction of sentence as leverage on Dean, the prosecutors were subject to the chain of command which went straight to the president. But a heavy sentence plus hope of reduction of sentence as a weapon for inducing a reluctant witness to turn is under the direct control of the court and not the executive—while a grant of immunity is just the reverse. But in practice, a reduction in sentence after conviction would not reach Petersen, and this may be another reason that Silbert and Glanzer decided to go the heavy-sentence route rather than a grant of immunity.

Nixon's conversation with Petersen also shows his basic confusion caused by the conflict between his duties as chief law enforcement officer and his vulnerability to Dean's testimony.

"That decision on immunity can certainly be viewed . . . as [Nixon's] major tactical error," Haldeman wrote. "If Dean had been granted immunity, he wouldn't have had to reach so high to try to obtain it, and Nixon would never have been dragged in." (Haldeman, *The Ends of Power*, p. 261)

Honoring his loyalty to the Justice Department, Petersen urged the president not to fire Dean as long as the prosecutors' negotiations with him were continuing. The prosecutors wanted nothing to happen that might interfere with turning Dean as a witness. Petersen's recommendation: Wait until Dean's testimony is complete.

Kleindienst later expressed surprise at Nixon's calm reaction to the news that John Dean was negotiating to turn and become a witness for the prosecution. Kleindienst believed the news was not "new" to the president. Petersen, in his later testimony before the Senate Watergate Committee, expressed the same conclusion.

Nixon asked Petersen to report further developments directly to him. If at that time Petersen regarded Nixon as a possible target of the prosecution, he should have refused the request.

Sunday night, April 15, the president summoned Haldeman to meet him at his offices in the Executive Office Building. Before Nixon arrived at the EOB, he had enjoyed dinner and a pleasant ride on the *Sequoia* with his friend Bebe Rebozo. Nixon loved the *Sequoia*; he could escape some of the worst pressures of his office while still enjoying one of the most luxurious presidential perks. An ex-navy man, he observed the traditional protocol. "Nixon stopped at the head of the short gangplank, returned the captain's salute, then turned, faced the ship's stern and with obvious feeling saluted the flag." (Colson, *Born Again*, p. 43)

Haldeman described Nixon as "very cheery about what a beautiful day it was . . . he had his second talk with Kleindienst and Petersen, and that Dean had been in an all-day meeting with the U.S. Attorney and that Petersen will report to the [president] tomorrow at noon on the full details of that. . . . He's now ordered Kleindienst out of the entire operation and is dealing directly with Petersen." (*The Haldeman Diaries*, p. 637)

That night the president phoned Petersen four times. (*Presidential Transcripts*, pp. 416-420)

The first time, Nixon asked Petersen if there were any new developments. Petersen said that Dean, on the advice of his attorneys, planned to plead not guilty. Petersen explained what this meant—a court trial. Petersen also suggested that Liddy would not talk unless "signaled" to do so by Mitchell.

"A signal from John Mitchell?" the president asked, clearly surprised.

"Yes, sir," Petersen replied, "and so indicated that he was going to stand firm."

Nixon wished Petersen a good night's sleep, hung up, and called him back in ten minutes.

"I am trying to reach Dean," Nixon said. "In the meantime, on Liddy—I don't know the man, of course, and have no control over him, but hell, you are to tell him the President wants everybody involved in this to tell everything they know. Okay?"

"I will get in touch with his lawyer [Peter Maroulis, Liddy's former law associate in Poughkeepsie] first thing in the morning," Petersen agreed.

"You might want to do it tonight," the president persisted. "I don't want to stall around."

Here, clearly, the president appeared to be fulfilling his duties as chief law enforcement officer and thus giving Petersen confidence. Just as clearly Nixon was acting without legal advice for his own defense and with a clear disadvantage for the safety of his administration, then under threat of impeachment.

Nixon repeated his disclaimer about Liddy and waited a little over an hour before calling back. Petersen was getting a thorough initiation into his new position vis-à-vis the president. This time Nixon said, "I talked to John Dean and haven't quite finished, but he stepped out for a minute. . . . " (Dean remained in the room and heard the president's remarks.) Nixon instructed Petersen to contact Liddy's attorney and reiterate that the president wanted Liddy to "tell everything he knows."

Two hours later—at 11:45—Nixon again phoned and told Petersen, "I hope I didn't wake you up."

The president and Dean had discussed Dean's resignation. "But what do you want me to do?" Nixon asked. Petersen advised Nixon to wait. "I would say two weeks or more." (*The Presidential Transcripts*, pp. 416-420) It was now almost midnight after a rough two days, but Petersen courteously said, "Thank you for calling, Mr. President."

Nixon misled Petersen during those conversations. Leon Jaworski later said, "Nixon had numerous conversations with Henry Petersen during which he obtained information that he then related to Haldeman and Ehrlichman in order that they could be prepared to meet the testimony of those who were cooperating. . . . He also attempted to prevent Petersen from giving Dean immunity for fear that Dean could then testify fully against Haldeman, Ehrlichman, and possibly Nixon himself." (Leon Jaworski, *The Right and the Power: The Prosecution of Watergate*, New York: Reader's Digest, 1976, p. 190)

Before coming to see Nixon in the Oval Office that Sunday night, John Dean had offered Watergate prosecutors everything he could think of that might be of interest to them. Of course, all of this represented a violation of Dean's loyalty to Nixon. That very afternoon, Dean had told Silbert and Glanzer about the break-in at Dr. Fielding's office. Furthermore, Dean said, photographic evidence existed in Justice Department files.

Silbert quickly recognized the temperature of what he had just been handed and on Monday he passed the hot potato to Henry Petersen.

During a two-hour meeting in the president's Executive Office Building office, Petersen filled Nixon in on the prosecution's case to date. He reported on Mitchell, Magruder, Hunt, Gray, Ehrlichman, and Colson. When he came to Liddy, Petersen said, "This man is crazy, Mr. President."

For the most part Petersen's voice comes through quite clearly on the tapes, but time after time Nixon's comments were transcribed as inaudible.

On April 18 the president phoned the prosecutor again, this time from Camp David. In his later testimony to the Watergate grand jury on August 23, Petersen gave this account:

"What else is new?" Nixon asked.

Petersen "dropped the next bombshell" and told the president about the Fielding break-in. But it was Petersen's turn to be surprised. The president said, "I know all about that. That's a national security matter. Your mandate is Watergate. You stay out of that."

Under the law, however, Petersen had no choice. As soon as he verified the raid on Dr. Fielding's office from police records—and after conferring with several people in the Justice Department—Petersen directed the prosecutor in the Ellsberg case to notify both Judge Byrne and Ellsberg's defense counsel.

After considering it overnight, Judge Byrne summarily dismissed the case against Ellsberg with prejudice. He said, "The bizarre events have incurably infected the prosecution of the case. The only remedy available . . . is that this trial be terminated and the defendant's motion for dismissal be granted. . . ."

Byrne's ruling had the effect of an acquittal. It also had the result of derailing the possible appointment of Judge Byrne as director of the FBI.

Nixon has since referred to the next fourteen days as the pivotal period in Watergate.

During the critical last two weeks in April 1973—and at Kleindienst's direction—Petersen advised and counseled with the president on his actions in Watergate matters. From April 15 to April 30, Petersen and the president had at least seven telephone conversations and four meetings. (*The Presidential Transcripts*, pp. vi-viii) "On this thing, for two weeks I saw the president more, probably—I'm guessing—than most Cabinet officers see him," Petersen later told Special Prosecutor Archibald Cox. (James Doyle, *Not Above the Law*, New York: Morrow, 1979, p. 55)

Why did the president rely on Petersen?

One answer may be found in Ehrlichman's *Witness to Power* (p. 381n): "[Petersen] had impressed Nixon at several Cabinet meetings in 1971 and 1972. With Mitchell under suspicion, Kleindienst unwilling to get involved and both Dean and [Ehrlichman] the subjects of probable prosecution, Nixon needed advice from some lawyer, and he chose the lawyer who might decide who else might be pursued. The president curried favor with the prosecutor, probably unaware that Petersen had strong alliances with people who were not Nixon's friends."

Although Petersen had not been in the inner circle of Nixon's advisers, he was the only lawyer at that time close to the president who had the necessary legal knowledge and criminal law experience to give such advice. But from Nixon's standpoint, Petersen was not a good choice as a personal legal adviser. Petersen was a career lawyer who—as far as I know—had never done any defense work, and he did not think like a defense lawyer.

A good defense lawyer would have probed the degree of Nixon's possible vulnerability and would not have made any recommendations until he had all the facts. Petersen assumed that the president was *not* vulnerable and did not question Nixon in detail about his personal vulnerability. Once he knew Nixon was vulnerable, Petersen was stuck in a serious conflict of interest.

A good defense lawyer—or, it would seem, any lawyer—would have recognized that there would be no way to stop a crumbling chain of command from cratering and pulling everyone down, including the president. I do not understand why Nixon himself did not see this immediately when Kleindienst first presented the information to him that Sunday afternoon.

Petersen was in charge of the prosecutors who vigorously were building a case against the administration and possibly against Nixon himself. Petersen should have faced up to the conflict of loyalties within himself and advised the president that he could not continue as the president's counsel. He should have told the president to employ a top-notch criminal lawyer to guide him through his personal vulnerability. And since the president had confided in him without having been given the Miranda warning, Petersen should not have continued in charge of the prosecution.

A lawyer's duty is to dig deeply into the facts with his client and to extract the truth from his client so as to advise him how to proceed. A good lawyer never simply accepts what he is told as truth: he continues to test it. This Petersen did not do with Nixon. Obviously he did not regard the job—imposed on him by Kleindienst—of counseling the president as including the duty to inquire into Nixon's personal vulnerability.

A sample of the relationship between Petersen and the president is illustrated by the following excerpt of a telephone conversation on April 16, 1973. (*The Presidential Transcripts*, pp. 473-474)

> President: And Kleindienst out? Because of allegations that have been made, Kleindienst has removed himself from the case, can we say that?—Well. How do you want me to handle Kleindienst?
>
> Petersen: Well, I think that's terribly sensitive, Mr. President.
>
> President: How do we—What do I say then about you? That Henry Petersen is acting as the President's Special Counsel? Can I say it that way?

> Petersen: Yeas, you can say it that way.

Petersen recognized that his relationship with the president was analogous to that of attorney-client, and said he did not feel free to reveal confidential conversations between the two.

Did Petersen slowly come to realize the president's possible vulnerability? Did he realize he had been used? In a later conversation with Archibald Cox and James Vorhenberg, "Petersen admitted to having suspicions about the president, saying he was a little ashamed of them. Petersen said, 'I'm not very good at cross-examining Presidents.' " (Doyle, *Not Above the Law*, p. 58)

By now President Nixon realized where Petersen was taking him and stated that he did not intend to see him anymore. But he did meet with Petersen one more time. The president called Petersen to come for a conference on a statement Ron Ziegler was preparing which would say that—in accordance with attorney John Wilson's recommendation—no immunity would be granted to any White House employee.

Petersen took exception to this and maintained to the president that he, Petersen, as assistant attorney general, Criminal Division, had the final statutory authority on granting immunity and that the president's statement would impair the negotiations with John Dean to become a witness.

The following conversation (*The Presidential Transcripts*, p. 675) between Petersen and the president on April 27, 1973, revealed this.

> President: I have applied that to others, and I don't want to—no. Do I make myself clear?
>
> Petersen: Yes. Now let me make myself clear.
>
> President: Yes.
>
> Petersen: I regard immunity authority under the statutes of the United States to be my responsibility, of which I cannot divest myself.
>
> President: Right.
>
> Petersen: . . . we take [opinions] but I would have to treat this as advisory only.

Petersen's statement to the president took a lot of guts.

President Nixon yielded to Petersen and watered down the statement on immunity for White House employees. Petersen also was firmly recommending that President Nixon should now require the resignation of all three: Haldeman, Ehrlichman, and Dean. The deciding factor seems to have been the following conversation with Petersen (*The Presidential Transcripts*, pp. 684-685).

> Petersen: But you see that's what I see has to get out to the public. But Mr. President, my wife is not a politically sophisticated woman.
>
> President: That's right.
>
> Petersen: She knows I'm upset about this and you know, I'm working hard and she sees it. But she asked me at breakfast—She, now I don't want you to hold this against her if you ever meet her, because she's a charming lady—
>
> President: Of course.
>
> Petersen: She said, "Doesn't all this upset you?" And I said, "Of course it does."
>
> President: "Why the hell doesn't the President do something?"
>
> Petersen: She said, "Do you think the President knows?" And I looked at her and said, "If I thought the President knew, I would have to resign." But, you know, now there is my own family, Mr. President. . . .
>
> President: Sure. Sure.
>
> Petersen: Now whatever confidence she has in you, her confidence in me ought to be unquestioned. Well, when that type of question comes through in my home. . . .
>
> President: We've got to get it out.
>
> Petersen: We've got a problem.
>
> President: Well, you know I have wrestled with it. I've been trying to. . . .
>
> Petersen: Mr. President, I pray for you, sir.
>
> President: I have been trying to get the thing. . . . Like even poor [Pat] Gray, there was nothing we could do. Ah—wrestling with Dean's covers. . . . But, ah. . . .
>
> Petersen: I wouldn't try to distinguish between the three of them.
>
> President: I understand, I understand. Well, I won't try to distinguish, but maybe they will be handled differently due to the fact that I am not communicating with Dean.
>
> Petersen: Mr. President, it is always easier to advise than it is to assume the responsibility.
>
> President: I will do it my way. And it will be done. I am working on it. I won't even tell you now how. . . .
>
> Petersen: I understand.

The president went on national television to announce the resignations of Haldeman, Ehrlichman, Kleindienst, and Dean. With his starting offensive players now permanently ineligible, Nixon faced the last quarter with a new, untried defensive team.

After the announcement, Nixon phoned Petersen and said: "You can tell your wife the president has done what needed to be done."

But what needed to be done—the president's full and candid statement of the facts of Watergate—had *not* been done. What had been done was done too late to alter the inevitable outcome.

Thinking in terms of a definition of loyalty, we can say that in handling his personal conflict Henry Petersen clearly remained loyal to the Justice Department and to law enforcement. In fact, when Nixon phoned Henry Petersen from Camp David on April 28, the president said he didn't want to "put any burden on you that you don't want now." Petersen replied: "That doesn't put any burden on me that I don't have by law." (Emphasis added.) (Kutler, *Abuse of Power*, p. 360) But he gave the president advice which contributed to Nixon's disaster. So far as I know, he did not bring up and discuss a general pardon of all concerned with the president at a time when this might have saved Nixon's presidency. Petersen was concentrating on making those obstruction of justice cases.

Petersen remained head of the Criminal Division until his resignation on November 4, 1974, taking effect the end of the year and bringing to a close a twenty-seven-year career with the Justice Department.

It has been three decades since I was in the Justice Department building and last saw Henry Petersen, but in my mind's eye somehow I still see him there—eager, intense, decisive, wreathed in cigarette smoke, and firmly in command. He was fiercely loyal to the Justice Department. He never varied from his dedication to the law and to his strong Jesuitical principles. In Watergate he did not extend his prosecutorial discretion from doing what was best for the Justice Department to what (I think) was best for the nation.

Still, I hope the Justice Department always has many such professionals as Henry Petersen.

CHAPTER 12

Agnew for President?

"Surely much of the controversy about the Vice Presidency could be quieted if we would accept the fact that the Vice President is the President's man."

—Spiro Agnew

FDR'S VICE PRESIDENT FROM 1933 to 1941 was John Nance Garner. The crusty old Texan, dubbed "Cactus Jack" by the press, is often quoted as having said his office was "not worth a bucket of warm spit." The vice president is the nation's standby, becoming important only if the president dies in office, is impeached and convicted, or resigns.

Lyndon Johnson once told me that the main criteria in selecting a vice president should not be his political contribution to the upcoming campaign but rather his competence to be president.

But the hasty, often last-minute choice for a vice-presidential nominee is far more likely to be a compromise between opposing ideologies within the party, an attempt at geographical balance, or an outright payoff for support and fundraising.

So how did Spiro "Ted" Agnew from Maryland emerge as the Republican vice-presidential candidate in 1968?

It had been Mitchell who first brought Agnew into the Nixon campaign. It had been Mitchell who urged that Agnew be allowed to place Nixon's name in nomination at the 1968 Republican Convention. Mitchell had suggested to Agnew that if he did a good job, he would be a contender for the number-two spot.

When Nixon and Agnew stepped out on the convention platform in Miami, Nixon stiffly spread his arms in an awkward "V" for victory. He had adopted the gesture from the triumphant Dwight

Eisenhower at the end of World War II, but "it became for many in the nation a detested gesture . . ." (Brodie, *Richard Nixon,* p. 246) Agnew just stood by, and it was the Republican minority leader of the House, Gerald Ford, who thought fast enough to grab Agnew's wrist and thrust his arm upward.

Soon after the Republican convention, Nixon wrote "Why I Chose Ted Agnew," as a Foreword to *Where He Stands: The Life and Convictions of Spiro T. Agnew.* Issued as it was—after the Republican Convention and before the November elections—*Where He Stands* must be recognized as no more than campaign literature.

"I consulted more than a hundred leading Republicans whose judgment I respected," Nixon wrote. "I seriously considered more than a dozen very able men, all of whom were of . . . vice presidential caliber."

Nixon added, "I was deeply impressed by [Agnew's] tremendous brain power, great courage and unprejudiced legal mind." The "brain power" disappeared as Agnew became the attack dog of the Nixon Administration, the "great courage" soon manifested itself in belligerent battles with the press, and the "legal mind" turned out to be full of prejudice.

Pointing to Agnew's "long experience at the local and state levels of government" and his record as "an effective administrator," Nixon declared his intention to ask Agnew "to assume responsibility for the development of more effective partnership between all levels of government in seeking solutions to our many domestic problems."

Agnew actually had had only ten or eleven years of political experience—and that in a small state. I find it hard to believe Nixon selected Agnew on the strength of his record as governor of Maryland. Maryland was a machine state and Agnew—like Truman from Missouri—was a product of big-city machine politics.

Nixon admitted that "no training . . . can prepare any man to be President or Vice President. . . . If the man has the *inner character, ability and dedication* he will grow in the office." (Emphasis added.)

Later events in the Nixon Administration revealed the darker side of the coin: A president or vice president lacking the qualities of "inner character, ability and dedication" can break and give way under the pressures, demands, and temptations of the office.

Agnew brought with him concealed baggage from his governorship of Maryland which was to help bring about his downfall and present Nixon with uncomfortable embarrassment.

Agnew had served in World War II. He returned home from Europe as a lieutenant and used the benefits of the GI Bill to complete his study of law in night school at the University of Baltimore. He lacked an academic degree but passed the bar in 1947.

When Agnew expressed an interest in politics, a friend advised him to run as a Republican in a state dominated by Democrats. The Democratic party was filled with ambitious young Turks; his adviser assured Agnew he would face less competition as a Republican.

"Agnew's very first significant act—joining the Republican party—did not stem from conviction but from personal ambition . . . he did not become a Republican because of any values the party stood for locally or nationally." (Robert Marsh, *Agnew*, New York: Evans, 1971, p. 166)

Agnew began his path into politics by volunteering. He licked stamps and helped canvass from door to door. He worked hard, met the right people, and eventually gained appointment to the three-man Baltimore County Zoning Board of Appeals, where he served from 1957 to 1961.

Agnew progressed from the zoning board to county executive. In 1966 he successfully ran for governor and carried out some rather liberal programs. At the National Conference of Governors he began to look toward national politics. He became a supporter of New York's governor, Nelson Rockefeller.

A number of writers have described how Agnew ordered a color television set to be brought to his gubernatorial office so he could watch Rockefeller announce his candidacy for president. Instead, the New Yorker said he was not interested in becoming president and withdrew his name from possible consideration. Agnew was hurt and humiliated.

A couple of days later John Mitchell hopped in his car, drove to Annapolis to talk to Agnew, and immediately got him involved in Nixon's campaign. (Strober and Strober, *Nixon: An Oral History*, p. 22) Agnew switched his wholehearted loyalty to Richard Nixon.

Nixon had not done his homework. Undeniably, Agnew captured both national attention and his own popular following. But after the nominating convention, the campaign was barely under way before Nixon's workers began talking about "the Agnew problem." Agnew could be coarse, tactless, and insensitive. He made a poor showing, they said, compared with Edmund Muskie, the suave and polished Democratic vice-presidential candidate.

Nixon's negative criteria for selecting a running mate is reflected in a comment he made to an aide: "The vice president can't help you. He can only hurt you." (Ambrose, *Triumph of a Politician*, p. 163) Nixon defended his choice of Agnew, although he did shoot off a quick note to the man whose political future was now linked with his own: "Dear Ted: When news is concerned, nobody in the press is a friend—they are all enemies." (Ambrose, *Triumph of a Politician*, p. 192)

The Republican ticket was successful, due in part to the unfortunate events of the Chicago Democratic Convention. Although Nixon won, he did not win by the margin he believed was necessary to claim he had a mandate from the American people. His efforts to explain or rationalize his squeak-through win is reflected in one of his early memos (Oudes, *From: The President,* p. 4) to Haldeman and Ehrlichman. He asked: "How much did Agnew hurt us?"

Shortly after the 1968 election, LBJ advised Agnew not to try to fight the media. The new vice president either felt he could win where others had failed, or else he believed that the fight alone—win or lose—was good strategy and sure to gain favor with middle-Americans.

Agnew had a sense of humor. He was quite capable of making fun of himself. In May 1969 he joked about his role as Nixon's chief spokesman. At a gathering in Phoenix, after paying tribute to Arizona's Barry Goldwater, Agnew quipped, "My speech tonight is the one President Nixon approved for this occasion. It's somewhat short—beginning with my name, mentioning my office, and concluding with my serial number." (John R. Coyne, *The Impudent Snobs, Agnew vs. The Intellectual Establishment*, New York: Arlington House, 1972, p. 204)

Nixon declared his intention to ask Agnew "to assume responsibility for the development of more effective partnership between all levels of government in seeking solutions to our many domestic problems." Nixon apparently started with good intentions, assigning his vice president an office in the White House and involving him in Cabinet meetings.

"The idea," Agnew wrote (*Go Quietly . . . or else,* New York:

William Morrow, 1980, p. 36) was "to use presidential staff with my own staff . . . to better serve the President. . . ." Eventually Agnew was asked to give up his White House office. He spent more and more of his time in his offices in the Old Executive Office Building. After that, there seems to have been little direct communication between the president and his vice president.

The rift between the two became apparent in late February 1972. Nixon's China initiative was a crucial part of his foreign policy. The president returned from his visit to Peking exhilarated by the experience—the culmination of many months of secret negations involving Nixon and Kissinger but not Secretary of State Rogers.

"At that point," Nixon wrote (*Memoirs,* Vol. 2, p. 13) in a particularly apt metaphor, "a bull in the form of Ted Agnew inadvertently careened into the diplomatic China shop."

Agnew certainly noticed the drop in temperature. "I presume that my firm opposition to the policy of cozying up to Communist China was the main reason the White House froze me out of the Nixon decisions in that area." (Agnew, *Go Quietly,* p. 34)

Agnew continued to be an outspoken advocate for the domestic agenda, taking a strong stance for law and order—as he interpreted it—against civil dissent along with the print and broadcast media.

The vice president was a favorite of the White House speechwriters. Agnew had a good delivery, a relaxed physical stance (in contrast to Nixon's awkward stiffness) and the ability to toss off alliterations such as "nattering nabobs of negativity." (Safire, *Before the Fall,* p. 323) And to the administration's approval, Agnew could attack the "liberal press" while at the same time his immense popularity with the American people forced full newspaper coverage of every one of his appearances.

In a speech to the Mississippi State Republican dinner at Jackson on May 18, 1971, he defined and defended the "Southern Strategy." He said, "It is a political phenomenon that is born in the suspicious minds of the liberal pundits and flung at an unsuspecting public via tons of newsprint and network rhetoric whenever a national administration attempts to treat the South on equal terms with other regions of this country." (Coyne, *Impudent Snobs*, p. 245)

But Nixon began to fret as the election of 1972 drew near. He wanted an anointed heir to his throne, a vice president who would be a shoo-in for election in 1976.

White House insiders were familiar with Nixon's tendency to have "pets"—men who quickly came into and abruptly went out of presidential favor. Haldeman and Ehrlichman watched the rise and fall of several such favorites. Nixon's close friend and confidant, John Mitchell, had lost much of his clout with Nixon when his suggestions for Supreme Court nominations failed of confirmation. "After 1970 we didn't see the Mitchells much for dinner," Julie Nixon Eisenhower said. (Safire, *Before the Fall*, p. 270)

"Connally came in like a comet, bedazzling and enthralling Nixon," wrote Brodie in *Richard Nixon* (p. 476). Connally appeared to have all the attributes Nixon admired but lacked.

At a Cabinet meeting in late 1970, Nixon announced the resignation of David Kennedy as secretary of the treasury and Connally's nomination to the post. Someone made certain the press took due notice of Nixon's choice of a Democrat (which Connally still was—nominally at least) to fill an important slot in the Republican administration.

Shortly after Connally took office as secretary of the treasury, I paid an official call on him. John and I knew each other, of course; we had long been political rivals. Connally had defeated me in the race for governor of Texas in 1962. But our meeting was characterized by scrupulous courtesy on both our parts with no references to the bygones of Texas politics.

The Treasury Department had contributed highly trained, skilled personnel to our strike forces. I explained the important role treasury agents played in our crime-fighting program and asked Connally for his department's continued cooperation. As I recall, he gave me some noncommittal answer about looking into the matter. Treasury involvement in the strike forces did continue.

Connally's appearance on the Washington scene brought my disillusionment with and mistrust of Johnson/Connally politics rushing back to mind. Troubled, I discussed with Marjorie whether I would resign and return to Texas—but I had become so involved in the work of the Organized Crime Section which I headed that I decided to stay on a while longer.

Rumor soon made the rounds that Nixon was grooming Connally not only to be his running mate in 1972 but to be the Republican party's candidate for president in 1976. Nixon and Connally "had made a deal—a deal for the vice presidency, the stepping stone, for Connally, to the presidency." (Ann Fears Crawford and Jack Keever, *John B. Connally, Portrait in Power,* Austin: Jenkins, 1973, pp. 346-347) When he heard of it, Mitchell was decidedly negative about getting Agnew to step aside.

Agnew was not unaware of the palace intrigue. In *Go Quietly* (p. 38) he wrote: "Indeed, the President had toyed with the idea of dropping me in 1972 and substituting the former Governor of Texas, his new favorite, who had become the star of the Cabinet as Secretary of the Treasury.

"At first, I didn't believe the reports that the President was thinking of dumping me. He would often volunteer for my benefit in the presence of others, 'That's just a lot of political talk. The biggest game in Washington is to create a fight between the President and the Vice President.'"

In public, Agnew made jokes about Nixon's attitude. Once he apologized for arriving late at a luncheon: "I did my best to hurry, but John Connally had me down on his ranch for a barbecue, and it took me an hour and a half to cut myself down from the spit." (Agnew, *Go Quietly,* p. 39)

Just as Eisenhower had wanted Nixon to take a Cabinet position instead of the vice presidential slot on the second term ticket, Nixon at one time hit upon the scheme of making way for Connally by appointing Agnew to the Supreme Court.

Nixon's tough political realism told him neither man had a gosling's chance of being confirmed.

When Connally had high-tailed it to Washington, his saddle bags were packed with political enemies. Old-guard Texas Democrats viewed his desertion as treachery of the lowest kind. The recently organized Republicans looked on Connally as "an implacable enemy of the Republican party in Texas. . . ." (James Reston, Jr., *The Lone Star: The Life of John Connally,* New York: Harper & Row, 1989, p. 380)

John Connally began to position himself for possible advancement. On April 30, 1973, he formally left the Democratic party to become a registered Republican—but not until after the death of his political mentor, Lyndon Johnson.

But not even the wealthy rancher from Texas possessed the necessary skills to change horses in midstream. Nixon, who could be a hard-eyed realist when the circumstances arose, realized Connally could never again serve him in a position requiring congressional confirmation.

Even though a "dump Agnew" campaign seemed to be underway, the vice president received support from conservative Republicans. Senator Barry Goldwater declared it was "an absolute necessity" to keep Agnew on the ticket. (*Go Quietly*, p. 39) Kissinger also lined up behind Agnew—he did not want John Connally, "whose headlong foreign policy views made up in fervor what they lacked in subtlety." (Isaacson, *Kissinger*, p. 595)

Nixon did not decide definitely on his running mate until June 12, when he "asked Mitchell to tell Agnew. . . ." (*Memoirs*, Vol. 2, p. 169) Several weeks later (July 26, 1973), and a month before the Republican Convention, Haldeman wrote an ACTION MEMORANDUM (Oudes, *From: The President*, p. 523) to Agnew: "The Vice President should knock off golf and use of the White House tennis courts. We should not look leisurely as we go into the campaign."

Once again, Nixon had shown his concern for public image over substance. And apparently the president communicated with Agnew only through Mitchell or Haldeman. Nixon's inability to deal directly with his staff is another example of his lack of executive ability.

Little wonder that Agnew could say (in *Go Quietly*, p. 34) he wished he had served under Lyndon Johnson "because if anything had gone wrong, probably he himself would have picked up the phone and said, 'Agnew, what the hell are you doing?'" And he would have, too.

Agnew could not have drawn much comfort or reassurance from the campaign committee to "Re-elect the President" but not to "Re-elect Nixon–Agnew" as might have been expected.

Nixon did not make his choice official until the 1972 convention. In his acceptance speech Agnew said, "Surely much of the controversy about the Vice Presidency could be quieted if we would accept the fact that *the Vice President is the President's man.*" (Emphasis added.)

Above all, Agnew was totally loyal to Richard Nixon.

On the face of it, it is hard to imagine how any president could have had a more loyal henchman. Agnew—articulate, smiling, shaking hands, posing for photos, always immaculately groomed and superbly tailored—somewhat balanced Nixon's dark moods, dour reclusiveness, and physical stiffness.

Agnew stumped vigorously. He and John Mitchell's wife, Martha, became the two most popular, sought-after Republican personalities in the country. There was no love lost between them. In one of her highly publicized phone calls, Martha told UPI correspondent Helen Thomas: "I don't like Vice President Agnew, but by God, I think he's better than Mister President." (Ervin, *The Whole Truth*, p. 256f)

From Nixon's standpoint, the spontaneous ovations Agnew received from the crowds may have been among the vice president's least likable attributes. Nixon himself made few public appearances during the campaign. His campaign advance men carefully orchestrated applause and cheers for his own appearances, but Nixon must have been uncomfortably aware how much the people enjoyed the show Agnew put on.

The McGovern campaign collapsed. In the November 1972 election Nixon finally got the overwhelming mandate that he wanted from the people. Nixon was prepared to overlook the fact that his mandate was due more to the work of Agnew and Martha Mitchell than his own.

Agnew thought that because he had worked so "hard to insure our reelection by a huge majority . . . [he would] get a very big, important assignment." (*Go Quietly*, p. 37) Instead, Agnew was assigned to work with the Bicentennial planners for the 1976 celebration.

Nixon immediately called for resignations in his administration. Secretary of State Rogers, goaded perhaps by his rivalry with and resentment of Kissinger, immediately began negotiations to stay on for at least six months.

John Dean saw a clear and present danger in the wholesale forced resignations. "One guy we need. . . . that's Henry Petersen," said Dean in an urgent phone call to Haldeman. "I don't think we should let Henry worry about his future." Until his rise to head of the Criminal Division, Petersen would have been protected under Civil Service. But after his appointment he served at the president's pleasure—just like other appointees.

Kleindienst received an unexpected summons to Camp David, where he met with Haldeman and Ehrlichman.

"From here on out," Haldeman told Kleindienst, "only people loyal to the president are to be running the government for the next four years." Haldeman followed that up with a startling directive. Kleindienst was ordered to "replace every lawyer and department head [in the Justice Department] not protected by Civil Service" within ninety days.

Kleindienst argued the impracticality, not to mention the sheer irrationality, of replacing some 2,000 Justice Department lawyers. He finally lost his temper, made a crude suggestion, and stalked out.

That night Kleindienst phoned John Mitchell, described the meeting with Haldeman, and heatedly declared his intention to resign. Mitchell talked him out of it. "They want you to resign," Mitchell told him. "Then they can put in someone else, like Ehrlichman." All of this is put forward in detail in Kleindienst's book, *Justice*.

Kleindienst stayed, but some department people did resign, among them my close friend and former colleague, Solicitor General Erwin N. Griswold. He requested to be allowed to remain in office until the end of the Supreme Court session, so his replacement, Robert Bork, actually did not take office until June 1973—just in time to become embroiled in Agnew's resignation and in the Saturday night massacre.

Nixon must have believed that his re-election had somehow erased the threat of Watergate. Now he was free to turn his entire attention and energy toward ending the cold war and ushering in an era of world peace—or so he must have thought.

After we had left Washington and Marjorie and I were back home in Austin, stories began to appear in the media suggesting Agnew's possible involvement in corruption.

Agnew, the stories said, had accepted bribes while in office as a member of the zoning board, as executive of Baltimore County, later as governor of Maryland—and even in his vice president's office in the basement of the White House. He was under investigation by Maryland U.S. Attorney George Beall.

I was not surprised. My own involvement in prosecuting former Senator Daniel B. Brewster (D.–Maryland) had prepared me to believe corruption and bribery at that time were deeply entrenched traditions in Agnew's home state.

Robert Marsh (*Agnew: The Unexamined Man*, New York: Evans, 1971) described Brewster as "one of the most promising of the young Democrats in the state." Marsh must have completed his manuscript prior to Brewster's indictment on ten counts of having accepted payment in return for being influenced in his Senate vote and before allegations of Agnew's corruption surfaced.

In August 1973 the *Wall Street Journal* reported that Agnew was under investigation. Elliot Richardson—who had replaced Kleindienst as attorney general only a few months earlier—brought the matter to the president's attention and then issued the expected statement: The Justice Department was watching the Maryland investigation closely. "That turned out to be bad news for me," Agnew wryly observed in *Go Quietly* (p. 59).

Agnew maintained he was innocent of bribery and wanted to defend himself. He said, "My acceptance of contributions was part of a long-established pattern of political fund-raising in the state [of Maryland]. At no time have I enriched myself at the expense of my public trust."

Agnew's lawyers tried to halt a grand jury investigation on the grounds that a sitting vice president could not be indicted. Solicitor General Robert Bork filed a brief in the Baltimore federal court that a sitting vice president *could* be indicted and tried on a criminal charge. Bork contended that vice presidents were different from presidents, against whom the only remedy was impeachment. (Emery, *Watergate*, p. 382)

Agnew seemed eager for an opportunity to defend himself and wanted a forum from which to speak out. On September 25 he submitted a letter to the office of Carl Albert, Speaker of the House of Representatives, asking the House to initiate impeachment proceedings against him. The Democratic majority leader, Tip O'Neill, decided to turn this down and so advised Speaker Albert. Perhaps O'Neill considered this a diversion from his own main target: Richard Nixon.

Failing in that tactic, four days later Agnew began "a full-throated attack on Henry Petersen [of the Justice Department], who had been brought in to supervise the Agnew case." (Doyle, *Not Above the Law*, p. 131) Agnew accused Petersen of attempting to rescue his own reputation—tarnished by the bungled Watergate investigation—by destroying Agnew's.

The vice president soon discovered that his loyalty to the president did not enjoy a reciprocal trade agreement. "The saddest thing about [my] case is that . . . the people I was depending on to help me immediately assumed I was guilty." (Agnew, *Go Quietly*, p. 83)

Nixon could scarcely repudiate the vice president he had so strongly praised—but neither could he be seen as protecting Agnew if the charges against him were founded on hard evidence.

Agnew clearly recognized that his own situation had possible advantages for the president. In *Go Quietly* (p. 130), he wrote:

> Mr. Nixon did not seem to realize that I was his insurance policy against his own ouster. The left-wingers who despised us both would never push him out of the White House until they were certain I would not be around to take his place. What would be the point of exchanging a weakened Nixon for a President whose ideas seldom meshed with theirs, and who could be stubborn? Therefore, logic dictated that I must be moved aside first, by fair means or foul.

Actually, Nixon did realize that Agnew was impeachment insurance. In a taped conversation (Kutler, *Abuse of Power*, p. 559) with Secretary of State Rogers, Nixon said, "What the hell are you going to do? Turn the [reins] over to Agnew? Huh? [Chuckles.] Is that what they want?"

In his *Memoirs* (Vol. 2, p. 344), Nixon simply said, "I was very concerned at the prospect of Agnew's being dragged through the mud unfairly, but in view of all the other problems and *our strained relations with Capitol Hill*, I did not see how we could do anything to help him." (Emphasis added.)

Clearly, Nixon thought that Watergate had given him all he could handle. He evidently believed he could not afford to reach out a helping hand to his floundering vice president. Neither did Nixon see loyalty as reciprocal. He turned the matter over to the new White House chief of staff, Al Haig.

Nixon may have had another compelling reason to distance himself from Agnew. Investigators, in addition to looking at the charges of accepting bribes, were also examining Agnew's profitable real estate deals. Articles about Nixon's luxurious San Clemente house had begun appearing in the *Los Angeles Times* and other newspapers. Nixon was not eager for close and comparative scrutiny of his own real estate deals. (Lukas, *Nightmare*, p. 403)

If Vice President Agnew had been under indictment in Maryland—and Dick Kleindienst had remained as attorney general, with Bob Haldeman and John Ehrlichman still firmly in place in the White House—Nixon would have had a briar patch between himself and his own impeachment. He might have succeeded in stonewalling the Watergate cover-up investigation and avoiding the threat to his presidency until after the conclusion of Agnew's trial.

Even if Agnew had been allowed to fight his case in the Maryland courts there is no certainty that he would have been convicted. This case depended upon the testimony of two civil engineers who, in return for grants of their own immunity, would testify they had paid bribes to Agnew.

My own experience as Dallas County district attorney had taught me how very difficult it is to convict a popular local official. I tried the Dallas County treasurer for stealing cash from the County—cash he had lost betting on horse races. In spite of his confession, a jury still found him not guilty in a trial where he blamed one of his employees for stealing the money and charged me with political motivation in prosecuting him.

Later, as Texas attorney general, I tried several county sheriffs for bribery but found it very difficult to get a favorable jury verdict. Another example: Look at the not-guilty verdict by the Senate in the impeachment trial of President William Clinton.

Fred Emery, in an article entitled "Watergate—Worse Than You Thought" (*The New York Times*, Sunday, June 19, 1994), suggested that Nixon's greatest strategic blunder was in not first serving up Vice President Agnew to Congress for impeachment—which Emery said Agnew would have preferred to a criminal trial. Emery wrote that "in pushing instead for the Vice President's resignation . . . Mr. Nixon made perhaps his worst tactical mistake, greater even than failing to destroy the incriminating White House tapes. Congress might not have had the stomach for another impeachment the following year."

In considering the impeachment of Nixon, every congressman would first look to see who would succeed Nixon as president—and every congressman would study his own situation to analyze how the impeachment verdict would affect his own re-election. Agnew was a strong and articulate hawk on Vietnam. He had been an administration hatchet-man in attacking and smearing liberals. Probably none of the Democrats would have wanted Agnew to succeed to the presidency—especially while under indictment on charges of bribery. Most senators, if forced to choose between Nixon or Agnew for president, would have selected Nixon.

Every impeachment vote is a choice between the president and the vice president.

If President Nixon had left the vice presidency vacant after Agnew's resignation, and if Nixon himself had been ousted by impeachment, the mildly alcoholic Speaker of the House Carl Albert, a Democrat from Oklahoma, would have been next in line. Not only did Albert himself have no desire to be so elevated, but the result would have been an exchange from an elected Republican administration to a non-elected Democratic one. Most senators would have seen that as a dangerous prospect.

The danger of such a possible shift would have strengthened Nixon in his own fight against removal from office.

While Agnew was doing all he could to defend himself publicly, Attorney General Richardson was pushing hard for Agnew to resign. In *Go Quietly* (p. 189), Agnew states he was finally forced into resigning as vice president by a threat to indict Mrs. Agnew for income tax violations. (Agnew was the second vice president to resign from office. The first, John C. Calhoun, resigned as Andrew Jackson's vice president but returned to Washington as a senator from South Carolina.)

If he had to go, Agnew was determined to avoid serving time in prison. Richardson was equally determined that Agnew must acknowledge the validity of the government's case against him. On October 10 Agnew appeared in federal court and faced a forty-five-page bill of particulars against him by the Baltimore prosecutor.

In entering a plea of nolo contendere, Agnew was aware that "a full legal defense of the probable charges against me could consume several years. I am concerned that intense media interest in the case would distract public attention from important national problems, to the country's detriment." (Agnew, *Go Quietly*, p. 16)

Agnew announced his resignation the same day.

Meanwhile Connally waited in the Mayflower Hotel for the

president's call. He believed—as did the rest of Washington—that "Connally as the new vice president was a done deal." (Reston, *The Lone Star*, p. 458) But when Congress learned of the president's plan, the outpouring of opposition quickly persuaded Nixon that Connally could not expect confirmation. The president instructed Al Haig to call Connally with the disappointing decision.

Haldeman suggests that "if there had been no Watergate. . . . John Connally would have been appointed Vice President after Spiro Agnew's resignation and would have been nominated by the Republican Party for President in 1976." (Haldeman, *The Ends of Power*, p. 323) But Haldeman's conjecture overlooked Connally's indictment July 29, 1974, and subsequent acquittal for offenses in connection with the 1971 "milk fund" scandal unrelated to Watergate.

Nixon, who had learned to play poker as a young navy man, now decided to check to what looked like a cinch. Under the provisions of the recently adopted Twenty-fifth Amendment to the Constitution, on October 12, 1973, President Nixon appointed Gerald Ford to fill the second slot, believing that the popular Michigan congressman was virtually an automatic confirmation. However, thirty-eight congressmen voted against his confirmation—largely, I believe, because they had not forgotten his previous efforts to impeach Justice Douglas.

If Nixon wanted to avoid impeachment, the appointment of a popular congressman as his vice president was exactly the wrong move. Since impeachment charges are brought by the House of Representatives and must be passed by a two-thirds vote, why would a president under such an attack want his probable successor to be popular with Congress?

But Nixon did not see it that way. Until Ford took the oath of office on December 6, Speaker Carl Albert was the *de facto* vice president. After Agnew resigned, Nixon should have left the vice presidency open. That would have presented a far more complicated situation for Tip O'Neill, who expected to succeed Carl Albert as Speaker.

Just as Nixon never wanted to fire anyone directly—he did it through his staff—he seemed to feel the same reluctance to hire anyone. He handed off to Haig, who broke the news to Ford.

Nixon did not easily give up his vision of himself and Connally as an all-powerful team. Nixon made it clear to Ford that he did not expect him to be the party's next candidate. "I'm supporting John Connally for president in 1976," Nixon told Ford. (Reston, *The Lone Star*, p. 460)

The Agnew controversy weakened Nixon at a time when he needed all his strength. It is tempting to move the chess pieces around on the board and play "What if?. . ."

Had Kleindienst not resigned as attorney general, there would have been no confirmation hearing for Elliot Richardson and hence no Archibald Cox as special prosecutor, and had Nixon not fired Haldeman and Ehrlichman, Nixon's team would have been intact. Had he let Agnew's criminal trial in Maryland go forward, the whole subject of impeachment might have been delayed until near the end of Nixon's last term.

A contrary view is expressed by William D. Ruckleshaus in a memorial, "Elliot Richardson's choice":

> The overwhelming nature of the case against the vice president eventually left Elliot no choice but to pursue his [Agnew's] resignation. The criminal trial or impeachment (his other two choices) of a sitting vice president serving under a besieged president was almost unthinkable. Under the circumstances, the vice president's resignation was good for the country and created a stable situation, with Gerald Ford in office, for the presidential resignation that followed. (*Austin American–Statesman,* January 7, 2000, p. 15)

With the controversy about Vice President Agnew safely out of the way, Nixon now turned his attention to another burr under his saddle—Special Prosecutor Archibald Cox.

CHAPTER 13

Fire the Special Prosecutor!

"Now . . . we can get rid of Cox."
—President Richard Nixon

WITH SPIRO AGNEW OUT and Gerald Ford in as vice president, Nixon apparently believed his administration once more had dodged the bullet. "Now that that's over," he said, "we can get rid of Cox," the special prosecutor who had been brought in by Elliot Richardson.

Nixon had named Richardson as attorney general to replace Dick Kleindienst. Richardson's qualifications to fill the slot were many. He had been a U.S. attorney and had a reputation as a vigorous prosecutor. In 1964 he had been elected lieutenant governor of Massachusetts and two years later he won the office of state attorney general. Nixon had brought Richardson into his administration with earlier appointments as undersecretary of state, secretary of the Department of Health, Education and Welfare, and secretary of defense.

So when Richardson came to the Justice Department he had a proven track record as a good administrator.

Both Richardson and Cox apparently were quite prepared to take the proviso "independent" literally. Nixon soon realized he had closed one avenue of attack on himself only to open another.

It is passing strange that in selecting Elliot Richardson as his nominee for attorney general and in delegating to Richardson the authority to select a special prosecutor, Nixon had delivered the fate of his administration into the hands of the Eastern establishment, the "elitists" whom he had spent his political life fighting in the Republican party.

If you stand back and review the whole situation, Nixon's allowing Kleindienst to resign—thus making necessary the appointment of a new attorney general requiring Senate confirmation—was probably one of the biggest procedural mistakes Nixon made in all of Watergate. Selecting as Kleindienst's replacement an attorney general whose home state was Massachusetts enhanced the mistake because it not only gave Senator Ted Kennedy control of the confirmation but also the virtual selection of the special prosecutor, Archibald Cox.

Nixon said: "If Richardson had searched specifically for the man whom I would least have trusted he could hardly have done better." (*Memoirs*, Vol. 2, p. 910)

As it turned out, the Eastern elite—which President Nixon so disliked and distrusted—carried a sharp knife.

Cox (perhaps not coincidentally) had served as solicitor general under President Kennedy. For five years Cox had been responsible for all federal litigation before the Supreme Court. He had earned a reputation as a skilled negotiator and arbiter in labor disputes. His professional colleagues recognized his dedication to the law; his personal integrity was unquestioned. He was known as a persistent and determined advocate.

How very different things might have been had Nixon accepted representation from the beginning by a criminal defense lawyer with Archibald Cox's same qualifications. Richardson had announced that the president could no longer depend on the Attorney General's Office for legal advice. Now Nixon faced Cox as an independent prosecutor without being able to exercise the same command authority he had held over a Henry Petersen bearing the double burden of divided loyalties.

Cox employed a staff in the main hostile to Nixon. They remained in place under Cox's successor, dedicated to Nixon's impeachment and criminal conviction.

The new prosecutor knew the power of public opinion. After all, it was public opinion that had forced the appointment of an independent prosecutor. Cox determined not to conduct his investigations in secret, but to communicate directly with the press and the people. Everything was to be out in the open.

Congress appropriated a $2.8 million budget. More than any other single act, the money spoke to Congress's determination to support the special prosecutor in his investigation.

The team set up offices at 1425 K Street—a "civilian" building outside of the White House, outside of the Justice Department. Cox asked for security equal to "the inner reaches of the FBI."

His first task was to put together a large staff of some seventy or eighty competent men and women. Many of them were young—with a median age of about thirty—and some of them had worked for the Kennedys. None of them were Nixon people. The Kennedy connection was certain to rankle Nixon, and it did so. In his *Memoirs* (Vol. 2, p. 464) Nixon wrote:

> No White House in history could have survived the kind of operation Cox was planning. If he were determined to get rid of me, as I was certain that he and his staff were, then given the terms of their charter it would be only a matter of time until they had bored like termites through the whole executive branch. The frustrating thing was that while I saw them as partisan zealots abusing *the power I had given them* in order to destroy me unfairly, the media presented them and the public largely perceived them as the sacred flame of American justice against a wicked President and his corrupt administration. (Emphasis added.)

Then came the problem of breaking the entangled cases apart into manageable chunks. This is the way Cox and his assistants laid them out:

The first priority was the Watergate break-in and cover-up. Following in order came the Plumbers cases, the money trail, the International Telephone and Telegraph Corporation (ITT) investigations, and finally the "dirty tricks" during the 1972 political campaigns. (Doyle, *Not Above the Law*, pp. 60-81) A task force leader was assigned to each of the five areas of inquiry.

On his own, Attorney General Richardson attempted to follow some leads of "shoddy, disruption-sowing 1972 campaign operations." Somewhat startled to discover the federal penal code did not cover "dirty tricks," he sent President Nixon a memorandum suggesting certain corrective steps that could be taken. "The President, it seemed, could not or would not take positive steps to restore confidence in his administration. As time went on, it became clearer and clearer that his strategy would be defensive." (Richardson, *The Creative Balance,* New York: Holt, Rinehart and Winston, 1976, p. 16) "Still giving him the benefit of the doubt, I charged this off to an error of judgment. I should, of course, have realized that Richard Nixon was more likely to be guilty than stupid."

Following Haldeman's and Ehrlichman's forced resignations, Nixon brought Gen. Alexander Haig back into the White House on May 4, this time as chief of staff. Although Haig was not a lawyer and had no political experience outside of his service on Kissinger's staff, Haig was to become Nixon's closest adviser and defense advocate.

"One of the biggest mistakes related to Watergate—and I know I've said this to you before—was letting Haldeman go," Nixon said, looking back many years after his resignation in disgrace. (Crowley, *Nixon Off the Record*, p. 149) "He was loyal and tough. Haig was good, but he was nothing like Haldeman."

Haig had graduated from West Point in 1948, ranking 214 in his class of 310, and was sent to Japan to join Gen. Douglas MacArthur's staff. The young second lieutenant married Patricia Fox, the daughter of his commanding general, Alonzo Fox. Fox was one of MacArthur's favorites, and Haig soon found promotion. He became an aide to his father-in-law and, after that, an aide to a corps commander in the rapidly developing Korean War.

Haig returned home for an assignment to West Point, classes in several service schools, and a post as a military aide. He later saw action in Vietnam as a battalion commander.

Joseph Califano, general counsel of the army and former domestic adviser in the Johnson Administration, noticed Haig's abilities. Califano recommended Haig as a good staff man. Kissinger had never met Haig, but Califano's recommendation was good enough.

When Kissinger picked him up at the beginning of the Nixon Administration, Haig was a holdover from a Democratic administration. He had by then become a smooth and polished regular army aide-de-camp—which meant that he was skilled at getting along with temperamental patrons in positions of great power. Haig—who said he saw scant difference between "soldiering and politicking"—had little training in foreign policy, none in running for elective office, nor any service as a political activist, public relations man, or congressional assistant.

He was a professional army aide.

That proved to be exactly the right experience Haig needed in the narrow valley where he found himself between Nixon and Kissinger—two craggy peaks of pride, secrecy, and deviousness.

Folk wisdom has it that a triangle is good geometry but a poor structure in human relations. Haig's rapid progress altered the configuration of the Nixon-Kissinger team. By hard work and skillful manipulation of staff members, Haig gradually changed his office manager's job into that of Kissinger's deputy.

President Nixon liked to roam the White House corridors before going to bed. His own tendency toward isolation—constantly reinforced by his gatekeepers, Haldeman and Ehrlichman—created a loneliness and a need to talk to someone. Al Haig was a workaholic who often stayed at his desk until late evening. "When you see lights burning in Kissinger's office," Nixon observed, "it's usually Haig." (Anthony J. Lukas, *Nightmare: The Underside of the Nixon Years,* New York: Viking, 1976, p. 438) The president enjoyed stopping in for a chat.

These nocturnal visits enabled Haig to establish a separate and direct relationship with the president—to Kissinger's detriment. Kissinger suspected that Haig made fun of him and mimicked his thick accent behind his back. Kissinger eventually became so jealous and mistrustful of Haig that sometimes he was reluctant to leave Washington for fear of giving Haig unobstructed access to Nixon. Thus a triangle was established which ultimately was to prove uncomfortable for Kissinger and damaging for Nixon.

One cannot be anything but dumbfounded by the success of Haig's ambitious ascendancy. He was promoted from lieutenant colonel to brigadier general in November 1969. Just sixteen months later, in March 1972, he jumped from brigadier to major general. In five more months he rocketed from major general to four-star general—in the process vaulting over the heads of 240 senior officers. Working in the White House, Haig had made the leap from colonel to four-star general in three years and nine months.

Isaacson commented wryly, "[Haig] was decorated for his heroism—and earned a battlefield promotion to colonel—by taking over command of a brigade in a fierce two-day battle close to the Cambodian border. But each of his subsequent promotions, up to four-star general, came for valor behind a desk at the White House." (Isaacson, *Kissinger,* p. 186)

In late April 1972, Haig was at Camp David with Nixon while Kissinger was in Moscow on a mission so hush-hush than even the American ambassador to the Soviet Union was unaware of the meeting between the national security adviser and Leonid Brezhnev. Haig, "to Kissinger's discomfort, was becoming one of the Nixon insiders. . . ." (Stephen E. Ambrose, *Nixon: The Triumph of a Politician*, New York: Simon & Schuster, 1987, pp. 531-532)

White (*Breach of Faith*, p. 242) described the situation: "As Haig first settled behind his desk as Chief of Staff in the gold-carpeted room through which the President's business flows, he could not escape Watergate, the crisis of authority and credibility. Thus, immediately, Haig invited to join him a Pentagon lawyer, Fred Buzhardt, a West Point contemporary of his, who arrived on May 10th to be named President's special counsel on Watergate matters, while [Leonard] Garment shifted to prepare the defense before the Senate committee."

Thus once again the two lawyers who were to bear the brunt of defending Nixon against impeachment were chosen on the basis of friendship and not on a record of defending criminal cases.

"Yet the two lawyers—Buzhardt and Garment—were not enough," White continued. "What Haig needed was a full legal team, headed by someone of the eminence of a Supreme Court judge, to take overall charge of the case."

Early in his career Fred Buzhardt had left the army. He attended law school in North Carolina and practiced law in that state for several years. He then became a legislative assistant to Senator Jesse Helms (R.–North Carolina). Buzhardt had moved from there back into the army, where as counsel to the Defense Department he was assigned to prosecute cases involving Ellsberg and the Pentagon Papers. Those had collapsed through the disclosure of Liddy's illegal acts and the raid on Ellsberg's psychiatrist's office, so Buzhardt was free to accept Haig's offer to be Nixon's counsel.

Garment, Nixon's friend and former law partner, described himself as "almost the first person" Nixon worked with when he began his concerted drive to the presidency; Garment was acting legal counsel to the president. Buzhardt and Garment were joined by Charles Alan Wright, a University of Texas law professor skilled in constitutional law, for special assignment to the tape situation and its litigation. The men had a half dozen young lawyers working for them. (Ambrose, *Ruin and Recovery*, p. 146)

So now Nixon had legal counsel competent as far as their expertise went to advise him and work on his behalf—but not skilled in criminal defense. Haig soon proved himself to be equal to Haldeman as a gatekeeper, so Nixon remained isolated. His lawyers did not have direct access to him but had to go through Haig—who became stingy with his client. And Nixon continued to operate on an intensely private internal level. He still believed he was capable of directing the course of his Watergate defense without the advice of other lawyers skilled in the criminal law.

With the advent of Haig, a new set of presidential advisers came into being: Haig himself, former Secretary of Defense Melvin Laird, Attorney General Richardson, Len Garment, Fred Buzhardt, and Ron Ziegler.

The special prosecutor, Cox, wanted access to certain White House files. He arranged a meeting on June 6 with Nixon's lawyers. Predictably, the lawyers replied that the files contained highly sensitive items, that acquiescing to such a request would establish "a bad precedent," and finally that the files were protected by executive privilege.

Cox put forward several rebuttal arguments, but in the end he walked away from the White House empty-handed.

On June 25, the day John Dean began his public testimony before the Senate Watergate Committee, Cox told the three assistant U.S. attorneys who headed the original Watergate prosecution team—Earl J. Silbert, Seymour Glanzer, and Donald E. Campbell—that he was now ready to receive their resignations. Cox had asked the men to remain in place and assist with the transition. In accepting their resignations, he noted that the trio had developed many of the details of the cover-up that finally emerged in the Senate hearings. (Doyle, *Not Above the Law*, pp. 79-80) Petersen claimed that the prosecutors had already broken the case.

Nixon's thinking was still focused on public relations, of "getting the story out." In a rather lengthy memo to Haig from "The Western White House, San Clemente," dated July 7, Nixon wrote: "The strategy of both the Committee and Cox is clear—they want to drag on these hearings and maintain public interest in them as long as they can." Over and over he repeated the need "to get out our stories."

He apparently viewed his lawyers largely as just additional PR spokesmen. In the same memo (Oudes, *From: The President*, p. 592) Nixon suggested that "a statement from the White House—perhaps by Buzhardt—might be in order."

That same month, some of Cox's team began gathering background information about the president's real estate holdings—specifically, expenditures of federal money related to San Clemente. Cox asked his press officer to request newspaper clippings from the *Los Angeles Times*, which knew a good story when it was handed to them. News about the prosecutor's inquiry broke in the *Times* while Nixon happened to be at San Clemente.

Nixon, infuriated, raged at Haig—who phoned Richardson who phoned Cox.

The prosecutor's response was calm and reasoned as he spoke to his former student: "Elliot," he said, "do you really think it's proper for you to call me up. . . . the first time that something hostile to the President appears in print?"

Haig called Richardson back to say that the president "wanted a tight line drawn [in the scope of Cox's investigation] with no further mistakes. If not," Haig concluded, "we will get rid of Cox." (*The Impeachment Report*, p. 99)

This is how Nixon viewed the investigation, as later recorded in his *Memoirs* (Vol. 2, pp. 461-463):

> Unfortunately, in my April 30 speech I had said that I was giving Elliot Richardson "absolute authority to make all decisions bearing upon the prosecution of the Watergate case and related matters." I had, in essence, and as events turned out, put the survival of my administration in his hands. From the time Richardson's confirmation hearings as Attorney General began it was clear that the Senate would hold his nomination hostage until an independent Watergate Special Prosecutor was appointed. Richardson felt compelled to yield to the pressure and began conducting a search for a candidate to fill the position. It took him two weeks and several refusals before he finally selected Professor Archibald Cox of the Harvard Law School. . . .
>
> Appointing Archibald Cox was bad enough. But Richardson then compounded the mistake by approving a charter for the Special Prosecutor Forces that, instead of limiting its responsibility to the area of Watergate, gave it a virtual carte blanche to investigate the executive branch. . . .
>
> The partisan attitude that permeated the top ranks of the

> Watergate Special Prosecution Force was exceeded by the fervor of the junior members of its staff, most of whom were brash young lawyers intoxicated with their first real taste of power and with the attention being paid to them by a flattering and fawning press. Reports came back to me of arrogant young men using unsubstantiated charges to threaten and intimidate my personal friends and members of my staff.

Bits and pieces Cox had heard from various sources caused him to wonder if some kinds of verbatim records might have been kept of the president's meetings with his staff. A similar hope had been growing in the mind of Donald Sanders, a former FBI agent familiar with wiretapping and at the time a minority counsel for the Ervin Committee.

On July 13 (a Friday, and an unlucky day for Nixon) Sanders popped the question to Alexander P. Butterfield, a former White House aide to Haldeman and a witness before the Watergate Committee.

"Well . . . yes, there's a recording system in the president's office," Butterfield responded.

From that defining moment, Nixon's loss of the presidency was predictable. The tapes became the target of the special prosecutor, the courts, the Congress, and the press. It opened the opportunity for the prosecution to catch Nixon in a big fat lie.

Al Haig, sitting in Haldeman's old office, watched Butterfield's testimony on television and reacted with shock. He ordered the taping system to be ripped out immediately. (Strober and Strober, *Nixon: An Oral History*, p. 393)

Over the weekend after Butterfield's revelation, Republican chief counsel Fred Thompson talked to Buzhardt. "You guys had better plan on gathering up your tapes and getting them down here," Thompson said. "We know you have them." Thompson could not tell from Buzhardt's vague reply if he had been aware of the taping system.

The president's legal advisers—Buzhardt and Garment—tried to assess the pros and cons: "Do we keep them or get rid of them?" Garment believed that "destroying the tapes would be a felony, and could be count number one in an impeachment petition." (Strober and Strober, *Nixon: An Oral History*, p. 393)

The president's other close advisers—including Connally, Kissinger, Agnew, and Rockefeller—urged Nixon to destroy the incriminating White House tapes at once. Connally and Kissinger must have been aware that their own conversations with Nixon undoubtedly had been recorded. As additional White House tapes are released, as some were in November 1996, other men may be embarrassed by the frankness of their "private" conversations with the president.

Connally told the president to burn the tapes in a giant Rose Garden bonfire. Nixon chose to disregard that bit of advice.

Why did Nixon ignore the many warnings and refuse to destroy the incriminating tapes? He may have believed his own constant statements that he had done nothing wrong. He may have forgotten or failed to realize how potentially damaging the tapes were to him. He may have believed his "executive privilege" argument would hold up. He may—as some writers suggest—have wanted to keep the tapes for the books he planned to write after he left the Oval Office. He also may have hoped to donate some of them for income tax deductions, as he had done with his vice-presidential papers.

Haldeman supplied his own answer to the question: "One reason is that, by a stroke of bad fortune, Nixon was ill in [Bethesda Naval] hospital with pneumonia when the news of Butterfield's revelation arrived at the White House." (Haldeman, *The Ends of Power*, p. 205)

Whatever Nixon's reasons for preserving the tapes, the whole issue became moot on the afternoon of July 23: Cox issued subpoenas for nine tapes. The subpoenas were hand-delivered to the White House. Until then, the tapes had not been "evidence." Thereafter, destruction of the tapes would have constituted a criminal offense. The ten-day window of opportunity to destroy the tapes was gone.

Throughout August and September, Nixon fought one delaying action after another.

The president had been ordered by the U.S. Circuit Court of Appeals to turn over the nine tapes. Nixon issued a statement on Thursday, October 19, with the offer of a compromise: the so-called Stennis proposal. Nixon would prepare summaries of the Watergate tapes in question, supply Judge Sirica with the summaries, and allow Senator John Stennis (D.–Mississippi) to listen to the tapes and to verify the transcripts. Cox was to make no further attempts to subpoena any additional materials.

Nixon must have viewed his offer as a "heads I win, tails you lose" scheme. If the courts agreed to his plan, the president still had control over what he released. If Cox refused the president's offer, Nixon probably thought he had the grounds he needed to fire the special prosecutor.

A good defense counsel would have told Nixon that no self-respecting prosecutor could accept such a proposition. Nixon's offer was a thinly disguised effort to cover up the tapes, that it was not going to be accepted, and that making it only weakened his position. But Al Haig, who was acting as the president's adviser, apparently did not say any of that to him.

Cox took the position that Nixon could not pick and choose what evidence he would supply and what he would withhold. To have done so would have been to defeat the fair administration of justice. That was a sound legal and public position. The next day, Friday, October 20, Cox cited continued frustration with the job but said he had no intention of resigning.

By this time the angry president must have seen himself in the role of the beleaguered King Henry II railing against "this turbulent priest," Archbishop Thomas Becket. But Nixon could not take action directly. He had to operate through the attorney general.

Here's the batters' lineup in the Justice Department at the beginning of the ninth inning: after Attorney General Richardson came the deputy attorney general, William Ruckelshaus. Third in line was the new solicitor general, Robert Bork.

On Nixon's orders, Al Haig phoned Richardson and told him the president had decided to fire the special prosecutor.

Cox's independence had been a condition of Richardson's congressional confirmation; Richardson himself had publicly reaffirmed the special prosecutor's freedom to take the investigation wherever it led.

Richardson felt "that if he fired Cox he too would have to resign for breaking his promise to the Senate." (*Memoirs,* Vol. 2, p. 929)

A veteran of the D-Day landings in World War II, Richardson later said the spot he was in was like putting down one foot after another in a mine field. Richardson notified Cox of the president's plan. There was little either man could do.

On Friday evening Richardson received a letter from the White House officially demanding that Cox make no further attempts by judicial process to obtain tapes, notes, or memoranda of presidential conversations.

At home Richardson discussed the letter with his wife, Anne. She compared his situation to being buried in a mahogany coffin—it was elaborate, but he was just as dead.

Saturday, October 21, Richardson received the expected call from the White House: Fire Cox! Clearly Richardson could not comply. He refused and resigned. "I'm sorry that you insist on putting your personal commitments ahead of the public interest," the president told him. (Emery, *Watergate*, p. 398)

The buck passed to Ruckelshaus, former acting FBI director and now acting attorney general. Ruckelshaus himself had not given any promises to Congress concerning the special prosecutor but said he felt "duty bound" by Richardson's promise since Richardson had been the one who hired him. Ruckelshaus, too, refused to fire Cox. He submitted his resignation.

Nixon, in a pique at being thwarted twice by his own executive branch appointees, refused to accept the resignation and instructed Haig to fire Ruckelshaus.

"I think Bork may be your man," Ruckelshaus volunteered to Haig.

Before appointment, Bork had been a law professor at Yale, specializing in constitutional and antitrust law. As a constitutionalist, Bork agreed with the president's argument that "the Government . . . cannot function if employees of the Executive Branch are free to ignore . . . the instructions of the President."

As acting attorney general, Bork agreed to wield the headsman's ax. The president sent his lawyers, Garment and Buzhardt, in a White House limousine to pick up Bork before he could rethink his position and change his mind.

Bork signed a short, two-paragraph letter drafted by the White House, sent it to Cox, and the deed was done. Nixon, by way of appreciation, made a comment that could have been interpreted as offering Bork the job of attorney general. Bork brushed it off with a quick comment: "That would not be appropriate."

Bork has been remembered primarily as the only Justice Department official willing to fire Cox. On closer examination, Bork appears to be a more complex player in the drama. As solicitor general, he was "the government's lawyer at the Supreme Court, a job he had always wanted." (Emery, *Watergate*, p. 381) After Butterfield disclosed the existence of the White House tapes, Al Haig sounded Bork out about becoming the president's counsel. Bork thought it over and said no, thanks.

Before he agreed to follow Nixon's order and fire Cox, Bork discussed his position with both Richardson and Ruckleshaus. Perhaps he should follow suit and resign? His erstwhile Justice Department colleagues pointed out the obvious fact: if Bork left too, the department would be rudderless.

As soon as Cox was fired, the White House press secretary, Ron Ziegler, announced that "the office of the Watergate Special Prosecutor has been abolished as of approximately 8 P.M. . . ."

At Haig's orders, the FBI swept into the special prosecutor's suite of offices at 1425 K Street, closed them, and secured all files and records, including any personal mementos such as family portraits. Haig also sent the agents to secure the Justice Department offices of Richardson and Ruckelshaus.

When the news of the multiple firings—quickly dubbed the "Saturday Night Massacre" by the outraged press—reached the American public, a firestorm erupted unlike anything Nixon could have imagined. Stunned, people watched on their television sets as scenes unfolded reminiscent of some of Hitler's Nazi Germany.

Why, the public asked, had the firing of the special prosecutor and the two top Justice Department men been necessary if the president was innocent of any wrongdoing? What was the president hiding?

"Three million [of the American people] sent angry messages to their senators and representatives. No such enormous outpouring of public protest had ever been seen in this country." (Elliot Richardson, *Reflections of a Radical Moderate*, New York: Pantheon, 1996, p. 14)

Nixon lost all chance of avoiding impeachment.

The pressures on President Nixon were enormous. During the month of October 1973 he had made critical foreign relations decisions while preoccupied with the worsening Watergate affair. The Yom Kippur War had begun on October 6 when Egypt and Syria attacked Israel on the very day of one of the most important Jewish religious holidays. The fact that the United States had tied itself into a knot over Watergate may have had something to do with this war starting when it did. The United States, under Nixon's active direction, sided with Israel, furnished planes and munitions to the Israelis, while the Soviets supplied weapons to Egypt and Syria. A serious world crisis loomed. Less than two weeks later, Nixon held important talks at the White House with several Middle Eastern ministers.

On the Saturday night of the "massacre," Henry Kissinger—no longer national security adviser but by then officially secretary of state for almost a month—was in Moscow on an extremely sensitive diplomatic mission. Annoyed that one of his cables had been ignored, Kissinger chose that night to phone Al Haig.

"Get off my back," Haig snapped at his former boss. "I've got problems of my own."

"What problems could you possibly have in Washington on a Saturday night?" Kissinger demanded in his deep, heavily accented voice.

"The president has just fired Cox," Haig replied. "Richardson and Ruckelshaus have resigned, and all hell has broken loose." (Isaacson, *Kissinger*, p. 525)

Meanwhile, in the absence of a special prosecutor, the whole Watergate investigation—at least temporarily—fell back into the hands of Henry Petersen.

CHAPTER 14

NOT SINCE TEAPOT DOME

"Congress [may] follow the precedent it adopted in respect to the Teapot Dome matter."
— Senator Sam Ervin

TO THOSE AMERICANS OLD enough to remember—or those who knew the nation's political history—the mounting indications of fraud, deception, and lying in the Nixon Administration began to sound like the scandals associated with the administration in 1921-1923 of President Warren G. Harding.

It is not an overstatement to say that a large segment of the public expected more revelations from the Watergate investigations.

The Monday following the Saturday Night Massacre was the Veterans Day holiday. Henry Petersen had been out on Chesapeake Bay in his boat but returned to Washington when he heard that Acting Attorney General Bork wanted him.

Petersen and Bork held a hastily called meeting in the Justice Department with Henry Ruth, deputy special prosecutor and a longtime friend of Petersen's, and Philip A. Lacovara, counsel to the special prosecutor. They all were uneasily aware of the spotlight of publicity and negative public opinion focused on them as they tried to determine how best to proceed.

Petersen became angry at Lacovara's mention of a Justice Department official; for an anxious moment it seemed likely the two might come to blows. Ruth and Lacovara returned to their offices, depressed and discouraged.

Bork decided to throw the Watergate investigation back into

Petersen's hands, "apparently unaware that the special prosecutor, because of Dean's testimony, planned to call Petersen as a witness in the main obstruction of justice trial." (Emery, *Watergate*, p. 402)

The special prosecutor's press spokesman, James Doyle, had already issued a statement that the prosecutors would continue their investigation if the Justice Department would allow them to do so. Doyle also had received a tip that "Petersen was raring to crack down on Cox's whippersnappers, who had stolen 'his' investigation." (Emery, *Watergate*, p. 402) The sentiment may have been Petersen's but I doubt if he used the oddly old-fashioned word *whippersnapper*.

At the White House "hubris reigned." Hubris, Colson observed in *Born Again* (p. 72) "was the quality Nixon admired the most."

The president failed to realize that in ridding himself of Cox, he had—like Macbeth—scotched the snake, not killed it. Nixon planned to respond to Judge Sirica's order with yet another offer of transcripts filtered through some third person.

Al Haig and Ron Ziegler were shielding the president from the public's outrage. Top Nixon aides were scurrying to leave the administration before being splattered by the scandals certain to come.

Monday Judge Sirica called the two grand juries into his courtroom to make it very plain that they "remained operative and intact." The judge, who had been among Saturday night's television viewers, pronounced himself to be "plain damned angry," and later said he had hardly slept that night. He was prepared to cite the president for contempt.

On that same hectic Monday, the Democratic leadership of the House of Representatives met. Speaker Carl Albert's apprehension was mounting: he genuinely did not want to become president. But if Nixon left office before Ford's confirmation as vice president, Speaker Albert was next in line of succession. Albert decided the time had come for a House Judiciary Committee investigation to determine if grounds for impeachment existed. The committee's chairman was Congressman Peter W. Rodino, Jr. (D.–New Jersey).

On Tuesday—in what Nixon had hoped and expected would be a conciliatory statement to the press—the departed Richardson and Ruckelshaus praised Petersen. But Richardson added: "I think the situation is fraught with great difficulty for him, and I think that whoever is attorney general and Mr. Petersen would both be in a better position if a new special prosecutor were appointed."

Probably as much to his own surprise as anyone's—and again without good legal advice as to his own vulnerability—Nixon was swinging around to the same conclusion. By this time, since Acting Attorney General Bork had officially abolished the Watergate Special Prosecution Force, Nixon was faced with demands from his own Republican party to appoint a new special prosecutor.

Tuesday, October 23, Charles Alan Wright, Nixon's special counsel for Watergate, and Len Garment, counsel to the president, appeared in court. Wright told Judge Sirica that President Nixon was prepared "to comply in all respects with the order of August 29 as modified by the Court of Appeals" to turn over certain materials. "The president does not defy the law," Wright said.

The people gathered in the courtroom clearly were surprised by Nixon's apparent about-face. Sirica may also have been surprised, but he confined his comments to a proper "Mr. Wright, the court is very happy."

Nixon had not squarely faced the problem of his own vulnerability—a thing he was never able to do for himself and a thing which he would eventually dump on his successor, Gerald Ford.

That same afternoon Henry Petersen accompanied Acting Attorney General Bork on a visit to Cox's headquarters at 1425 K Street. Apparently Petersen wanted the Justice Department to finish the job by prosecuting Haldeman, Ehrlichman, Dean, and numerous staff workers. But someone would have to be selected and turned to furnish the direct testimony.

The initial confrontation between the Justice Department officials and Cox's staff was not an especially cordial one. To the loyal survivors of "Cox's army," the red-bearded Bork must have resembled a pirate boarding their ship on the high seas: How many of them would also be forced to walk the plank?

In his raspy, cigarette-hoarse voice, Petersen quickly assured the staff that they were not to be fired. (Doyle, *Not Above the Law*, p. 226) "And for you to quit would be a moral and professional disservice to yourselves and your country. This case can't stand another change in personnel," he added.

Of course, President Nixon would not have allowed Petersen

to say that if he had known about it. Nixon wanted to get rid of all the Kennedy people on Cox's staff, along with Cox himself.

Petersen did want one change in personnel, however. He wanted James Doyle, the special prosecutor's press secretary, *out.* "If this were my office," Petersen told Doyle, "you wouldn't be here."

"That's right," Doyle shot back. Unlike Nixon's press secretary Ron Ziegler, Doyle had been one of the "working press" and was respected by his media colleagues. Under Cox he had enjoyed a degree of responsible autonomy that Petersen would have been unlikely to approve.

Bork then announced that since the Office of the Watergate Special Prosecution Force no longer existed, it could not continue as a separate unit but would become an office within the Justice Department with Henry Petersen in charge.

So exactly what was Henry Petersen's position in the interim?

Until a new prosecutor took over, Watergate and related cases reverted to Petersen, who had supervised the first investigation from June 17, 1972, until Cox's appointment as special prosecutor in May 1973. Petersen may have been somewhat mollified by the return of the investigation to the Justice Department, where he felt it rightly belonged. And to his credit, Petersen's reaction was that of a responsible lawyer.

Petersen "requested the [tapes and documents concerning the Plumbers' activities] in a letter to Buzhardt, and at the same time asked for tapes and logs and recent dealings with the Watergate cover-up and other actions under investigation." (Jaworski, *The Right and the Power*, p. 20)

The deposed attorney general, Elliot Richardson, could not understand why the White House "resisted the production of documents. . . . The American people, I thought, would be more than likely to forgive and forget." (Richardson, *Reflections,* p. 17)

Ten days was not enough time for Petersen to accomplish what Cox's army had been unable to do in five months. Petersen did not get the requested materials. How stunned he would have been had he heard the March 21 tape during which Nixon and Dean had coldly planned to use him in their cover-up.

But Petersen's investigation was far from being the only one. Two grand juries, the U.S. attorneys, Judge Sirica, the House Committee under Peter Rodino, the Senate Select Committee under Sam Ervin, the IRS, and the press all were engaged in investigating various aspects of Watergate.

By that time Nixon had so many hound packs baying after him that no tree was tall enough, no stream wide enough to cover the scent trail leading straight to the White House.

Judge John Sirica is an interesting player in the Watergate investigations. The grandchild of Italian immigrants, Sirica delayed his formal education and became a boxer. Jack Dempsey, former heavyweight champion, was a friend of his.

Sirica had actively campaigned for Republican candidates Eisenhower and Nixon in 1952 and 1956. He became a judge for the U.S. District Court for the District of Columbia on April 2, 1957, and chief judge on April 2, 1971, just in time for Watergate. As a judge, Sirica could no longer take an active role in political campaigning, but as a private citizen he voted for Nixon in 1968 and 1972. It is interesting that this second vote was after the indictment of the Watergate burglars, which was then pending in his court.

On September 15, 1972, the five Watergate burglars, plus E. Howard Hunt and G. Gordon Liddy, had been indicted on federal charges. After consulting some of his brother jurists, Judge Sirica assigned himself to the case. As chief judge, he had the time. As a Republican, he could scarcely be accused of a political bias. Sirica ruled that nothing further should be made public in the proceedings until after the November election. (Emery, *Watergate*, p. 217)

Before the trial began, reporters Woodward and Bernstein visited the five burglars, their families, and their attorneys in an Arlington, Virginia, apartment house. The defendants told the reporters that the raid on the Watergate offices had been approved by "high government officials" and was, therefore, an "authorized mission." (Bernstein and Woodward, *All the President's Men*, p. 299) The men believed that such authorization supported their pleas of not guilty.

The trial, the *United States v. George Gordon Liddy, et al.*, began in Judge Sirica's sixth-floor courtroom on Monday, January 8, 1973, with the selection of a jury. The prosecution team—Earl Silbert, Seymour Glanzer, and Donald E. Campbell—were the assistant U.S. attorneys who had investigated the break-in from the beginning. In his chambers, Sirica (*To Set the Record Straight*, New York: Norton, 1979, p. 58) told Silbert, "You've got a great opportunity in this case if you go right down the middle, let the chips fall where they may. Don't let anyone put any pressure on you."

As a defendant, Liddy was thoroughly uncooperative, defiant, and unrepentant in court with the prosecutors.

As the trial proceeded, Sirica examined some of the witnesses himself. He had a reputation as an activist judge and at one point told Liddy's attorney, Peter Maroulis, that he had "on many occasions and in the presence of the jury examined witnesses where I thought all the facts had not been brought out by counsel on either side." He might be reversed on appeal, he conceded, but in his courtroom he would do what he thought was right. (Sirica, *To Set the Record Straight*, p. 80)

Sirica had gained his nickname, "Maximum John," partly because he did not believe in giving light sentences to those convicted of white-collar crime. As he considered sentences, he decided to give provisional sentences to the five who had pleaded guilty, dependent on their cooperation with the grand jury, the prosecutors, and the Senate Select Committee.

But Liddy, who had clowned around and had made no effort to take the case or the Court seriously—ah, Liddy would feel the full brunt of Sirica's sentencing power.

From Gordon Liddy's standpoint, there was little left of the Nixon Administration to command loyalty. Nevertheless Liddy did not bargain, did not testify, and did not plead for mercy. He was what the Mafia would call a "stand-up guy." He never wavered in his dedication to the code of James Bond. He followed to the bitter end Shakespeare's "to thine own self be true" in exhibiting to the Court his prickly personality.

Judge Sirica sentenced Liddy to "a firm twenty years and a fine of $40,000." (Emery, *Watergate*, p. 271) But Sirica had not broken Liddy. He still had his pride. The judge then turned his attention to James McCord. McCord would not get off lightly either.

March 19, 1972, was Judge Sirica's sixty-ninth birthday. The judge was about to receive a totally unexpected gift from a totally unlikely source.

The next day McCord waited in the judge's outer office, asking to see Sirica. The judge quite properly refused to see the defendant alone. He sent for McCord's probation officer, who delivered an envelope to the judge. Still observing legal propriety, Sirica called his court reporter and two law clerks into his chambers before he opened the envelope from McCord.

He removed and read McCord's letter, silently at first, then aloud.

The letter spoke of political pressure, perjury, and other persons involved in Watergate who had not been identified during the trial. Unlike the other defendants, McCord was not willing to go to jail to protect anyone. McCord wanted to talk to the judge privately in chambers because "I cannot feel confident in talking with an FBI agent, in testifying before a grand jury whose U.S. Attorneys work for the Department of Justice, or in talking with other government representatives. . . ."

Almost everyone who has studied and written about Watergate has a favorite *if.* The Watergate case would never have been broken, Sirica has said, "if McCord had elected to stand pat and had not written the letter to me."

Senator Ervin went further than that. "If President Nixon had entrusted his campaign for re-election to the Republican National Committee, *there would have been no Watergate.*" [Emphasis added]

Nixon, Haldeman, Ehrlichman, Dean, and Mitchell met in the president's EOB office on the afternoon of Thursday, March 22, 1973. Among other things, they discussed Pat Gray's inadvertent bean-spilling performance before the Senate confirmation hearing to become director of the FBI. Dean and Ehrlichman had given Gray a fake telegram found in McCord's wall safe in the Plumbers' old quarters in the basement of the White House, with the clear intent that it should be destroyed. It purportedly involved President Jack Kennedy in the death of South Vietnam President Ngo Dinh. Indeed, the poisonous and ill-conceived document cried out to be destroyed. Pat Gray—apparently believing that he was acting in loyalty to Nixon—did so. He admitted as much in his confirmation hearings.

How can Gray's blunders be explained? Was he naively offering his testimony of the destruction of evidence as proof of his loyalty to the president and his ability to carry out covert activities? Gray had really opened the sluice gates and had brought John Dean directly into the path of the onrushing torrent.

But the facts were that Gray's Senate confirmation hearing "began the second largest catastrophe of all for Nixon: the transformation of John Dean from the White House point man on Watergate to the leading informer against Nixon." (Haldeman, *The Ends of Power*, p. 232)

Dean had been steadily asked by Nixon to write a report on Watergate which would show "no White House involvement." Dean was having great difficulty getting down to it. He promised to "sit down this evening and start drafting."

"I think you ought to hole up for the weekend and do that and get it done. . . . Give it your full attention and get it done," Haldeman said.

"I think you need . . . why don't you do this?" Nixon suggested. "Why don't you go up to Camp David. . . . Completely away from the phone. Just go up there and [inaudible]. I want a written report." (*The Presidential Transcripts*, p. 160) Nixon made a mistake in asking John Dean for a written report because Dean could not write anything which would not turn into a confession implicating Nixon.

That conversation took place on March 22. The following day, Friday, Sirica read McCord's letter in open court.

McCord's letter came as a complete surprise and shook Dean badly. Dean knew better than anyone how much damage McCord —whom Haldeman had described as a "low-level security man"— could do to John Dean on the post-June 17 cover-up. But McCord had not had access to Nixon and could not furnish testimony directly implicating Nixon.

Evidently Dean concluded that putting a report in writing showing no White House involvement would be fatal to his own defense. To save himself, Dean needed to implicate Haldeman and Ehrlichman. Moreover the report could be used as a tourniquet to cut him off from the president's protection and to set himself up as the scapegoat.

Instead of writing a report, on Friday, March 30, Dean met with his personal attorney, Charles Shaffer—who recommended that Dean break off all contact with his fellow conspirators and make no effort to prepare the report which Nixon had requested. "Although he did not know it, [Nixon] was about to undergo the slow torment of his betrayal by John Dean. . . . [Dean] was scrambling to save his own skin." (Emery, *Watergate*, p. 290)

Dean was at first reluctant, all too keenly aware that any communication with the prosecutors would go straight to Petersen and from Petersen to the president. Dean's lawyer Shaffer told Dean that Seymour Glanzer was the one to approach. In Dean's presence, Shaffer phoned Glanzer. "You need to talk to me," he said. "Put on a pot of coffee."

Dean's willingness to talk was relayed to the prosecutors on April 2. On Saturday, April 7, Haldeman noted (*The Haldeman Diaries*, p. 628) that "Dean called later today, said his lawyers had met with U.S. Attorneys again, that they only want to get to the facts on the Watergate and they do not expect to go beyond that."

Right here is when Nixon needed the advice and counsel of a criminal defense lawyer in the worst way. Instead he got a soothing brush stroke from non-lawyer Haldeman. Apparently, Haldeman had not yet figured out that Dean had selected him (Haldeman) to be a fall guy and that Nixon may have concurred in this.

The following day, Haldeman briefed the president: "I just wanted to post you on the Dean meeting. It went fine. He is going to wait until after he's had a chance to talk to Mitchell and to pass the word to Magruder through his lawyers that he is going to appear at the grand jury." (*The Presidential Transcripts*, p. 227)

The news that Dean was willing to talk was wonderfully exciting to the two prosecutors, Earl Silbert, and Silbert's assistant, Seymour Glanzer. This was the second big break in their case following McCord's letter and can be directly attributed to McCord's letter.

Dean took the action partly because he had exhausted ways of meeting the increasing demands for money by the burglars. The Watergate break-in had been expensive from the first day, but in mid-March 1973 one of the burglars, E. Howard Hunt, demanded an additional $130,000 in cash. Poker went up. The implication—"or else"—was quite clear. Following McCord's letter to the court, Dean saw the cover-up collapsing. Determined not to be a scapegoat himself, Dean decided to terminate his loyalty to Mitchell and to shift the blame for Watergate onto the shoulders of the president's chief gatekeepers, Haldeman and Ehrlichman.

On the surface, John Dean's becoming a witness for the government seems an act of great disloyalty to the president because up to that moment Dean had been acting as the president's lawyer. Years later, referring to a White House problem in the Clinton Administration, Nixon (Crowley, *Off the Record*, p. 193) wryly observed: "They can't hide behind attorney-client privilege because [John] Dean knocked that out in Watergate."

But Dean's decision must be judged against the general background created by Nixon and against Nixon's decision in June 1972 to cover up instead of making a complete public disclosure.

Nixon should have realized Dean was too young and inexperienced to handle the assignment he had been given. Under these circumstances, Dean was justified in expecting immunity if not a pardon from Nixon. Since Nixon would not consider a pardon for what appeared to be political reasons, Dean believed he had a right to protect himself even if his actions breached his loyalty to Nixon. Dean started negotiating for a plea bargain, which was the only way for him to stay out of jail. That was what Dean's lawyer advised him to do.

After the Saturday Night Massacre, the printed *Presidential Transcripts* clearly document Nixon's efforts to perpetuate the Watergate cover-up. Judge Sirica (*To Set the Record Straight*, p. 205) found the whole thing disgusting when he "actually listened to [Nixon's own voice on the tapes] coaching his aides on the cover-up, and realized he was displaying no outrage, not even the normal anger one would expect from a politician whose aides had gotten him into trouble."

The evidentiary phase of the burglars' trial in the district court was over, but obvious serious questions remained. There was widespread belief that the Justice Department had done a poor job in the Watergate prosecution in not uncovering the real higher-ups behind the burglary. (Samuel Dash, *Chief Counsel: Inside the Ervin Committee*, New York: Random House, 1976, p. 25)

If the Senate planned to launch an investigation into President Nixon's possible involvement with Watergate, was there a precedent?

Indeed there was: the Teapot Dome scandal of 1922.

In that scandal Republican president Warren G. Harding made the mistake of delegating too much responsibility to his subordinates and failing to keep close tabs on them. Harding's Administration was marked by a number of scandals, including the misuse of $200 million of Veterans' Bureau funds appropriated for World War I veterans and a plan to return to Germany assets seized during the war.

The most notorious, Teapot Dome, involved the lease of federal naval oil reserves to private investors—for which Interior Secretary Albert B. Fall received an unsecured "loan" of $125,000.

Just in time to escape political embarrassment, President Harding died in August 1923 apparently of a heart attack. The vice president, Calvin Coolidge, succeeded him. President Coolidge's own integrity was never in question. He set about cleaning up the mess he had inherited from Harding.

In that protracted six-year investigation, the two special counsels appointed by President Coolidge were not connected with the Justice Department; they remained under Coolidge's direct authority and complete control. But they were not investigating a sitting president. They were investigating Cabinet officers who had been appointed by a former president, the late President Harding.

Harding's attorney general, Harry M. Daugherty, was accused of criminal conspiracy and avoided conviction only by invoking the Fifth Amendment. He was acquitted but President Coolidge requested his resignation. (Gunderson and Smelser, *American History at a Glance*, p. 186)

Interior Secretary Fall was "convicted for accepting a bribe, thereby achieving the distinction of being the first Cabinet officer in American history to go to jail." (Kenneth C. Davis, *Don't Know Much About History*, New York: Avon, 1990, p. 263) Charles R. Forbes, head of the Veterans' Bureau, also went to jail.

The two cases—Teapot Dome and Watergate—were not analogous. In Teapot Dome, greedy administration officials had stolen millions of dollars from the federal government for their own enrichment. In Watergate, while perjury, subornation of perjury, conspiracy, and obstruction of justice are all very serious offenses, they were committed by a score or so of men who apparently believed they were acting on behalf of the president. But none of them stole any money. At first, greed for money was not involved.

Teapot Dome had been about personal profit; Watergate was about political power, getting elected, staying in office, and covering friends.

The Senate Select Committee—with Senator Sam Ervin, Jr. (D.–North Carolina) as chairman—was created February 7, 1973, by a vote of 70 to 0. Ervin was selected because he was "the most nonpartisan Democrat" in the Senate and had no presidential aspirations of his own.

The formation of the committee was duly but briefly noted in Haldeman's *Diaries*. The official White House position was that "we welcome a nonpartisan investigation." On the following day, February 8, Nixon's attention was focused on a possible Nobel Peace Prize for himself. ("It's a bad situation to be nominated and not get it." *The Haldeman Diaries*, pp. 575-576.)

The president and his staff then left Washington for a ten-day stay at San Clemente to discuss, among other things, Watergate strategy. Haldeman noted (*The Haldeman Diaries*, p. 577), "[The president] thinks we should play a hard game on this whole thing regarding the Ervin investigation." Haldeman summed up the "Watergate strategy" this way: "[W]e should keep the outward appearance of total cooperation but our objective internally should be maximum obstruction and containment, so as not to let the thing run away with us."

This strategy was sure to lead to disaster. Haldeman, not a lawyer, was giving the worst possible legal advice. At this critical time Nixon badly needed a good criminal defense lawyer. He still had the pardoning power. He still could have fought his way out of this situation and saved his presidency if he had had the right lawyer.

Meanwhile, in Washington, the Senate Select Committee proceeded with the first task: setting up membership and staff. The majority members, in addition to Ervin, were Herman E. Talmadge of Georgia, Daniel K. Inouye of Hawaii, and Joseph M. Montoya of New Mexico. Minority (Republican) members were Howard H. Baker of Tennessee, Edward J. Gurney of Florida, and Lowell P. Weicker, Jr., of Connecticut. In an interview with the press, Senator Baker said he favored "a full, thorough, and fair investigation . . . let the chips fall where they may."

Senator Ervin set about trying to find someone to serve as majority counsel. "This is too important a job for me to worry about motive," he said, so "anyone seeking the job won't get it."

Samuel Dash, who was teaching a course in criminal procedure at Georgetown University, did not seek the job; however, when Ervin approached him, Dash admitted that "any red-blooded trial lawyer would be thrilled to have [the part of chief counsel to a congressional committee]—me included."

Dash was given freedom to select his own staff and to follow the trail of facts as far as it took him. Dash—a lawyer, after all—asked for the agreement in writing.

The areas of investigation included the Watergate break-in and cover-up, the political espionage and campaign dirty tricks, and illegal campaign-financing practices. Each of three task forces would be headed by an assistant chief counsel and a team of young lawyers, investigators, and research assistants.

As Dash set about finding his staff, he was determined to look for trial lawyers who had experience not just as prosecutors but as defense counsel as well, because he believed defense experience strengthened a prosecutor and gave him a more balanced view of the testimony and evidence.

Senator Ervin, modestly claiming to be "just a country lawyer," agreed. "You know," he told Dash, "every prosecutor's criminal skunk is some defense lawyer's aggrieved client."

There were no vacant offices available for Dash's staff; they set up as best they could in the Senate building's auditorium. A decision was made to start the investigation with Donald Segretti. It was feared he might go into hiding and become unavailable for questioning. Nixon's appointments secretary, Dwight Chapin, had selected Segretti for the political dirty tricks.

Furthermore, Nixon's personal and family counsel, Herbert Kalmbach, had been Segretti's paymaster.

Investigators believed that Kalmbach, as the man who held the purse, had been aware of all the clandestine operations of the Plumbers and the Committee to Re-elect. His fundraising tactics were also open to question. In addition to hitting up the Republican party's own big contributors, Kalmbach approached government appointees as well as people who had no connection with the GOP. The special prosecutor's task forces on dirty tricks and campaign finances were especially interested in hearing what Kalmbach had to offer them.

After he had fired Archibald Cox, Nixon enjoyed a few brief moments of triumph before he realized he needed another special prosecutor. He instructed Al Haig to start sounding out some possible candidates for the job. The trick here would be to keep the offer of the special prosecutor's job from sounding like an invitation to become the second sacrificial lamb.

Haig phoned Houston lawyer Leon Jaworski and made an offer.

"After what happened to Archibald Cox?" Jaworski asked,

laughing. But General Haig had not attained his stellar rank as four-star general without learning to coax, cajole, and flatter. Haig talked Jaworski into flying to Washington, where he talked to several people, including William B. Saxbe, whom Nixon had nominated for attorney general to replace Richardson. (Using one of his father's expressions, Nixon described Saxbe as "independent as a hog on ice." *Memoirs*, Vol. 2, p. 505) Nixon's counsel, Garment and Buzhardt, both asked Jaworski to take the job.

Jaworski made it clear he expected real independence, not a sham.

As lawyers in Texas, Jaworski and I had enjoyed a cordial professional and social friendship over the years. During my last year in Washington, Jaworski served as president of the American Bar Association.

Jaworski was a trial lawyer; Archibald Cox was a law professor. Their styles differed, as one might expect. But Cox had earned the fierce loyalty of his team, and one of Jaworski's first moves as special prosecutor was to ask Cox's staff to remain in place—particularly Cox's deputy, Henry Ruth. Jaworski kept the special prosecutor's public relations spokesman, James Doyle, and he asked Cox's secretary to stay.

This infuriated Richard Nixon.

"Cox had selected [Florence Campbell] as his secretary," Jaworski wrote (*The Right and the Power*, p. 47), "and I had accepted her without even an interview. . . . I could feel her loyalty seeping under my office door."

Jaworski could have brought some of his own staff from his Houston offices, but he did not. That was a sound move on his part. Cox's army of young lawyers and paralegals had demonstrated vigor and persistence in their investigation as well as loyalty to the principal that no man is above the law. Jaworski was wise not to waste five months of good work.

Not surprisingly, Nixon saw Jaworski's actions from a different perspective. "The new special prosecutor, Leon Jaworski, kept in place the entire staff of lawyers recruited by Archibald Cox, further hardened in their attitude toward the case's ultimate defendant [Nixon]. Informed over dinner one evening that President Nixon had requested money from Congress to pay for twelve additional White House lawyers, Jaworski [said], "He'll need every one of them." (Christopher Matthews, *Kennedy and Nixon*, New York: Simon & Schuster, 1996, p. 333)

Early on Jaworski recused himself from any investigations that might involve Jake Jacobsen or John Connally of Texas, who had problems with milk pricing. Connally had been with a large law firm in Houston where the law practice is especially competitive. Jaworski also severed ties with his prestigious Houston law firm, Fulbright, Crooker. He worked for a government salary of $38,000 a year—far less than he was accustomed to earning.

Jaworski observed that Haig became noticeably less friendly as he began to realize Nixon's vulnerability. Haig and Buzhardt—the two men in the White House with whom Jaworski had the most contact—began to use the "national security" rationale to withhold certain documents, logs, and memos from Jaworski. Their ploy was unsuccessful. Jaworski still had his top-secret clearance from his days as a war crimes prosecutor; he had the right to see classified documents.

One of the first tasks for Jaworski was to familiarize himself with what the special prosecutor's task forces had already accomplished. He was especially interested in Herbert Kalmbach.

From the beginning Kalmbach had "adopted a posture of complete cooperation" with the special prosecutor's task force. Kalmbach's name had been one of those mentioned by Pat Gray in his disastrous confirmation hearing. Like Gray, Kalmbach may not have understood the degree and extent of his own vulnerability.

After Kalmbach realized the gravity of his situation, he entered into plea bargaining with the prosecutors. Jaworski allowed him to plead to having raised money illegally for the Republican campaigns in 1970 and to having promised an ambassadorship to one contributor in exchange for $100,000. The prosecutors agreed to drop other Watergate charges, and Judge Sirica accepted the plea on February 25, 1974.

Was Kalmbach guilty of violating attorney-client confidentially? Well, no. Kalmbach did very little legal work for Nixon. Money-raising seems to have been his primary function in Washington, and that does not fall within the lawyer-client privilege.

Jaworski (*The Right and the Power*, p. 78) reasoned that Kalmbach's title was "pure window-dressing." He had not initiated any of the wrongful acts, and "He was motivated more by a desire to continue to carry the title of the President's personal attorney than in engaging in a willful criminal pursuit."

Nixon might have felt even greater concern over the course of events if he had been aware that his own lawyers were seriously considering the president's resignation. Leonard Garment and Fred Buzhardt—shocked and alarmed by the firing of Richardson and Cox, the missing tapes, and the increasingly hostile newspaper editorials calling for the president to resign—felt that they must see Nixon right away. On November 3, 1973—a little less than a year since Nixon's triumphant re-election—Garment and Buzhardt flew to Key Biscayne. Both men believed it was their duty to try to get Nixon to recognize the extent of his vulnerability. Perhaps the time had come to urge the president to clear himself or resign.

Al Haig flatly refused them admittance to the president. Gerald Ford had not yet been confirmed as vice president, Haig argued. For Nixon to resign now would throw the nation into an unimaginable constitutional crisis.

Garment had "come aboard the good ship Watergate" on April 9, not long before the departure of Haldeman and Ehrlichman. Now another gatekeeper barred him from his client. "We had no access to our client, no access to the material. I wanted out," Garment later said. (White, *Breach of Faith*, p. 271) Buzhardt had joined the White House staff about a week before Cox was named as special prosecutor. Buzhardt was sick with worry that he might inadvertently have made false statements about the tapes to the special prosecutor, for which he could be disbarred.

Haig's lawyering is well illustrated from the following excerpts from Morris:

> . . . Haig had called [Leon] Jaworski to the White House Map Room for what the special prosecutor remembered as a talk "about the tapes." . . . [Haig said] "it was terrible beyond description." There was "no criminal offense involved," Haig went on. The White House lawyers had assured him. But Jaworski, shaking his head, answered, "I can't agree. . . . I'm afraid the President engaged in criminal conduct." Get a good lawyer and follow his advice, Jaworski told Haig. (Roger Morris, *Haig, The General's Progress*, New York: Playboy Press, 1982, pp. 269-70)

Leon Jaworski clearly meant that Haig ought to employ a top criminal trial lawyer and put him in charge of the coming impeachment and criminal trials.

Haig did some recruiting and decided upon James St. Clair, a Boston trial lawyer with impeccable credentials. Haig did not mention to St. Clair that the president's other lawyers, Garment and Buzhardt, wanted Nixon to resign. After Haig's interview, St. Clair was flown to San Clemente to meet Nixon.

St. Clair's appointment was announced January 4, 1974. He replaced Buzhardt, who remained on the legal staff. Garment had resigned as counsel to the president on January 1, but Buzhardt's heart attack on June 13 would bring Garment back.

On March 1, the grand jury indicted all of the president's men: Bob Haldeman, John Ehrlichman, John Mitchell, Robert Mardian, Charles Colson, Gordon Strachan, and Kenneth Parkinson. The president himself was named as an unindicted co-conspirator although the fact was not revealed publicly.

The next morning, according to Woodward and Bernstein (*Final Days*, pp. 122-123), St. Clair read in his newspaper that the secret report of the grand jury "contained evidence against the President and its recommendation that the material in the brief-case—tapes, testimony and documents—be forwarded to the House Judiciary Committee."

St. Clair, White points out in *Breach of Faith*, (p. 293), "was ignoring Rule One of his professional craft—he was defending a client of whom he could not ask the facts, from whom he could not expect true answers, whom he could see only at the client's will and hear from him only what the client chose to tell."

Meanwhile, Al Haig's constant polling of Congress showed a steadily diminishing support in Congress. Taking the polls was a mistake. To keep going back to congressmen and asking if they still supported Nixon was to encourage a negative response. Again, Nixon acted without good advice.

The final events came swiftly—ending what Nixon later described as "eight months of pure hell and agony." On July 8, 1974, the Supreme Court ruled 8-0 against Nixon in his battle to keep from turning over the White House tapes. (Haldeman, in *The Ends of Power*, said Nixon had been prepared to defy a majority decision of the Court. But he did not.)

Nixon's foul language on the tapes did the most damage initially. Efforts to control the effect by using the designation *(expletive deleted)* only made it worse because where a simple "damn" was deleted, the public imagined something far worse. The profanation involved in the use of "Jesus" and "Jesus Christ" as swear words offended millions of Christians who had been taught—as I was—never to use those names except reverently.

Release of the June 23, 1972 tape—the so-called "smoking gun"—created a national uproar when it was released on August 5, 1974. It proved that Nixon had been in on the cover-up from the very beginning and shocked even Nixon's staunchest Republican supporters. The president's party support ended abruptly. Senator Barry Goldwater said, "We can be lied to just so many times." (Emery, *Watergate*, p. 470)

In spite of public reaction, Nixon announced the next day that under no circumstances would he resign. Finally, he realized that his options had narrowed to two: resign or face impeachment. But so far as I can tell, his conclusion was reached without a thorough analysis of the law of impeachment or a legal analysis of available defense. For instance, an office holder can be impeached only for events occurring during the term from which he is being impeached. Most of the Watergate events and much of the cover-up occurred during Nixon's first term, but the impeachment proceeding was during Nixon's second term.

On August 7 Nixon phoned his stalwart former chief of staff as Haldeman and his wife were having breakfast.

"Bob, I want you to know I have decided I must resign."

After expressing his sadness and compassion, Haldeman said, ". . . before you leave office you should exercise your Constitutional authority and grant pardons to all those charged . . . with any crimes in connection with Watergate." To do so, Haldeman said, would enable the new president to start with a clean slate. This was good advice.

Haig had suppressed his own quick personal anger at Haldeman's suggestion of pardons—to him, it sounded like a threat.

Haldeman followed up through his own Washington lawyers to the president's counsel, St. Clair. But it was "too late—and the president too broken. . . . Twenty of the president's men who had thought they were acting in his behalf were convicted." (Haldeman, *The Ends of Power*, pp. 312-314)

Why was Nixon unwilling to exercise his executive power of pardon on behalf of his men? He may not have been—unwilling, that is. Woodward and Bernstein (*The Final Days*, pp. 451-457) suggest that the idea may have appealed to Nixon. "Haig said that the President felt that pardons would allow him to assume the entire burden of Watergate. He felt responsible for the plight of his old friends.

"All the guilt and responsibility and the public outrage falling on Nixon: [Leonard] Garment knew how that would appeal to [Nixon]."

Thursday, August 8, 1974, Samuel Dash returned to the Senate auditorium that served as the offices of the Ervin Committee special counsel but found it empty. The room "had been crowded with lawyers, investigators, research assistants and secretaries; witnesses accompanied by their lawyers, waiting to be interviewed; reporters, cameramen. . . ." (Dash, *Chief Counsel*, p. 263) Everyone had gone to watch Nixon announce to the nation on television that he would resign on the following day.

The resignation speech—which some have called an "abdication"—was "a good performance," but the text was "graceless . . . less an explanation, owed to the millions who had elected him . . . than it was a first building block for a new reputation. . . . It might have been impossible for a man of Nixon's pride and complexity to explain what he had done to bring it to pass." (Emery, *Watergate*, p. 478)

Even though St. Clair no longer represented Nixon—since Nixon was no longer president—he remained on the White House payroll for a few weeks to clear up any remaining legal problems.

The various avenues of investigation did not automatically cease once Nixon and his family left the White House for the last time as president. Jaworski, Judge Sirica, the Ervin Committee, and the House Judiciary Committee all continued to work at untangling the twisted lines of conspiracy and cover-up.

Ford had enjoyed good relations with the press as a representative and as a senator. Now the new president looked forward to his first formal press conference on August 28. He instructed his staff to rearrange the East Room to achieve a more informal, less "imperial" setting. He prepared himself to answer questions about the reorganization of the White House staff, the nation's economy, and the foreign relations initiatives he planned.

The very first question from the gathered members of the

media concerned Ford's attitude toward giving Nixon immunity from prosecution. The questions that followed were all along the same line.

"How long is this going to go on?" Ford demanded rhetorically when he re-entered his Oval Office. A long time, his advisers said—as long as Nixon's position remains in a legal limbo.

The nation's obsession with Nixon and Watergate was like a drug addiction, said one of his staff members. "We're all Watergate junkies," the aide said. ". . . We, as a nation, must go cold turkey. Otherwise, we'll die of an overdose." (Gerald R. Ford, *A Time to Heal*, New York: Harper & Row, 1979, pp. 156-160)

Ford said he wanted "to get the political monkey off my back," but in the final analysis, all he could do was shift the monkey from one shoulder to the other.

He had two choices, both of them fatal to his political career.

He could ignore the Nixon problem, thereby ensuring that Nixon would be indicted, tried, and probably found guilty. As I have said before, I believe that indicting and trying a former president would have been an act of national self-destruction. Or Ford could pardon Nixon, thereby infuriating many voters.

Ford asked his lawyers to research the question. Was there legal precedent for granting a presidential pardon to someone who had not even been indicted, much less tried and convicted? There proved to be ample precedent. Furthermore, the justices of the Supreme Court had held that a pardon "carries an imputation of guilt [and] the acceptance [of a pardon is] confession of it."

On September 4 Jaworski met with Ford's legal counsel, Philip Buchen. From Ford's home state of Michigan, Buchen had been a longtime friend of the new president. Buchen it was who had tried to get Chief Justice Warren Burger to return from Europe to administer the oath of office to Ford. Burger did not believe what was happening until Ford himself got on the phone.

Buchen had tried to do all he could to set up a smooth transition for Ford. He knew there were many details that needed attention: appointments, briefings, an inaugural speech, and all those matters that a new president normally has months to consider. (Woodward and Bernstein, *The Final Days*, p. 444)

In their meeting, Buchen asked Jaworski for an opinion as to how long it would take—assuming Nixon was indicted—before a trial could begin. Jaworski estimated it might take nine months to a year, just to bring the former president to trial. And even then, of course, there was no telling how long the trial itself might last.

A memo from Jaworski's deputy, Henry Ruth, listed ten areas of continuing investigation, including Nixon's tax deductions, his misuse of the IRS, and his handling of campaign contributions for personal use. But Ruth went on to say that if President Ford were inclined toward leniency, "I think he ought to do it early rather than late." (Ford, *A Time to Heal*, pp. 166-167)

Ford's advisers argued for a "statement of contrition" from Nixon. Haig, who knew his former commander in chief as well as anyone, said, "You'll never get it." He was right. (Ambrose, *Ruin and Recovery*, p. 458)

There remained the problem of getting *some* sort of satisfactory statement from Nixon—no easy task, under the circumstances. He was in seclusion in San Clemente, and Ron Ziegler—one of the few Nixon aides untouched by indictment—was now the former president's fiercely loyal gatekeeper.

"Let's get one thing straight immediately," Ziegler said. "President Nixon is not issuing any statement whatsoever regarding Watergate, whether Jerry Ford pardons him or not."

Ziegler finally agreed to submit a draft. The third draft, in which Nixon said, "I can see clearly now . . . that I was wrong in not acting more decisively and more forthrightly in Watergate," was about as good as Ford's legal team was going to get.

Ford decided to go ahead with a pardon. I think he did the right thing.

September 8, 1974—a month after Nixon's resignation—President Ford announced a pardon for the former president. Perhaps it is worthwhile to examine the language of the executive pardon.

> Now, therefore, I, Gerald R. Ford, President of the United States, pursuant to the pardon power conferred upon me by Article 2, Section 2, of the Constitution, have granted and by these presents do grant a full, free and absolute pardon unto Richard Nixon for all offenses against the United States which he, Richard Nixon, has committed or may have committed or taken part in during the period from January 20, 1969, through August 9, 1974.

Jaworski left the special prosecutor's office as soon as the pardon was announced. Some people criticized him for dropping the special prosecutor's investigation; they still wanted to see the former president tried in open court. But Jaworski realized that the wording of the pardon—covering acts from the date of Nixon's first inauguration and extending to "all possible Federal charges"—virtually eliminated any opportunity for prosecution.

As a lawyer I would have to say that Jaworski had no choice.

CHAPTER 15

IMPLACABLE HOSTILITY

"I said to myself somewhere in the 1972 campaign. . . . 'This fellow is going to get himself impeached.'"
—Thomas P. (Tip) O'Neill,
Democratic Majority Leader
(As quoted in Jimmy Breslin,
How the Good Guys Finally Won)

WHAT WAS IT ABOUT Nixon that would make an Irishman from Boston and an Italian from Newark, New Jersey, dedicate themselves to his impeachment?

Lyndon Johnson told me that when he was majority leader during President Eisenhower's Administration, he saw himself as standing behind an aging pilot in a big plane as it approached the runway for a landing. Some of the Democratic senators wanted Johnson to grab the pilot's arm and bring the plane down in a crash landing on the runway. Instead Lyndon placed his hand on the pilot's shoulder and gave confidence to make a landing.

In Watergate, the Democrats chose to grab the pilot's—Nixon's—arm and bring about a crash landing, destroying the Nixon presidency.

Although a possible conflict of loyalties existed for the Democratic leadership between what was good for the nation and what was good for the Democratic party, as far as we know no lofty philosophical debate occurred between House Majority Leader Thomas P. "Tip" O'Neill, Jr. (D.–Massachusetts) and Congressman Peter W. Rodino, Jr. (D.–New Jersey)—the two leaders of the impeachment movement in Congress.

From the start of the session, both were dedicated enemies of Nixon and all-out for impeachment.

Both Tip O'Neill and Peter Rodino were themselves the products of big-city political machines. Both had had unpleasant experiences with the Nixon Criminal Division.

Congressman Rodino had been elected to Congress in 1948 from the Tenth District—adjacent to Hugh Addonizio's Eleventh District—that included part of racially and ethnically mixed Newark. When Addonizio was congressman and later mayor, he cooperated with Congressman Rodino on projects beneficial to the city. It is doubtful that Rodino could have been returned to Congress term after term if Addonizio and the power structure of Newark had actively opposed his re-election.

Rodino was proud of his Italian heritage; he introduced the resolution that led to Columbus Day, October 12, being recognized in 1971 as an annual federal holiday. According to Jimmy Breslin, Rodino was very sensitive to the use of the word "Mafia" and felt that the adverse Mafia publicity worked unfairly against all Italian Americans.

Rodino enjoyed a long tenure and became a member of the House Judiciary Committee. When committee chairman Emanuel Cellar left Congress, Rodino became chairman in January 1973. There he was ensconced when he first discussed the Nixon impeachment with Tip O'Neill in Speaker Carl Albert's office. We do know from Jimmy Breslin's book, *How the Good Guys Finally Won* (New York: Viking, 1975), that Rodino—together with O'Neill—became an early and consistent worker in Congress for Nixon's impeachment. Obviously, he had formed his judgment upon Nixon's impeachment long before the committee hearings started, as had O'Neill.

Perhaps their perspective was influenced by the Justice Department's previous crackdown on organized crime. The link between crime and governmental corruption was so strong that when organized crime in a large city was successfully attacked, it altered the de facto political structure of the city itself. In that sense, our organized crime work was revolutionary.

Attorney General John Mitchell delivered a conference speech in Florida in late December 1969. He referred to an impending "massive indictment of public officials on the local level." No one outside the Justice Department was supposed to know the exact details, but I think it is safe to say Mitchell's words occasioned some sleepless nights, recurring ulcers, and hasty shredding of documents in a number of public offices.

The "local level" in this instance was the city of Newark, New Jersey. Newark had long been regarded by professional law enforcers as a racket-ridden, mob-controlled city. One writer described the city as "the Mafia capital of the United States since prohibition."

The Justice Department was aware of Newark's reputation. Strike Force Number Six was established in Newark in December 1968, near the end of Ramsey Clark's term as attorney general. The result of it was a sixty-four-count indictment against Mayor Hugh Addonizio and others.

Tip O'Neill had a saying that all politics is local. In that sense, much of the law enforcement work of our strike forces was political.

In due course, the impeachment of Nixon came before Rodino's committee. Rodino was a scholarly lawyer who followed the proper procedures and conducted himself in a restrained fashion during the long Watergate impeachment hearings and later during the unprecedented implementation of the Twenty-fifth Amendment. He was consistent in his drive toward impeachment.

Rodino took his time in employing a special counsel for the committee. He wanted a thorough and meticulous lawyer who could and would marshal all of the evidence and organize it carefully, while not seeking personal publicity for himself. He wanted someone who could penetrate the wall around Nixon, establish a conspiracy, and prove Nixon to be an actor in it. He wanted a Republican to make it bi-partisan. He found his man in John Doar and gave him plenty of office space, staff, and backing. Doar was a Republican who as a young man had been a member of Bobby Kennedy's civil rights team in Mississippi. Congressman Rodino wanted Nixon impeached, and he did everything he could to bring this about.

In 1985 members of the House rose to pay special tribute to Rodino. After retiring from his congressional seat, Rodino went on to have a career as a professor of law. Was he influenced by our strike force effort, which brought down the Democratic party in his hometown? He teamed early with O'Neill and was persistent in his efforts to accomplish Nixon's impeachment. I personally think that our Newark Strike Force case had a big influence on him.

But the Democratic members of Congress were patriotic people. Why did they insist upon impeachment when such a drastic action had so great a potential for damage to the nation?

Perhaps President Nixon's years of liberal-bashing and rough campaigning were as responsible as anything else. Obviously, his slashing congressional campaigns were not forgotten. Neither were his attacks on Alger Hiss, nor his attacks on Adlai Stevenson, nor his California-style dirty political tricks hidden behind a Quakerish piety. A politician draws his political label from his opponents. Nixon got his conservative label from having run against Jerry Voorhis and Helen Gahagan Douglas—and trashing them as "pinks"—plus his being the attack dog as Eisenhower's vice president in the race against Adlai Stevenson.

But if you define a liberal as a person who believes in an expansion of the federal government and an extension of its regulatory reach—which seems to be today's definition of a political liberal—then in that sense Nixon was a liberal. Nixon's formula was to run as a partisan Republican, to appoint conservative people to public office, and to submit liberal legislation to Congress.

A number of the cases handled by the Nixon Justice Department Criminal Division during Nixon's first term may have helped set the temper of Congress against the president.

Many of our cases—the Newark indictment of Mayor Hugh Addonizio, the Maryland indictment of Senator Daniel Brewster, the Washington indictment of Nathan Voloshen and Martin Sweig with the termination of Speaker John W. McCormack's career in Congress, the indictment of Judge Otto Kerner—undoubtedly produced swirls and eddies of hostility in Congress. Did the trial of Hugh Joseph Addonizio and his cohorts from the city of Newark and our drive against the Mafia in Newark produce a hostility in Congressman Rodino that existed before the impeachment process began? He worked slowly and carefully to build the case against Nixon, but he never wavered in his objective—which was to impeach Nixon.

Tip O'Neill was pure Boston Irish. He was more responsible for the impeachment vote than any other congressman.

Did our investigation of his mentor, Speaker McCormack, and the indictment and conviction of Martin Sweig create a great hostility in Tip O'Neill?

Breslin, who was a close friend of Tip O'Neill, wrote that methods used to collect donations to Nixon's 1972 campaign funds from Democrats primarily motivated O'Neill's hostilities.

Jimmy Breslin devotes the opening chapter of his book *How the Good Guys Finally Won* to proving that Tip O'Neill conceived the idea of impeaching Nixon during the activities of Republican fundraisers Maurice Stans and Herbert Kalmbach in the 1982 presidential campaign. The following quotations from Tip O'Neill in that book make this clear.

> "Now," O'Neill went on, "I was the Chairman of the Democratic Congressional campaign dinner in Washington, and because of that I got to know every big giver to the Democratic party in the nation. We had a guy every where to organize and to get you the money.
>
> "Well, I can tell you that I started hearing from a lot of them. There would be a guy who always was a big giver, and nobody was hearing from him. I'd go over the lists for our dinner and I'd say, 'Hey, where is so and-so? He always was a helluva good friend of ours. Why haven't we heard from him?' So I'd call the guy and he'd call me back and he'd say, 'Geez, Tip, I don't know what to tell you. Nine IRS guys hit me last week and I'd like to stay out of things for a while.' . . . So what does [George] Steinbrenner say to me? He said, 'Geez, Tip, I want to come to see you and tell you what's going on.' And he came into my office. He said, 'Gee, they're holding the lumber over my head.' They got him between the IRS, the Justice Department, the Commerce Department. He was afraid he'd lose his business.
>
> ". . . He said Stans' people wanted a hundred thousand dollars for Nixon's campaign. And then they wanted him to be head of Democrats for Nixon in Ohio.
>
> ". . . I told George to do what he had to do. George said he didn't think he was going to give in. Then he left the office and I don't know what he did. He went over to see this [Herbert] Kalmbach or somebody like that. I guess he had no choice. This Maurice Stans. He has to be the lousiest bastard ever to live. Now, I was getting this from all over. . . ."
>
> ". . . It was a shakedown. A plain old fashioned goddamed shakedown. . . . Now I don't remember when I said it, but I know I said to myself somewhere in the 1972 campaign. I said, 'This fellow is going to get himself impeached.' The strange thing about it is that I never gave much thought to the Watergate break-in when

it happened. I thought it was silly and stupid. I never thought it was important. I was concentrating on the shakedown of these fellas like Steinbrenner." (Breslin, pp. 14-16)

Breslin added (p. 34):

> . . . But by law or custom, there's no exact definition of the duties of the Majority Leader.
>
> When Tip O'Neill decided that his primary duty was to make rapid the removal of Richard Nixon he took on great power.

These quotations from Tip O'Neill clearly demonstrate his anger and a highly partisan personal dedication to impeachment. Our strike force investigation which brought down Speaker McCormack may have contributed to this anger. O'Neill regarded the Watergate break-in as only a misdemeanor.

I had left the Criminal Division before these campaign donations occurred, and I do not know anything about them. But I am convinced that our national drive against the Mafia contributed to the hostility against Nixon in Congress.

And I think that Nixon's political label had something to do with it. He ran as a conservative, but he actually initiated and approved much liberal legislation. This had the effect of cooling both sides of the liberal/conservative equation.

Paul Gigot, writing in the *Wall Street Journal* (May 24, 1996, p. A10), pointed out that "As conservatives remember, the Nixon years were Big Government's Golden Age. Affirmative action, the regulatory state (OSHA, EPA), runaway entitlements—all of these were embraced by Nixon as a way to win his own second term."

Nixon chose for himself neither the conservative nor liberal label; his domestic accomplishments were what he called "progressive."

Nixon met with economist Milton Friedman in November 1970. In an entry from Haldeman's *Diaries* (p. 212) we learn that "[Nixon] said after it was nice to have someone say we're doing things right. Friedman urges we stay on same economic course. Says we're in good shape if we stay with it." Friedman later noted that during the Nixon Administration the number of pages in the Federal Register more than doubled, rising from roughly 20,000 in 1969 to 45,000 in 1974 when Nixon resigned.

One who studies the content of Nixon's domestic program

will reach the conclusion that he was indeed an economic liberal. Joan Hoff has done just that (*Nixon Reconsidered*, p. 49):

> Nixon also exceeded the accomplishments of the New Deal and the Great Society in the areas of civil rights, social welfare spending, domestic and international economic restructuring, urban parks, government reorganization, land-use initiatives, revenue sharing, draft reform, pension reform, and spending for the arts and the humanities. In particular, his proposals on national health insurance and welfare reform were so far in advance of his time that *congressional liberals preferred to oppose them than to allow Nixon to take credit for upstaging them.* [Emphasis added]

Nixon, in addition to starting the Affirmative Action program and stepping up school desegregation in the South, created quite a number of departments or agencies during his tenure: Alcohol, Tobacco and Firearms; Consumer Protection Safety Commission; Drug Enforcement Administration; Environmental Protection Act; Legal Services Corporation; National Highway Traffic Safety Administration; National Oceanic and Atmospheric Administration; and the Occupational Safety and Health Agency.

Of school desegregation, Leonard Garment (*Crazy Rhythm*, p. 217) said: "More school desegregation took place during Nixon's first term than in all the preceding eighteen years following *Brown.* Historians consider this Nixon's most important domestic achievement; he said publicly that it was his most important achievement."

Nixon walked in the shoes of Presidents Grant, Teddy Roosevelt, Coolidge, and Hoover in establishing national parks and maintaining them. He expanded this into a general concern for the environment. Congressman Rick Lazio, writing in the *Christian Science Monitor* (August 8, 1996, p. 19), pointed out that:

> It is often forgotten that many of the advances to the early environmental movement were made by the Nixon Administration. Yet a number of key environmental laws taken for granted today, nearly two dozen in all, were developed and signed during those years.
>
> The National Environmental Policy Act (NEPA) of 1970 mandated the present environmental impact statement process, which requires the government to study the environmental effects of major Federal projects. The Clean Air Act seeks to reduce various emissions and pollutants and improve outdoor air quality.

> The Clean Water Act of 1972 is responsible for protecting water quality in our nation's rivers, lakes and coastal waters. The 1994 Safe Drinking Water Act required the EPA to set and enforce national standards to ensure the safety of our tap water. The Endangered Species Act of 1973 strives to prevent extinction of endangered plants, animals and habitat.

Here we might pause to ask how a Republican president could push such a tremendous legislative program through a hostile Congress where both the House and Senate were controlled by a Democratic majority.

Well, the answer is that much of Nixon's program *was* liberal and one which the most liberal Democrats could support. And here is a paradox: After McGovern's Democratic campaign collapsed in 1972, had Nixon diverted some of his political war chest to his party's candidates and succeeded in electing a Republican Congress, he might have experienced a much more difficult time getting congressional acceptance of his liberal legislative programs.

You might imagine that the Democratic liberals in Congress would have thought twice before voting to impeach such a liberal or progressive president. But storm-laden clouds of implacable hostility hung over Congress. You might imagine that the great liberal constituencies which contributed to the 1972 Nixon landslide would come to Nixon's aid when he came under attack. Their leaders hated him.

Many other factors—in addition to the Justice Department's prosecutions of Democratic officials—were causing an incendiary build-up of animosity among the members of Congress.

Early in his first term, Nixon created the Ash Council. The Ash Council's recommendations became known as "New Federalism." Hoff (in *Nixon Reconsidered*, p. 66) described it this way: "In a word, under the New Federalism Nixon addressed national problems by spending more and by redistributing power away from Congress and the Federal bureaucracy, toward local, state, and presidential centers of control."

As you might expect, this alienated much of the giant federal bureaucracy (Hoff, *Nixon Reconsidered*, p. 67):

> It is Haldeman's contention that reorganization in all its forms, including the New Federalism, constituted the "secret story of Watergate." According to Haldeman and others, as Nixon moved

"to control the executive branch from the White House . . . the great power blocs in Washington" turned against him and were ready to take advantage of Watergate in any way possible by the beginning of his second term.

Haldeman devoted a chapter to "The Hidden Story of Watergate" in *The Ends of Power*. In *Before the Fall*, Safire gave a picture of Nixon's plans to change the Cabinet. But the more I have read and studied about Nixon's reorganization aims, the more fault I find with them. This is just too much power and authority to be controlled by just one person. I believe that strong, skilled and independent men and women should compose the nation's Cabinet.

Nixon also planned to break the power of the entrenched and protected bureaucracy—the Civil Service. The bureaucracy *was* unwieldy—that was not just Nixon's imagination. Maurice Stans, whom Nixon appointed as secretary of commerce in 1969, later wrote: "I found Commerce to be a massive conglomerate of 25,400 people working in sixteen diversified agencies, their relationships to Commerce not at all well known because many of them . . . deal autonomously with the public." (Stans, *The Terrors of Justice*, p. 103)

Most of the career people were Democrats who regarded a Republican administration as a passing aberration: hold out long enough and they would be gone from Washington. No matter how hard Nixon scratched the layers of bureaucracy, he quickly struck impenetrable permafrost and could go no farther. Nixon was infuriated that executions of his simplest orders often were delayed by bureaucrats making a great show of compliance with memos, feasibility studies, impact reports, and so on.

Nixon's fight against the bureaucracy alarmed Congress as well. Haldeman wrote "these two power blocs—Congress and the Bureaucracy—reacted to save their lives. And they had a common cause. It's little known that the greatest power centers in Washington are the liaisons between Congressional Committee Staffs and the Federal bureaucratic departments they deal with." (Haldeman, *The Ends of Power*, p. 171)

In December 1970 Ash presented his recommendations "to a frigid Congress, each member afraid of losing access to the President." (Safire, *Before the Fall*, pp. 260-261)

"We're going to do great things with the Cabinet," Nixon told Safire. Safire reminded the president of his earlier determination to let the Cabinet run their own departments. Nixon shrugged off the reminder. "I know [government reorganization] has no sex appeal," Nixon admitted. "And we're not going to get it this year or the next from Congress—maybe the natural resources part, but certainly not the rest; it'll upset too many apple carts. But it's a start, and it fits in with the whole approach."

If Nixon wanted to change the direction of government, Safire observed in *Before the Fall*, he "was presented with Hobson's choice—that is, no choice at all." But Safire soon saw that Nixon had a plan: "infiltration of the departments with Nixon men, trained by Haldeman and Ehrlichman in the first term to take command of the substructure in the second term."

Haldeman addressed this plan: "In the middle of his first term Nixon had introduced a reorganization bill to accomplish that revolution. It was hastily rejected by a nervous Congress. Talk of power accruing to "a small handful of White House aides" filled congressional halls with fear; even more so when Nixon angrily said he would accomplish the reorganization by executive order and to hell with Congress—if he won the election." (Haldeman, *The Ends of Power*, p. 168)

Nixon and Nelson Rockefeller had a meeting in 1971. Here's how Safire (*Before the Fall*, p. 261) reported it: "We're going to reorganize the government come hell or high water. That's why we have [John] Connally—not for Texas politics but for national politics. He'll be pitching those congressmen hard as hell and sitting on top of Treasury he'll be able to pitch pretty hard. Now we're down to the nut-cutting."

As a step in that direction, on November 5, immediately after the victorious 1972 election, Nixon met briefly with his Cabinet and other top officials, thanked them, walked out, and left Haldeman to instruct everyone to offer their resignations. The action amounted to a splash of cold water in the faces of the team which had just contributed to winning Nixon's landslide re-election.

Nixon's actions seemed precipitous to those who lost their appointed positions, but Nixon secretly had been planning the firings since at least September 15. "You've got to do it right after the election," Nixon said. "You've got one week, and that's the time to get all those resignations in and say, 'Look, you're out, you're out, you're finished, you're done, done, finished.' Knock them the hell out of there." (Haldeman, *The Ends of Power*, p. 171)

Of course, all presidential appointees serve at the president's pleasure, and it is not uncommon for a second-term president to want to start off with a fresh team. The record of accomplishments in his last four years in office is often what history will remember him for.

Although Nixon's speechwriter, William Safire, said the scene was not as cold as it is usually presented, he referred to this as the "hail-and-farewell" meeting.

One person to whom Nixon was especially eager to bid farewell was Charles Colson. Time and again after the Watergate break-in, the president had been heard to mutter: "Colson must have done it.... There's no way he's not involved." (Haldeman, *The Ends of Power*, p. 156)

In his *Memoirs* (Vol. 2, pp. 290-291) Nixon observed that "Colson was a lightning rod for political reasons quite apart from Watergate and Ehrlichman in particular urged that he leave as soon as possible." Now Nixon saw the perfect cover for getting rid of him.

"Colson's got to go," the president told Haldeman, and Colson must go under the cover of the other departures. Much better, Nixon reasoned, "for Chuck to leave now . . . and appear to be doing it on his own initiative, than for him to be forced to leave under a cloud at some future date." (Haldeman, *The Ends of Power*, p. 163) The deal—although Colson may not have been aware of it—was that his resignation was to become effective March 10, 1973, after his official visit to the Soviet Union.

But adroit as all these political moves were, they left Nixon with no real friends in Congress. When the Democrats struck, he had as a practical matter very little support in Congress.

O'Neill's strategy was to delay the impeachment vote in Congress until Nixon was politically dead. It worked.

CHAPTER 16

THE COSTLY LEGACY OF WATERGATE

"As Nixon left the White House in disgrace, the presidency was weaker, relative to Congress, than it had been at any time in the forty-one years since Franklin Roosevelt had been inaugurated."

—John Steele Gordon

THE IMPEACHMENT OF NIXON was a mistake for the nation, although it was caused by Nixon's own mistakes in handling Watergate. I believe that it would have been better for the nation to impose some sanction—short of impeachment—upon Nixon, and one not as costly to the nation as impeachment turned out to be.

Justice may be blind, but it is not cheap. Nixon's removal from the Oval Office was an expensive victory—or defeat, depending upon your perspective.

Watergate was costly to the nation in many ways—some apparent, some hidden, some delayed.

As you might expect, Watergate had a negative impact on the stock market. As recently as March 30, 1999, the *Wall Street Journal* reported: "the oil shock of 1973, Watergate and the stagflation ushered in the worst bear market since the Depression and soured a generation on stocks. Not until 1982 would the average finally break through 1000 and stay through."

Of course, the oil shock of 1973 was directly related to Watergate.

One of the most obvious—but often overlooked—costs was

the time and money spent on the many different cases arising from Watergate. This was a total of more than $8 million—much of it from the public coffers. Nixon's defense against Watergate charges cost $290,000. Thirty new White House jobs were created to work on the cases. These costs were included in the federal budget. (Congressional Quarterly, Inc., *Watergate: Chronology of a Crisis*, Vol. 2, p. 236)

Determining costs to the individual defendants who were caught up in Watergate is more difficult, unless they chose to tell us.

Nixon knew his costs would not end when he left the Oval Office. Money—in the form of thousands of dollars in annual benefits paid to living former presidents—may have been a factor in Nixon's decision to resign rather than to face impeachment, possible conviction, and forfeiture of benefits.

In late November 1974 Nixon's close friends and advisers, "Bebe" Rebozo and Robert Abplanalp, went to California to try to help the former president. Nixon had known bitter poverty as a child; now, for the first time in many years, he again "became conscious of what it costs to live." Nixon faced $23,000 in medical bills, $500,000 in further legal defense, $148,000 to the IRS, and $75,000 in back state taxes. (Ambrose, *Ruin and Recovery*, pp. 474-475)

"By far the hardest blow was the pardon," Nixon wrote in 1990 (*In the Arena*, pp. 20-21) But his lawyer "knew my desperate financial situation." He pointed out that attorneys' fees and other costs of defending actions against me would bankrupt me." Apparently, Nixon finally got good legal advice.

The other Watergate defendants also faced enormous legal costs. In addition, those of the president's men who were attorneys were disbarred and lost for a time the right to practice their professions—a significant source of income for their families and themselves.

Watergate defendants shouldered another heavy load—the loss of reputation. Although some were able to rehabilitate themselves in the public's eyes, the disgrace would follow most of the president's men to the grave and into the history books.

One must add to the cost of Watergate the squandering of the most lavishly financed presidential campaign in history up to that time. Reports from a non-partisan research foundation show "the total cost of the Nixon campaign was $35,000,000. Of that amount, some $12.7 million was spent for Mr. Nixon's television appearances." Nixon's 1972 landslide election was costly. There should have been results. The nation and the world lost the enormous opportunity to bring about a more peaceful world.

Watergate forced Nixon to abandon his innovative and far-reaching domestic plans. When he took office in 1969 the economy was weak, large numbers of Americans were demonstrating and protesting, and as a nation we were belatedly recognizing that our vast natural resources are finite. Nixon envisioned a grand program of reorganizing the government, reducing the size of the Cabinet, reforming welfare, and introducing such revolutionary ideas as a guaranteed annual income for the working poor.

Were it not for Watergate and the continuing unsavory and shocking revelations of the cover-up, I believe that Nixon might well have been regarded historically as one of the outstanding presidents of the twentieth century, comparable to Franklin Roosevelt. During the depression years of 1932 to 1938, Roosevelt restored the country's hope and confidence. The most comprehensive domestic legislative program since Roosevelt's was put through between 1969 and 1972, during President Nixon's tenure.

President Nixon was totally committed to a program of law enforcement against organized crime. Speaking as an insider in the Criminal Division of Nixon's Justice Department, I know that his administration assigned funds and personnel to achieve its goals. We increased the strike forces from six to eighteen. No other administration during the last half of the twentieth century has done as much as Nixon's in effectively fighting organized crime. No restrictions were placed upon me in looking for and hiring good prosecutors. Had Nixon not been cut down by Watergate, I believe the administration would have so damaged organized crime by the end of his second term that it would not have remained such a large factor in the exploitation of our inner cities. During my time with the Criminal Division, there was not one White House attempt to interfere with any action of the division.

Nixon's conduct and his resignation with two and a half years of his second term remaining diminished much of the prestige and respect for the office of the presidency.

Watergate reduced the power and authority of the Cabinet. President Gerald Ford (*A Time to Heal*, pp. 131, 235) said: "A Watergate was made possible by a strong chief of staff and ambitious White House aides who were more powerful than the Cabinet but who had little or no practical political experience or judgment." Determined to reverse this trend and restore the Cabinet to its former position, Ford began by asking Nixon's appointees to remain in place—at least until the new president had time to deal with replacements. This did not prove to be a simple task. "Normally," Ford wrote, "a President has little difficulty finding qualified people to head key departments and agencies." In the wake of Watergate, however, many of the people Ford approached were reluctant to accept appointments that no longer carried honor and prestige, and, looming large, the possibility of indictment for some trivial offense.

Arguably the most critical cost of Watergate was the distraction of the government and its citizens for the twenty-six months from the break-in to the president's resignation. From June 18, 1972, to August 9, 1974, the nation's newspapers, magazines, television, political cartoons, and private conversations all were concentrated on conjecture about who knew what and when they knew it.

Nixon was described by Russell Baker (*New York Times*, November 23, 1996) as an "egghead," a "lonely intellectual whose understanding of a dangerous world was such that he never even felt inferior to Henry Kissinger." But Watergate distracted the Nixon Administration from diplomacy and foreign affairs at a crucial time.

One of the greatest losses was in the field of foreign relations. Nixon opened relations and established full communication with both the Soviet Union and China. This split the Communist world block and make a new and more peaceful relationship between Russia and the United States an imperative for Russia. Had it not been for Watergate, Nixon could have ended the cold war in 1973. This would have been more than fifteen years ahead of its actual end. Nixon's opening of China was the first big step toward ending the cold war and establishing a new world order based on a global economy. Had he served out his second term without Watergate, Nixon could have relieved our nation of twenty years of defense build-up and saved the Soviet Union from bankruptcy and collapse—an event proving to be an extremely costly thing for the United States.

While no one was minding the store, in 1973 the Arab nations —members of OPEC (Organization of Petroleum Exporting Countries)—chose the time when the presidency and the country were paralyzed to cut off oil shipments to the United States. During the 1960s, OPEC had nationalized U.S. oil holdings around the Persian Gulf. The event was one of immense economic consequences to the United States. It was perhaps one of the greatest transfers of wealth in the history of the world. In 1990 we fought—at great cost to us—the Gulf War (Operation "Desert Storm"), mainly to stabilize the status of this oil.

The Arab boycott of 1973 plunged the United States into an energy crisis—the worst since the rationing days of World War II—and did nothing to improve the country's already strained economy and low employment. That year Americans lined up at service stations, cut back on heating and cooling at work and at home, and left their outdoor Christmas light displays packed away.

In a letter to the author, a former official of the Gulf Oil Company, J. Neil Miller, Jr., had this to say about Watergate:

> The government was in such disarray it was virtually comatose. Before nationalization Gulf Oil produced 1,000,000 bbl/day in Kuwait. We provided energy for Eastern Europe and Japan.
>
> I know firsthand that Watergate led to the demise of Gulf Oil Company. It spawned the political contribution scandal which led to the discharge of several of our top officers including the chairman. . . . When good organizations show a sign of weakness someone is going to step in and exploit it as happened to the U.S. during Watergate.

One political cartoonist linked the Watergate scandal and the energy crisis. Above a drawing of the White House the caption read: "Will the last man indicted please turn out the lights?"

Nixon knew when he resigned there was no one to step in and carry out his proposed new world order. That made a resignation due to Watergate more than ever an agony for him. Witness a May 11, 1973, conversation (Kutler, *Abuse of Power*, p. 453) with Ron Ziegler. Nixon said: "The fact that at the present time in world history, the United Sates had an opportunity, either if you win or lose, the greatest chance that history has ever had to build a structure of peace in the world. . . . *Only us.* And I'm the only man to do it. There isn't anybody coming along the pike."

The windup of the Vietnam War overlapped this period and some have suggested that the confusion about accounting for all of the American missing in action, prisoners of war, and other military personnel was partially caused by the paralysis in the presidency brought on by Watergate.

One of the costs of President Ford's pardon of Richard Nixon —as opposed to the probable monetary costs of a possible impeachment trial before Congress or a trial in a federal court—was that many people believed Nixon "got away with it." But what would the cost of a trial have been?

Far better for us all, I believe, was President Ford's pardon of Nixon and Nixon's own vigorous and determined quest for personal rehabilitation, which author Monica Crowley describes as "Nixon's third term." After pulling out of a period of deepest depression, Nixon continued to campaign as hard for the restoration of his reputation as he had campaigned all his political life. Although not a big enough man to admit his guilt, through his writings, his public appearances, and his continued interest in America's foreign relations he succeeded in keeping himself occupied and served his countrymen as well as he could.

Nixon was followed by two presidents—Gerald Ford and Jimmy Carter—who were handicapped by the diminished power of the Oval Office. Ford seemed to be just what the country needed after Nixon, but his administration's failure to end the cold war fell so far short of the lofty potential of Nixon's second-term landslide vote that Watergate seems even more costly. Carter was a good and moral man whose only experience in governing had been as chief executive of Georgia. He was unable to reverse the nation's existing foreign and domestic problems.

Neither Ford nor Carter was able to carry out his programs during a single term in office.

When you consider the enormous cost of Watergate, the actions of Congress in confronting Nixon with impeachment seem harsh. My personal view is that because of Nixon's vast potential to end the cold war, he should not have been impeached. Congress might well have done better to have allowed Nixon to serve out his term, wind down the cold war fifteen years earlier than it finally ended, create a peace dividend in the 1970s, and speed up the emergence of a global economy.

Watergate brought about a drastic change in the method of selecting presidential nominees—the so-called election "reforms." You might think a reform would be an item for the credit side of the ledger, but I believe these particular reforms are debits. They changed the way candidates raise money, the way politicians campaign, and the way citizens perceive their candidates.

The attempts at reform created the political action committees (PACs) as vehicles for campaign donations. These PACs enable money donations to flow directly to the candidates from special interests to the detriment of the general public. Some contend that they have become a vehicle for legalized bribery.

Not the least of the election reforms was the drastic change in the method of selecting presidential nominees. At least partially as a result of Watergate, the old brokered national party conventions which once selected the party's candidate as a judgment call by the top city bosses and incumbent officeholders have been replaced by early statewide primaries. The outcome is heavily influenced by who hires the smarter advertising agency to compose the best sound-bites, targeted TV spots, and saturation advertising. Someday historical perspective may establish that the old system provided more heavyweight presidents and fewer lightweight presidents.

The national conventions—once a forum for hammering out the party's platform while reaching compromise and consensus—have become lavish extravaganzas designed to launch the campaign of the pre-selected candidate and to advance the interests of one-issue lobbying groups.

Watergate diminished forever the relationship of trust, confidence, and camaraderie between the president and the press corps. With Watergate, the white gloves were off. President Nixon told his staff that the press was the enemy, and from the Oval Office that must have appeared to be the case. The media swung around completely in its attitude toward the president and all other elected officials. Press and government relations became adversarial. Governmental scandal is the stuff of which Pulitzers are made. Young journalism school graduates longed to become the next Woodward or Bernstein. Every reporter's dream was to expose and topple a public official—not excepting even the president.

Watergate was a personal disaster—and not only for the president. It was a personal disaster for the members of his administration who went to prison, a disaster for numerous other individuals whose personal and professional lives were tainted by their peripheral involvement, a disaster for the Republican party, and a disaster for the nation.

Nixon often fell short of intellectual honesty and he easily slid into telling less than the truth. He frequently failed to complete his sentence, leaving the thought hanging in the air. His language to outsiders was controlled, proper, conventional, but often awkward, trite, and wordy. He used low-brow profanities to insiders when he was angry and off-guard. He probably learned the first pattern from his mother and the second from his navy experience.

From his father Nixon inherited a basic tilt toward the underdogs of life. In his own mind he was always a barb jousting with the fraternity boys who turned into the Eastern elite and who became flesh in the person of Special Prosecutor Archibald Cox and his hated staff.

He was rigidly self-disciplined and he was acquisitive. He was a loner always. Sometimes he drank too much, usually gin, usually late in the evening, always privately. He demanded and inspired full and complete loyalty from his subordinates but seemed incapable of giving loyalty in return.

He was courageous. He was a practitioner of the political maxim that today's friend is tomorrow's enemy—and conversely, today's enemy is tomorrow's friend. He saw life as encircling danger and combat, and believed in the warfare of open maneuver, placing little confidence in ramparts. He tried for the bold stroke and knew the value of a surprise attack. In the crises of his life, when defeat loomed, his first strategy was to counterattack—again and again.

Although he campaigned as a conservative Republican, he called himself a progressive. If one judges his first-term legislative program by the number of pages he contributed to the Federal Register and by his spending programs, he was a closet liberal. It is a paradox that a nominally conservative Republican could put through Congress in one term a liberal program which in the twentieth century was second only to Franklin Roosevelt's New Deal and surpassing in its reach Lyndon Johnson's War on Poverty. Had Nixon been able to put through his negative income tax proposal, he probably would have been recognized as a liberal. Yet he appointed to the Supreme Court a conservative majority which controlled decisions for many years.

It is a paradox that a professional anti-Communist could establish détente with Russia and open China. Perhaps a true-blue anti-Communist is the only type of political figure who could have pulled that off.

On his last presidential trip abroad, streets were lined with enormous crowds eager to greet the American leader.

Until Watergate, Nixon was a good president, guiding mankind toward his grand vision of a peaceful planet and moving the United States toward a greater prosperity, more equally distributed.

After Nixon's death, a postage stamp with his portrait on it was issued in his honor in April 1995. His enemies, still articulating hostility after twenty years, turned this honor into a jab at his supporters. Someone printed envelopes with a set of iron bars around a small blank rectangle left for a stamp. When a Nixon stamp was affixed, Nixon appeared to be peering out of a prison cell.

At his funeral, long lines of people passing by his coffin were a testimonial to his widespread following.

Historian George Macauly Trevelyan, speaking in 1945, said: "It is still too early to form a final judgment on the French Revolution." If we cannot fully evaluate an event of three centuries ago, how can the enigma of Watergate be solved in a mere three decades?

CHAPTER 17

Devil Take the Hindmost

At Nixon's death in 1994, Jimmy Breslin, perhaps in an excess of journalistic generosity, wrote: "To look at him objectively, as now you must, is to understand that Richard Nixon, not the Kennedys, is the greatest American story—he ranged the furthest, from grocery store to world leader, and he ended in enormous, self-inflicted tragedy."

PRESIDENT RICHARD NIXON'S was a tragically flawed character, well suited for a Greek drama or a Shakespearean play. The deceitful, secretive and vengeful side of him—his political Original Sin, if you will—and the enormous good for which he strove were so pitted against one another as to make his downfall seem inevitable.

John Mitchell, indicted and awaiting trial, still loyal to Nixon, made a desperate effort to save the president. He began negotiations with the special prosecutor and agreed to plead guilty and take the total blame if the special prosecutor would give up going after Nixon. The prosecutors turned this proposal down. Mitchell continued to deny any criminal guilt. He never did sign a paper approving the Liddy plan, although it became obvious that he did not stop Liddy. Magruder maintained that Mitchell had approved Liddy's plans. And Mitchell did read some of the printed reports of the wiretaps. He admitted to Nixon that he had not supervised the Committee to Re-elect closely enough, which might be called the major understatement of the whole Watergate affair.

As Watergate special prosecutor, Leon Jaworski headed the office in charge of gathering the incriminating evidence that sent

John Mitchell to prison. Jaworski, in *Confessions and Avoidance* (pages 227-228), gave a poignant picture of him:

> I felt sympathy for some of the men around Nixon, especially John Mitchell. He was a gruff bear of a man who had been outstanding in the narrow field of bond law. He was an interesting fellow, cordial, in contrast to the cold and forbidding image many had of him. He went off to prison without a whimper, with a certain poise and dignity. . . .
>
> [T]he costliest mistake John Mitchell ever made was taking the job of Attorney General. He simply was not qualified for it. He did not have enough experience in politics, or in life, and even his legal training was so narrow as to be useless in terms of that office.

Leonard Garment (*Crazy Rhythm*, pp. 120-121) makes this judgment of Mitchell:

> . . . Mitchell got in over his head, tragically so. He did many generous and useful things about which history has been silent. But he was asked to serve as a political adviser to a very political president and at the same time fulfill the constitutional responsibilities of an attorney general; he was given, in other words, the task of reconciling irreconcilables. He was not nearly so tough as most people (including himself) thought, and in the end he was no match for his own bad judgment, his president's worst side, and the small army of Chuck Colsons, Gordon Liddys, and John Deans scurrying around the halls of the Nixon Administration.

The trial of Mitchell and the others before John J. Sirica, chief judge, U.S. District Court for the District of Columbia, took place late in 1974. Mitchell did not testify against any of his companions and never turned against Nixon. As Fred Emery pointed out, Mitchell stayed loyal to Nixon to the end, even as his close friend, Nixon, had decided to cast him adrift.

The jury came in late in the afternoon on New Year's Day, 1975. As a prosecutor, I've spent many an hour in courtrooms waiting for the jury to return its verdict. But never, I'm sure, with the internal suffering and humiliation John Mitchell must have felt.

Judge Sirica's courtroom was bleak enough that afternoon in spite of the sunny first day of the new year. With Nixon in California remaining aloof from the trial, John Mitchell must have felt betrayed. As Mitchell sat with the other defendants—Haldeman, Ehrlichman, Magruder and Mardian, a small, scared remnant of the once powerful Nixon Administration—that courtroom must have seemed the loneliest place in the world.

Mitchell was found guilty of conspiracy, obstruction of justice, and perjury. "The Rose Bowl game in 1975 was interrupted on television by an announcement of the conviction of John Mitchell and my other top aides," Nixon wrote. (Nixon, *In the Arena*, pp. 20-21) "I could no longer even take refuge in my favorite avocation, watching sports on television." A self-centered remark, to say the least.

On February 21, 1975, Judge Sirica sentenced Mitchell to two-and-a-half to eight years in prison. Nothing can excuse Mitchell's subornation of perjury. I can't even imagine John Mitchell coaching perjury. Of course, he had been under tremendous pressure to save the president and himself from the bad judgment of a White House staffer he secretly despised. He must have decided he would do almost anything.

As a result, he stood alone by himself in front of a federal judge being sentenced while receiving no help or support from Richard Nixon.

As he left the courtroom, Mitchell wisecracked: "It could have been a hell of a lot worse—they could have sentenced me to spend the rest of my life with Martha." (*Facts-on-File*, 1975, p. 118) This gallows humor showed spunk, but it also showed the depth of his despair over his ruined marriage. And it does not alter the fact that had he followed Martha's insistence that "you can't throw McCord to the wolves," he would not have been in Judge Sirica's court at all.

Mitchell's lawyers petitioned the Supreme Court for a rehearing, but the petition was denied. John was still in the appeals process when Martha became seriously ill.

Why did Nixon refuse to pardon John Mitchell? Mitchell had been his best friend, his campaign manager, and had carried out the cover-up under Nixon's direction. Mitchell, like Liddy, was what the Mafia would call "a stand-up guy." It is true that Liddy's bad judgment broke through on Mitchell's watch. But it is also true that Mitchell was, as the president said, distracted out of his mind by domestic problems.

I wonder if Nixon felt that issuing pardons to his key staff would tend to focus guilt upon himself and imperil his own chances for a pardon? If that were his reason, Nixon failed what could have been his finest hour. But he did not go to the penitentiary. He emerged from his ordeal with a secure financial base for his remaining fifteen years. Haldeman rationalized Nixon's refusal to grant him and others a pardon by saying that by that time Nixon had become a broken man. In his *Memoirs*, Nixon said that accepting his pardon was the most difficult thing he ever had to do because that acknowledged his guilt—again, a self-centered reaction.

I think as a basic duty of loyalty Nixon owed John Mitchell a pardon. The same applies to Haldeman and Ehrlichman. What they did, they did for Nixon with his knowledge and consent in an effort to bail Nixon out of a situation Nixon had created and they had not. In view of Nixon's accepting a pardon for himself, I think his failure to pardon his three trusted lieutenants was an unforgivable breach of loyalty.

Failing to receive help from Nixon, John Mitchell still held out some hope for a presidential pardon from Gerald Ford. He realized none would be forthcoming in November 1976, when Ford lost the election to the Democratic candidate, Jimmy Carter.

When Mitchell entered the federal prison camp July 4, 1977, at Montgomery, Alabama, news magazines reported that he seemed as composed as ever. He faced a minimum of thirty months before he could ask for a parole.

He was the first U.S. attorney general to serve a prison sentence and the last of the Watergate defendants to be jailed. And yet apparently Nixon never gave serious thought to pardoning John Mitchell nor any of the others who had served him so loyally. Nixon could have issued a pardon before his own August 9 resignation, but he did not.

John Mitchell announced plans to write a book while he was in prison. After his release in January 1979, it was again reported that he was working on a book. My feeling is that he was too private a person to have done so. As far as I have been able to determine, he never wrote one—nor have I been able to find any full-length books about John Mitchell in the numerous publications spawned by Watergate.

In describing Mitchell's appearances before the Ervin Committee, Fred Emery (*Watergate*, p. 366) said: "For people who liked the man, Mitchell's appearance, yielding nothing, standing by the president, was a tonic after the squealing of Magruder and Dean. But any relief was temporary."

As the Nixon Administration crumbled, Bill Handley said of Mitchell: "I knew . . . there was one thing John Mitchell would never be is a fink. He didn't have a fink bone in his body, you know. And it aborted; that was the end of that. Jim [Neal] was not prepared to run up the American flag for Nixon and Mitchell was not prepared to be a fink, so nothing came of it basically." (*Watergate,* p. 487)

After the Watergate ordeal was over, and Mitchell was released from serving nineteen months in jail, Nixon gave a party for him. "The uncomfortable story is told by close Mitchell friends of a woman going up to him and saying 'Oh, Mr. Mitchell, I'm so sorry.' To which Mitchell is said to have replied: 'No more than I deserved, my dear.' That he was unable to be the salvation of his close friend at the time of his deepest trial was a secret regret he took to his grave in 1988." (Emery, *Watergate,* p. 492)

When John Mitchell died in 1988, whatever thoughts, beliefs or feelings he had about "the Watergate thing" died with him. When we were working together, John used to talk to me about his American Bar committee work. He was very proud of his standing in the association. I still grieve for John Mitchell.

It was unfortunate that both Dean Griswold and I had left the Justice Department before Watergate mushroomed. I feel quite sure that between us we could have persuaded Mitchell and Nixon to handle it differently.

The Nixon story says everything there is to say about loyalty and the breach of it.

In defining loyalty, one might look back to medieval times. A knight undertook missions assigned by the king or other lord to whom he owed fealty. He was a heavily armed warrior who moved among unarmed civilians. He pledged to right wrongs and do justice as he saw it. He performed no labor at all but spent much of his time jousting in tournaments with other knights. Those battles—not always mock—were conducted for the entertainment of the nobility. In addition, the proper knight searched for the Holy Grail, the legendary cup used by Christ in the Last Supper.

This knight of old lived an incredibly violent life. Nothing in our modern life compares to such institutionalized violence—unless it be professional football or presidential politics.

Camelot is the symbolic name the Kennedys chose for the glamour and the very special ambiance they brought to the White House. Perhaps it is appropriate that we look back through the dark and violent centuries of the Middle Ages to King Arthur himself for an ancient definition of loyalty.

Here is King Arthur's charge (Knowles, *Legend of King Arthur*, p. 102) to his knights of the Round Table:

> Then rose the king and spake to all the Table Round and charged them to be ever true and noble knights, to do neither outrage nor murder, or any unjust violence, and always to flee treason; also by no means ever to be cruel, but give mercy unto him that asked for mercy, upon pains of forfeiting the liberty of this court forever more. Moreover, at all times, on pain of death, to give all succor unto ladies and damsels; and lastly, never to take part in any wrongful quarrel, for a reward or payment. And to all this he swore them, knight by knight.

Loyalty must always be reciprocal. To build a team within the federal government and hold it together requires a steady two-way flow of loyalty between the members of the team and the team captain. Nixon never really understood this. He was basically a loner.

Watergate was a high-stakes drama testing many gradations between loyalty, betrayal, and treachery. For me, a fascinating aspect of the Watergate story is the almost classical interplay of conflicting loyalties.

Shakespeare's *Hamlet* (1:3) contains a frequently quoted definition of loyalty:

> This above all: to thine own self be true,
> And it must follow, as the night the day,
> Thou canst not then be false to any man.

As Watergate developed, the small circle of people surrounding Nixon had great difficulty in defining the parameters of their loyalty. Determining how to be true to oneself, true to Nixon, and true to the federal government was not an easy task. When by the steady pressure of events all the president's men were propelled into the practical world of plea bargaining, *to thine own self be true* might swiftly turn into *every man for himself.*

Of course, there was both duty and compulsion to tell the truth under subpoena. But because of their own involvement in the activities under investigation, most of those called to testify could legally have taken the Fifth Amendment. Taking the Fifth does something to a person's pride, and they may have feared that anyone who *did* take the Fifth might draw a more severe penalty if later to be found guilty. Furthermore, the public often regards seeking the constitutional protection from self-incrimination as tantamount to a confession of guilt.

To add to the confusion was the fact that any plea bargain had to be approved by Henry Petersen—a Nixon appointee subject to being fired.

My years as a criminal prosecutor and public official caused me to watch the unfolding legal and political blunders in stunned disbelief.

I had another reason to be interested.

One of the advantages of growing old is that you can look back over your shoulder and clearly see some of life's hazards that somehow missed you. But for chance, I might have been there.

I left Nixon's Washington to return to Texas in the late fall of 1971 before the Committee to Re-elect was established. John Mitchell had offered me the position of the Committee's general counsel—a job that later went to G. Gordon Liddy under Jeb Stuart Magruder. Magruder had been brought into the White House as deputy communications director in August 1969 by Bob Haldeman and was running the Committee to Re-elect as chief of staff.

Unquestionably, Nixon had surrounded himself with loyal supporters. How, then, did their actions lead inexorably toward his resignation to avoid impeachment? How were the prosecutors able to make their impeachment case entirely out of the testimony of Nixon's own people?

Both the cover-up and the bungled legal response to the aggressiveness of the prosecutors were Nixon's own doing. Nixon created a situation in which Haldeman, Ehrlichman, Mitchell, Kleindienst, Gray, Dean, Magruder, and Petersen were forced to determine whether their dominant loyalty lay between a personal loyalty to President Nixon, an institutional loyalty to the office of the presidency, a loyalty to the federal government, or a personal loyalty to themselves and their family. At stake were not only their own fates but the reputations of their families as well.

The Nixon Administration crumbled when Magruder and

Dean became convinced that Nixon was not going to pardon them. They faced what Edward O. Wilson, in his book *Consilience: The Unity of Knowledge*, calls "The Prisoner's Dilemma." In writing about the origin of moral and ethical rules, he states:

> Two gang members have been arrested for murder and are being questioned separately. The evidence against them is strong but not compelling. The first gang member believes that if he turns state's witness, he will be granted immunity and his partner will be sentenced to life in prison. But he is also aware that his partner has an option to do the same thing. That is the dilemma. Will the two gang members independently defect so that both take the hard fall? They will not, because they agreed in advance to remain silent if caught. By doing so, both hope to be convicted on a lesser charge or escape punishment all together. Criminal gangs have turned this principle of calculation into an ethical precept. Never rat on another member; always be a stand-up guy. Honor does exist among thieves. If we view the gang as a society of sorts, the code is the same as that of a captive soldier in war time obliged to give only name, rank, and serial number.

Had it not been for the turning of Magruder and Dean and the discovery of the tapes, there would have been little impeachment evidence against Nixon. And Henry Petersen was right. The Justice Department had broken the case before the special prosecutor Archibald Cox was appointed.

Bob Haldeman, Nixon's chief of staff, was totally and unswervingly loyal to the man he had admired for almost two decades. "My 'cause'," Haldeman wrote in the Foreword to *The Ends of Power*, "was neither the Presidency, as an institution, nor the man, Richard Nixon. It was a unique combination of the two: President Richard Nixon. . . . It was neither the office nor the man, but the two together that captured my loyalty, dedication and energy."

But there was a possessiveness about Haldeman's gatekeeping which grew into a form of captivity for Nixon. Haldeman constantly was striving to protect Nixon from Nixon's own character flaws. This succeeded so well that when the publication of the tape transcripts exposed Nixon's foul language, the public was surprised and shocked.

Haldeman drew the defensive lines so tightly that when Nixon needed sound criminal law advice there was no competent legal adviser in his inner circle and no friend of sufficient independence and stature to insist upon his employing a criminal defense lawyer.

The president's first legal counsel, John Ehrlichman, wrote in *Witness to Power* that when he left that job to take charge of the Domestic Council, Mitchell recommended Dean for the job of president's legal counsel. The recommendation of Dean showed that Mitchell had no real conception of the kind of lawyer needed for that job.

The president's legal counsel is the president's personal lawyer whose primary function should be to keep the president out of trouble. The last thing the president's legal counsel should be is an eager-to-please yes-man. This lawyer should be a mature person, with some twenty to thirty years of experience as a litigator of both civil and criminal cases. Added to his knowledge of the law should be an innate understanding of the political system gained through running for and holding a local public office or a seat in Congress. He should have a fair knowledge of the structure of the federal government and be able to spot legal trouble a mile away and head it off. In addition, he should have the realism and internal steel in his spine that comes from having faced numerous jury verdicts.

Dick Kleindienst understood this and tried to talk John Dean out of accepting the appointment. In *Justice* (p. 142), Kleindienst recorded the interchange when John Dean came to tell him of his proposed promotion:

> I'll never forget the afternoon in July, 1970 when Dean came into my office and said, "Boss, Haldeman and Ehrlichman want me to go to the White House to be counsel to the President. What do you think?"
>
> "Junior," I replied with brusque incredulity, "you've got to be kidding. To be counsel to the president you have to be a peer of the president. Presidents aren't the easiest persons to deal with. A counsel has to be able to say no to a president in a very adroit way if he is heading down the wrong track. You are a very bright, able young man and you have a good future ahead of you. Forget about being *the* counsel to the president at this time in your life."
>
> Dean looked at me for a moment, smiled, and replied, "I guess you're right."

Kleindienst thought he'd convinced Dean. But Dean returned to him, saying, "I know how you feel about it, Dick, but the honor is just too great. I'm going to do it."

Again Kleindienst attempted to dissuade him:

> "You're not going to be counsel to President Nixon. You'll have the title, and a big office and all you'll be is a runner for Ehrlichman. Seriously, John, you'll regret it for the rest of your life if you go there assuming that you will be counsel to the President."
>
> "I'm sorry you feel that way, Boss. The honor is just too great to pass up."

Kleindienst gave up, deciding he had no right to stand in Dean's way. Later he regretted his decision, concluding that "Dean took to the White House with him, talents (for duplicity and ambition) that enabled him to implement, if not conceive, the cover-up." (Kleindienst, *Justice*, p. 142)

But, because he was inexperienced, Dean did not take with him the knowledge and skills of a trial lawyer.

Nixon approved the fateful choice. John Dean was promoted from the Justice Department to the White House. It was a major blunder of Nixon's administration.

Gordon Liddy was a lawyer who did have some political experience, but his judgments were even less sound than Dean's. In a later conversation between Nixon and Haldeman, Nixon asked Haldeman who initiated the break-in. "Is it Liddy? Is that the fellow? He must be a little nuts."

"He is," Haldeman replied. (Oudes, *From: The President*, p. 504)

After the raid on Dr. Lewis Fielding's Los Angeles office turned into a disaster, an urgent need existed to get Liddy out of the White House. He had become a liability. But by that time the president's men were afraid to fire him because he knew too much. At Dean's suggestion, Liddy—in another kicking upstairs—was transferred to the Committee to Re-elect as general counsel under Jeb Magruder.

Jeb Magruder was part of Haldeman's "bargain-basement manpower" consisting of young, intelligent, handsome, and obedient but inexperienced men. Haldeman maintained that he could buy "young brains and energy" for less money. (Clark Mollenhoff, *Game Plan for Disaster: An Ombudsman's Report on the Nixon Years*, New York: Norton, 1976, p. 38)

Magruder had started his business career as a specialist in the mass merchandising of cosmetics. From there he went to a Los Angeles advertising agency where he became a trusted lieutenant of Haldeman. Although he had experience working under Haldeman as an advance man in Nixon's campaign, he had never made a race of his own and was unqualified by experience to make the judgment calls in a national campaign.

Nixon's chief criterion for choosing his people seems to have been their loyalty to himself. Often the men who started with unswerving loyalty to Nixon were unfitted for the jobs to which he had called them.

President Nixon had appointed John Mitchell—a man who had never been a litigator—to head the largest litigation office in the world. He nominated L. Patrick Gray—a navy man who had no law enforcement or prosecutorial experience—to head the FBI. He approved John Dean—an inexperienced young lawyer unqualified to advise him—as his own personal legal counsel.

Of the other lawyers having easy access to the president—Mitchell, Dean, Ehrlichman, Colson, and Mardian—all started out loyal to Nixon. But not one of them had any personal experience as a candidate for office nor as a prosecutor. None had any experience as a criminal defense counsel, unless it was Colson, who had already advised Nixon to employ a criminal defense lawyer.

Leonard Garment (in *Crazy Rhythm*, p. 264) had this to say of the legal team: "Nixon seemed never to have learned that his failure to assume responsibility for what his subordinates did for him—his failure to back them up—would sever and might ultimately terminate his subordinates' undivided loyalty to him."

The following "misguidance of loyalty" quotation is from Nixon's reply to Petersen in a telephone conversation.

> ". . . the misguidance of loyalty we can handle in an individual (inaudible)—but this message will get through."—President Nixon, Transcripts.

Petersen asked Nixon to publicly urge his staff to cooperate completely with the prosecutors, a thing all of Nixon's instincts should have told him he could not do. Nixon, striding a dilemma, refused. He was in fact vulnerable to staff testimony about the cover-up, and he knew it. He never resolved this dilemma, as one can see clearly in the two alternative speech drafts he prepared at the time of his resignation: one for his leaving office, and one for fighting an impeachment trial. In both, he attributed his sad situation to "mistakes." In neither draft did he acknowledge any fault on his own part.

Right from the start of Watergate, Attorney General Kleindienst backed off and kept his distance. After that, during the crucial ten days in April 1973, at Kleindienst's suggestion, Nixon turned for legal advice to Henry Petersen—the very prosecutor who was in charge of making the case against his administration and, of necessity, a man who was loyal to President Nixon but who was also a Justice Department career man. Petersen would never have any doubt that Shakespeare's charge, *to thine own self be true*, called for a dominant loyalty to the Justice Department and the United States government which would override any personal loyalty to Nixon. Petersen told the president that if material indicating Nixon's guilt came to him, he would "waltz it over" to the congressional impeachment committee and then resign. Thus in the crucial two weeks when Nixon still might have backed up Haldeman and Ehrlichman while pardoning Dean and easing him out, Nixon was looking primarily to Petersen for advice, and Petersen was concentrating on making criminal cases on Haldeman and Ehrlichman.

Nixon needed an attorney general whose prime loyalty lay in saving the presidency. Granting immunity for testimony was a decision of policy—not of legality or illegality—just as pardoning was a decision of policy. Petersen was backing up the court prosecutors, Glanzer and Silbert, who were focused on turning John Dean and producing the very testimony which would destroy Nixon's presidency. Nixon did not lift a hand to keep John Dean from turning state's evidence.

Although at one point he did consider hiring F. Lee Bailey, Nixon seems not to have realized that in the face of the terminal attack on his presidency he desperately needed the advice and guidance of an experienced criminal litigator whose undivided professional loyalty was to him alone.

Soon it was too late to do anything. Nixon resigned in disgrace. He refused to pardon anyone else while accepting a pardon for himself. He refused to acknowledge his guilt. He spent the remainder of his life rebuilding his public image.

Nixon's employees and associates all had to choose between conflicting loyalties.

As the Nixon Administration hit an iceberg, listed, split in two and sank, there were some who did not falter. The loyalty of Mitchell, Haldeman, and Liddy came shining through, even though Nixon did not back them up in their trials.

And I would remind you of my remark to my wife, Marjorie, when I first read the stories about Watergate and saw the statement: *Let the chips fall where they may*. I said to her, "Nixon can't do this. They were his men. They were doing it for him. He can't prosecute them. This will destroy him."

And so it did.

"I remember loyalty," Nixon said (Kutler, *Abuse of Power*, p. 634) but he seems to have meant only loyalty to himself. For some, loyalty is reciprocal. For others, it can turn lonely. In the very first conference on Watergate in the Justice Department, Petersen asked Dean to tell Nixon: "Let the devil take the hindmost." That old cliché seems to have become the prevailing sentiment in Nixon's second term. In the end, that meant no pardon for anyone but himself.

Those people who had tried to maintain their loyalty to Nixon—even at the risk of their own defenses—soon found themselves in a triple bind between loyalty to themselves or Nixon or the federal government.

As a result:

1. **John Mitchell** remained a soldier to the very end. As attorney general, Mitchell failed Nixon miserably when he worked with John Dean to accomplish the cover-up. He should have prevented the hush money and the perjury. Toward the end he offered to plead guilty and take all the blame if the prosecutors would forego pursuing President Nixon. This was turned down. He did not testify against Nixon or any of the others. Mitchell served his time in prison with no public comment. He emerged from prison a poised man, readily taking the blame for his part in the Nixon debacle. He was loyal to Nixon, but in the crisis Mitchell's professional standards failed him.

Both Nixon and Mitchell must have thought that they could make the cover-up work successfully. If so, they demonstrated a profound ignorance of the way federal prosecutors work their way up the food chain by turning witnesses. In my opinion, when you have as many as four potential witnesses, there is small chance of a cover-up not unraveling under the persistent pressure of prosecutors working hand-in-glove with a federal judge.

2. Bob Haldeman figuratively became Nixon's brother. He did not turn and become a witness against Nixon. He urged Nixon to pardon his employees right up to the day Nixon left the White House. After that he defended Nixon's failure to pardon his subordinates, saying that by then Nixon was a broken man. As to loyalty, Bob Haldeman was indeed a true soldier.

3. Richard Kleindienst was loyal to Nixon. At his confirmation hearing for attorney general before the Senate Judicial Committee, Kleindienst not only concealed but lied about President Nixon's order to him to dismiss the ITT antitrust appeal. For that Kleindienst was convicted on a misdemeanor charge of perjury, kicked around, and embarrassed. He was Joseph Conrad's Lord Jim of Watergate, not stepping into his big opportunity. Had he seized command that first Sunday morning at Burning Tree golf course, he could have saved the presidency in spite of Nixon. As it happened, Kleindienst distanced himself from Watergate because of John Mitchell's involvement and—in the midst of the crisis—abandoned ship, swam for the safety of shore, and resigned rather than face taking part in John Mitchell's prosecution.

4. Pat Gray was crucified before the Senate confirmation committee for destroying a piece of paper that was purported to be a copy of a telegram damaging to President Kennedy. There was no such telegram. This was not evidence of anything. It had obviously been prepared by some employee, probably McCord. The piece of paper should have been promptly destroyed as soon as it was discovered, and Pat Gray's destruction of it was an act of loyalty to the Nixon Administration. This incident was grossly exaggerated in importance. However, the president disowned Gray and allowed him—in Ehrlichman's words—"to twist slowly in the wind." Gray did not testify against Nixon.

5. John Ehrlichman, keeping his silence while growing desperate, called on Nixon for help but received none.

6. **John Dean** turned hostile, sold his testimony for leniency in sentencing, and became the principal witness against Nixon and his team. He chose loyalty to himself and to tell the truth. Dean was entirely too young and inexperienced for the job of counsel to the president.

7. **Jeb Magruder and Chuck Colson** turned to religious careers in their search for answers. Magruder became a Presbyterian minister and Colson was born again into the service of the prison population.

8. **Gordon Liddy** received a twenty-year prison term, was fined $40,000, and declared bankruptcy. Liddy was to serve fifty-two lonely months—the longest sentence of any of the Watergate defendants. In April 1977 President Jimmy Carter commuted Liddy's twenty-year sentence to eight years, thus making him eligible for a parole hearing. In September 1977 he walked out of Allenwood Prison, a free man emerging with his pride intact. As to loyalty, he was a stand-up guy. He became a radio commentator, expressing advice and opinions on public affairs.

9. **Elliot Richardson and William Ruckleshaus** were knights in shining armor in refusing to fire Special Prosecutor Archibald Cox. Robert Bork did the right thing in holding the house together and in preventing a constitutional crisis by serving as acting attorney general, firing Cox, and turning the whole Watergate investigation back to Henry Petersen until Special Prosecutor Leon Jaworski was appointed. Bork demonstrated loyalty to both Nixon and the federal government. For that he paid his price in being rejected by the Senate for appointment to the United States Supreme Court.

At least two women also found their lives irrevocably changed.

Rose Mary Woods, Nixon's loyal personal secretary, denied that she had deliberately erased eighteen and a half minutes from Nixon's June 20 tape. Not everyone believed the erasure had been accidental. Jokes about the Woods incident persist to this day.

Woods, like others of the president's close circle, was willing enough to blame the entire Watergate incident on Martha Mitchell. In a taped conversation between Woods and her boss on June 19, 1973 (Kutler, *Abuse of Power*, p. 614), the secretary said: "Well, [Martha Mitchell] is a nut. She is a nut, you know, as far as I'm concerned."

Martha Mitchell, in the minds of some, remains the tragic woman in Watergate. While some people viewed her as a pitiable alcoholic, others praised her as one of the few willing to breach the stone wall surrounding Watergate.

Although John and Martha never got a divorce, they remained separated and Martha hired a succession of attorneys to force support payments from her husband. When the money was not forthcoming, Martha began a desperate round of public speaking, paid television appearances, and magazine articles bearing her by-line. She continued to fulfill her role as a celebrity. In July 1974 some first-class mail from the Chicago area turned up with stamps bearing her likeness.

Her health continued to deteriorate. Jay Jennings, Martha's son by her first marriage, learned of his mother's critical condition too late to reach her hospital bedside. On May 31, 1976, Martha died of cancer—alone, estranged from her husband and her daughter Marty.

When Martha died, "Mister President" had been out of office for twenty-one months—forced out by Watergate. Mark Goodman, writing in the *New Times* magazine, said: "With a telephone receiver in one hand and a glass of whiskey in the other, [Martha] first sounded the alarm. . . . We did not listen to Martha Mitchell and we paid for it."

In a televised interview with David Frost in September 1977, Nixon said: "If it hadn't been for Martha, there'd have been no Watergate, because John wasn't minding the store [Committee to Re-elect]. John was practically out of his mind about Martha in the spring of 1972. *He was letting Magruder and all these boys, these kids, these nuts, run this thing.*" (Emphasis added.)

Nixon had it backwards, sort of. Martha was not the prime cause—she was just the whistle-blower. The break-in and burglary were Liddy's compulsion. The men who empowered Liddy to act caused the Watergate break-in.

At Martha's services in Pine Bluff, Arkansas, a large spray of white chrysanthemums spelled out the words: MARTHA WAS RIGHT.

I remembered the time when that vibrant, animated woman had served as barmaid for our Georgetown party. After sending a wreath to her funeral, I received a warm and friendly note of thanks from John Mitchell. That was our last communication.

Among all the lives forever altered by Watergate, two men who had been in the heart of the maelstrom escaped with their reputations intact.

Gen. Alexander Haig served as chief of staff in Gerald Ford's administration for six weeks. He went on to command NATO, became an unsuccessful candidate for the presidency, and found a seat as secretary of state in President Ronald Reagan's Cabinet.

Henry Kissinger, who had become Nixon's secretary of state in September 1973, remained in that position through the Ford Administration. He continues to act as an adviser, consultant, and senior statesman on foreign affairs.

Robert Bork was not so fortunate. He is remembered as the man who wielded the headsman's ax in the Saturday Night Massacre. Recommended by President Reagan for the U.S. Supreme Court in 1987, Bork failed to gain confirmation while enduring one of the nastiest smear jobs in Senate history.

In the end, Petersen's remark, "Let the devil take the hindmost," became a more accurate definition of political loyalty during the Nixon Administration than Shakespeare's "To thine own self be true." As the prosecution effort devoured its way up the food chain it turned out that the "hindmost" was the president himself.

In thinking about the Nixon presidency, an old nursery rhyme came to my mind:

> For want of a nail, the shoe was lost;
> For want of a shoe, the horse was lost;
> For want of a horse, the kingdom was lost.

First Dean was lost, then the Agnew situation was lost, then the kingdom was lost.

The "nail" needed by Nixon was a skilled trial lawyer, knowledgeable in criminal law, who could break through the gatekeepers, brush aside the amateurs surrounding Nixon, communicate with and guide his client. Nixon needed a lawyer who could quarterback the case in order to win it. Nixon had himself—plus Haldeman and later Haig—calling the shots, but neither Haldeman nor Haig was a lawyer, and Nixon had not been in a trial court for many years.

How, you ask, could it be that a president who was himself a lawyer with thousands of lawyers under his command lost the presidency because he had no one on his immediate legal staff who had practiced criminal law? Nixon did not have such a lawyer until far too late, and then he did not give him command of the case or a full knowledge of his own personal vulnerabilities.

There came a time when Nixon realized that Special Prosecutor Cox, using John Dean as a government witness, would expose Nixon's participation in the cover-up. He did not foresee the firestorm of public protest that firing Cox would produce nor the problems that would follow the resignations of Richardson and Ruckelshaus.

After that, the path to resignation or impeachment was as inevitable as the logic in college algebra.

Toward the end of his life, during the Clinton Administration, former President Nixon watched with great interest the unfolding of the Whitewater investigation. He could see that all of the explosive ingredients were present. Crowley (in *Nixon Off the Record*, p. 213) wrote:

> The appearance of stonewalling, the obstruction of investigations, the policy of appeasement in assenting to a special prosecutor, and the repeated denials of wrongdoing flowing from the White House brought back enough negative memories for Nixon that he felt compelled to ask . . . a desperate question:
>
> Didn't anyone learn anything from Watergate?

Epilogue

PRESIDENT CLINTON SURVIVED impeachment because the Democrats stayed behind him and because he followed the advice of skilled attorneys.

President Nixon did not survive impeachment because the Republicans abandoned him and because he did not employ a skilled criminal lawyer until too late. He was not found guilty in an impeachment because he resigned. He was not indicted because he was pardoned by President Gerald Ford.

Because of their adherence to the law, Gerald Ford and Jimmy Carter were not confronted with impeachment.

Ronald Reagan was not charged in an impeachment because he was out of office by the time Special Prosecutor Lawrence E. Walsh completed his cases on the hostages-for-arms swap with Iran and the use of federal money to finance the contras in Central America. He was not charged before a grand jury because by that time he had Alzheimer's disease.

Bill Clinton was impeached, tried, and acquitted by Congress for violating the social mores governing sexual conduct and then lying to the public and under oath about such conduct.

This use of what a prosecutor would consider more or less minor violations of the criminal law to impeach a sitting president has become a standard practice of partisan warfare in the United States.

Future presidents should think hard about greatly reducing the size of the White House staff. It may be better to govern through Cabinet officers who would serve as a barrier against the malfunction of operational employees. This should reduce the debilitating search of the presidency for possible criminal violations by the president.

And as for the original Camelot of old, solemn oaths of loyalty and fealty dissolved in jealousy.

Such is the nature of kingdoms and governments supported by the passions and needs of human beings.

Watergate's Cast of Characters

Spiro T. Agnew: Former governor of Maryland; vice president in President Richard Nixon's administration from 1969 until his resignation in 1973.

Howard H. Baker, Jr.: Republican senator from Tennessee; vice-chairman and ranking minority member of the Senate Watergate Committee. Coined the phrase: "What did the president know and when did he know it?"

Carl Bernstein: One of the *Washington Post* reporters who, with Bob Woodward, helped keep the public's focus on Watergate.

James J. Bierbower: Jeb Magruder's trial lawyer.

William "Bill" Bittman: Formerly a prosecutor in Attorney General Robert Kennedy's Justice Department; later Howard Hunt's lawyer in the Watergate case.

Robert Bork: Followed Erwin Griswold as solicitor general; became the acting attorney general following Nixon's firing of Elliott Richardson and William Ruckelshaus.

Alexander P. Butterfield: Former White House aide to H. R. Haldeman and a witness before the Senate Watergate Committee.

J. Fred Buzhardt, Jr.: General counsel of Department of Defense; later President Nixon's Watergate counsel.

W. Matthew Byrne: Federal district judge selected to hear the Daniel Ellsberg case (Pentagon Papers) in Los Angeles.

Donald E. Campbell: Aide to Earl Silbert; presented the government's evidence to the grand jury.

Dwight L. Chapin: The president's appointments secretary in Nixon's first term.

Charles "Chuck" Colson: Special White House counsel (1970-1973).

John Connally: Former Texas governor; later secretary of the treasury in Nixon's first term; he favored destroying the White House tapes.

Archibald Cox: Harvard Law School professor; solicitor general in President John Kennedy's administration; later appointed as the first Watergate special prosecutor.

Samuel Dash: Georgetown University law professor; chief counsel to the Senate Watergate Committee.

John W. Dean, III: Formerly an administrative aide in the Justice Department; later (1970-1973) counsel to the president.

"Deep Throat": Name used to protect the true identity of the person who leaked Watergate information to *Washington Post* reporter Bob Woodward.

John Doar: Special counsel to the House Judiciary Committee's impeachment inquiry.

John D. Ehrlichman: One of Nixon's principal campaign aides; later chief domestic policy adviser to the president (1969-1973).

Daniel Ellsberg: Researcher; leaked the Pentagon Papers to the press.

Sam J. Ervin: Democratic senator from North Carolina; chairman of the Senate Watergate Committee.

Dr. Lewis Fielding: Daniel Ellsberg's psychiatrist; Dr. Fielding's Los Angeles office was broken into by a covert team known as the Plumbers.

Gerald R. Ford: Republican congressman from Michigan; minority leader of the House (1965-1973); Ford was appointed vice president to succeed Spiro Agnew (1973); became president when Nixon resigned (August 9, 1974).

Leonard C. Garment: Nixon's former law partner in New York; later White House adviser (1969-1974).

Seymour Glanzer: Aide to Earl J. Silbert; presented the government's evidence to the grand jury.

Katherine Graham: Publisher of the *Washington Post*; approved publication of the Pentagon Papers.

L. Patrick Gray, III: Acting director of the FBI (1972-1973); Gray withdrew his nomination to become the permanent director and resigned.

Erwin Griswold: As solicitor general, Griswold argued the government's case before the Supreme Court in an effort to halt publication of the Pentagon Papers.

H. R. "Bob" Haldeman: White House chief of staff (1969-1973).

William "Bill" Hundley: Former special assistant to Attorney General Robert Kennedy, retained by John Mitchell as counsel.

E. Howard Hunt, Jr.: Former CIA clandestine officer; member of the Plumbers, the covert operations team which broke into Los Angeles offices of Dr. Fielding and the Democratic National Committee's offices in Watergate.

Leon Jaworski: Appointed to follow Archibald Cox as Watergate special prosecutor.

Barbara C. Jordan: Black congresswoman from the Eighteenth Texas District. Her speech about the Constitution is credited with swinging votes of impeachment against Nixon.

Herbert W. Kalmbach: Nixon's personal attorney and fundraiser.

Robert "Bobby" Kennedy: Attorney general in President John F. Kennedy's administration, carried over into President Lyndon B. Johnson's administration; his "band of brothers" and "get-Hoffa" squad later played a part in the Watergate cases.

Henry A. Kissinger: Nixon's national security adviser (1969-1973); later Nixon's secretary of state, carried over into President Ford's administration (1973-1977).

Richard G. Kleindienst: Deputy attorney general; appointed attorney general (1972-1973) following John Mitchell's resignation.

Egil "Bud" Krogh: Deputy to John Ehrlichman; head of the White House Plumbers.

Fred C. LaRue: John Mitchell's chief adviser in the Committee to Re-elect the President.

Philip A. Lacovara: Aide to Special Prosecutor Leon Jaworski.

G. Gordon Liddy: Former FBI agent; counsel to the Committee to Re-Elect the President; Plumber; led the covert entries of Dr. Fielding's Los Angeles offices and the Democratic National Committee's Watergate offices.

James W. McCord, Jr.: Former CIA security officer; participated in the Watergate break-in; later turned state's evidence.

Jeb Stuart Magruder: Former aide to Haldeman; later deputy director of the Committee to Re-elect the President.

Robert C. "Bob" Mardian: Assistant attorney general (1969-1972); later, Committee to Re-elect the President.

John N. Mitchell: Attorney general (1969-1972); resigned to work full-time for the Committee to Re-elect the President.

Martha Mitchell: Wife of John Mitchell. Her outspoken criticism of "Mister President"—although not believed by everyone—called the public's attention to efforts by the White House to cover up Watergate.

Richard M. Nixon: Republican congressman from California (1947-1951); senator (1951-1953); twice elected vice president under Dwight D. Eisenhower (1953-1961); elected president (1969-1974); resigned from the presidency August 9, 1974.

Lawrence F. "Larry" O'Brien: Chairman of the Democratic National Committee at the time of the Watergate break-in.

Thomas P. "Tip" O'Neill: Democratic congressman from Massachusetts, majority leader of the House.

Henry E. Petersen: Career Justice Department official; at the time of Watergate, Petersen was assistant attorney general, Criminal Division.

"The Plumbers": Covert team operating out of the White House, created after the release of the Pentagon Papers and ordered to stop leaks.

William Rehnquist: Assistant attorney general (1969-1971); appointed by President Nixon to the Supreme Court (1971); appointed chief justice (1986) by President Ronald Reagan.

Elliot L. Richardson: Appointed attorney general following Kleindienst's resignation (1973); Richardson appointed Archibald Cox as Watergate special prosecutor and resigned during the "Saturday Night Massacre."

Hillary Rodham: Graduate of Yale law school; aide to John Doar, special counsel to the House Judiciary Committee. Later, as Hillary Rodham Clinton, she was First Lady (1992-2000).

Peter W. Rodino, Jr.: Chairman of the House Judiciary Committee.

William Ruckelshaus: Deputy attorney general under Elliot Richardson; Ruckelshaus resigned during the "Saturday Night Massacre." The president did not accept the resignation and insisted that he be fired.

Donald H. Segretti: One of the "dirty tricks" team for Nixon's 1972 campaign for re-election.

Charles N. Shaffer: Formerly a member of Attorney General Robert Kennedy's "get-Hoffa" team; represented John Dean in the Watergate investigations.

Earl J. Silbert: Chief assistant U.S. attorney for the District of Columbia; chief prosecutor in the original Watergate trial.

John J. Sirica: Chief judge, U.S. District Court for the District of Columbia; presided over break-in and cover-up trials; known as "Maximum John" because of his stiff sentences.

James D. St. Clair: Boston trial lawyer selected by President Nixon to handle his Watergate defense.

Maurice Stans: Fundraiser for the Committee to Re-elect the President.

Lowell P. Weicker, Jr.: Connecticut Republican senator, member of the Senate Watergate Committee.

Edward Bennett Williams: *Washington Post* attorney who, along with the publisher, approved the printing of the Pentagon papers.

John J. Wilson: Lawyer for former White House aides Bob Haldeman and John Ehrlichman.

Rose Mary Woods: Nixon's loyal personal secretary for many years; generally believed to have been responsible for the eighteen-and-a-half minute erasure of the June 20, 1972, White House tape.

Robert "Bob" Woodward: Investigative reporter for the *Washington Post;* author of *All the President's Men* and *Final Days.*

Charles A. Wright: University of Texas law professor; legal consultant to Richard Nixon.

Ronald L. Ziegler: Formerly in advertising; President Nixon's press secretary (1969-1974).

Bibliography

Agnew, Spiro. *Go Quietly or Else.* New York: Morrow, 1980.
———. *Where He Stands: The Life and Convictions of Spiro T. Agnew.* (With an Introduction by Richard M. Nixon.) New York: Hawthorne Books, 1968.
Allen, Steve. *Ripoff: A Look at Corruption in America.* Secaucus, New Jersey: L. Stuart, 1979.
Ambrose, Stephen E. *Nixon: The Education of a Politician, 1913-1962.* Vol. 1. New York: Simon and Schuster, 1987.
———. *Nixon: The Triumph of a Politician 1962-1972.* Vol. 2. New York: Simon and Schuster, 1989.
———. *Nixon: Ruin and Recovery.* Vol. 3. New York: Simon and Schuster, 1991.
Baker, Leonard. *Brandeis and Frankfurter: A Dual Biography.* New York: Harper & Row, 1984.
Berger, Raoul. *Impeachment: The Constitutional Problems.* Cambridge: Harvard University Press, 1978.
Bernstein, Carl, and Bob Woodward. *All the President's Men.* New York: Simon & Schuster, 1974.
Bradlee, Ben. *A Good Life: Newspapering and Other Adventures.* New York: Simon & Schuster, 1995.
Brashler, William. *The Don: The Life and Death of Sam Giancana.* New York: Harper & Row, 1977.
Breslin, Jimmy. *How the Good Guys Finally Won: Notes from an Impeachment Summer.* New York: Viking, 1975.
Brodie, Fawn M. *Richard Nixon: The Shaping of His Character.* New York: Norton, 1981.
Colodny, Len and Robert Gettlin. *Silent Coup: The Removal of Richard Nixon.* New York: St. Martin's, 1991.
Colson, Charles. *Born Again.* Old Tappan, New Jersey: Spire Books, Fleming H. Revell Co., 1977.
Congressional Quarterly, Inc. *Watergate: Chronology of a Crisis.* Vols. 1 & 2. Washington, D.C.: 1975.
Coyne, John R., Jr. *The Impudent Snobs: Agnew vs. The Intellectual Establishment.* New Rochelle, New York: Arlington House, 1972.
Crowley, Monica. *Nixon in Winter.* New York: Random House, 1998.
———. *Nixon Off the Record.* New York: Random House, 1996.

Dash, Samuel. *Chief Counsel: Inside the Ervin Committee—The Untold Story of Watergate.* New York: Random House, 1976.
Davis, Kenneth C. *Don't Know Much about History.* New York: Avon Books, 1990, 1995.
Davis, Kenneth S. *FDR: The New York Years, 1928-1933.* New York: Random House, 1985, 1979.
Dean, John W., III. *Blind Ambition: The White House Years.* New York: Simon & Schuster, 1976.
———. *Lost Honor.* Los Angeles: Stratford Press, 1982.
Demaris, Ovid. *The Last Mafioso: The Treacherous World of Jimmy Fratianno.* New York: Times Books, 1981.
Douglas, William O. *The Court Years, 1939-1975: The Autobiography of William O. Douglas.* New York: Random House, 1980.
Doyle, James. *Not Above the Law: The Battles of Watergate Prosecutors Cox and Jaworski.* New York: Morrow, 1979.
Ehrlichman, John. *Witness to Power: The White House Years.* New York: Simon & Schuster, 1982.
Emery, Fred. *Watergate.* New York: Random House, 1994.
Ervin, Sam, Jr. *The Whole Truth: The Watergate Conspiracy.* New York: Random House, 1980.
Ford, Gerald R. *A Time to Heal.* New York: Harper & Row, 1979.
Garment, Leonard. *Crazy Rhythm.* New York: Times Books, 1997.
Gunderson, Joan R., and Marshall Smelser. *American History at a Glance.* New York: HarperPerennial, 1994.
Halberstam, David. *The Powers That Be.* New York: Knopf, 1979.
Haldeman, H. R. *The Ends of Power.* New York: Times Books, 1978.
———. *The Haldeman Diaries: Inside the Nixon White House.* New York: G. P. Putnam's, 1994.
Higgins, George V. *The Friends of Richard Nixon.* New York: Little, Brown, 1975.
Hoff, Joan. *Nixon Reconsidered.* New York: Basic Books, 1994.
Hoover, Herbert. *The Memoirs of Herbert Hoover: The Cabinet and the Presidency, 1920-1933.* Vol. 2. New York: Macmillan, 1952.
Hougan, Jim. *Secret Agenda: Watergate, Deep Throat, and the CIA.* New York: Random House, 1984.
Ianni, Francis A., and Elizabeth Reuss Ianni. *A Family Business: Kinship and Social Control in Organized Crime.* New York: Russell Sage Foundation, 1972.
The Impeachment Report: A Guide to Congressional Proceedings in the Case of Richard M. Nixon, President of the United States. Compiled and edited by the staffs of United Press International and *The World Almanac.* New York: New American Library, 1974.
Isaacson, Walter. *Kissinger, A Biography.* New York: Simon & Schuster, 1992.
Jaworski, Leon. *Confession and Avoidance: A Memoir.* Garden City, New York: Anchor Press/Doubleday, 1979.
———. *The Right and the Power: The Prosecution of Watergate.* New York: Reader's Digest, 1976.
Kennedy, Robert. *The Enemy Within.* New York: Harper & Brothers, 1960.
———. *The Pursuit of Justice.* New York: Harper & Row, 1964.

Kissinger, Henry. *Henry Kissinger, The White House Years.* Boston: Little, Brown, 1979.
Klein, Herbert G. *Making It Perfectly Clear.* New York: Doubleday, 1980.
Kleindienst, Richard. *Justice: The Memoirs of Attorney General Kleindienst.* Ottawa, Illinois: Jameson Books, 1985.
Kutler, Stanley J. *Abuse of Power: The New Nixon Tapes.* New York: Free Press, 1997.
Liddy, G. Gordon. *Will: The Autobiography of G. Gordon Liddy.* New York: St. Martin's, 1980.
Lukas, J. Anthony. *Nightmare: The Underside of the Nixon Years.* New York: Viking, 1976.
McCarthy, Mary. *The Mask of State: Watergate Portraits.* New York: Harcourt Brace, 1974.
McLendon, Winzola. *Martha.* New York: Random House, 1979.
McNamara, Robert S., and Brian VanDeMark. *In Retrospect: The Tragedy and Lessons of Vietnam.* New York: Times Books, 1995.
Magruder, Jeb Stuart. *An American Life.* New York: Atheneum, 1974.
———. *From Power to Peace.* Waco: Word Books, 1978.
Marsh, Robert. *Agnew, The Unexamined Man: A Political Profile.* New York: Evans, 1971.
Matthews, Christopher. *Kennedy and Nixon.* New York: Simon & Schuster, 1996.
Mazlish, Bruce. *Kissinger, The European Mind in American Policy.* New York: Basic Books, 1976.
Mollenhoff, Clark. *Game Plan for Disaster. An Ombudsman's Report on the Nixon Years.* New York: Norton, 1976.
———. *Strike Force: Organized Crime and the Government.* Englewood Cliffs, New Jersey: Prentice-Hall, 1972.
Morris, Roger. *Haig, The General's Progress.* New York: Playboy Press, 1982.
———. *Richard Milhous Nixon: The Rise of an American Politician.* New York: Holt, 1990.
Muzzio, Douglas. *Watergate Games: Strategies, Choices, Outcomes.* New York: New York University Press, 1982.
Nixon, Richard M. *Beyond Peace.* New York: Random House, 1994.
———. *From: The President: Richard Nixon's Secret Files.* Bruce Oudes, editor. New York: Harper & Row, 1989.
———. *In the Arena: A Memoir of Victory, Defeat and Renewal.* New York: Simon & Schuster, 1990.
———. *RN: The Memoirs of Richard Nixon.* Vols. 1, 2. New York: Grosset & Dunlap, 1975.
Osborne, John. *The Fifth Year of the Nixon Watch.* New York: Liveright, 1974.
———. *The Fourth Year of the Nixon Watch.* New York: Liveright, 1973.
———. *The Third Year of the Nixon Watch.* New York: Liveright, 1973.
Oudes, Bruce. See Nixon, Richard M. *From: The President: Richard Nixon's Secret Files.*
Rangell, Leo. *The Mind of Watergate: An Exploration of the Compromise of Integrity.* New York: W. W. Norton, 1980.
Rather, Dan, and Gary Paul Gates. *The Palace Guards.* New York: Harper & Row, 1974.

Reston, James, Jr. *The Lone Star: The Life of John Connally.* New York: Harper & Row, 1989.

Richardson, Elliot. *The Creative Balance: Government, Politics, and the Individual in America's Third Century.* New York: Holt, Rinehart and Winston, 1976.

———. *Reflections of a Radical Moderate.* New York: Pantheon Books, 1996.

Roosevelt, Franklin D. *FDR: His Personal Letters, 1928-1945.* Vol. 1. New York: Duell, Sloan and Pearce, 1950.

Safire, William. *Before the Fall: An Inside View of the Pre-Watergate White House.* New York: Doubleday, 1975.

———. *Safire's Washington.* New York: Times Books, 1980.

Schlesinger, Arthur M. *Robert Kennedy and His Times.* Boston: Houghton Mifflin, 1978.

Sirica, John J. *To Set the Record Straight: The Break-in, the Tapes, the Conspirators, the Pardon.* New York: Norton, 1979.

Stans, Maurice H. *The Terrors of Justice: The Untold Side of Watergate.* New York: Everest House, 1978.

Strober, Gerald S., and Deborah Hart Strober. *Nixon: An Oral History of His Presidency.* New York: HarperCollins, 1994.

Voorhis, Jerry. *The Strange Case of Richard Milhous Nixon.* New York: Paul S. Eriksson, 1972.

White, Theodore H. *Breach of Faith: The Fall of Richard Nixon.* New York, Atheneum, 1975.

———. *The Making of the President, 1964.* New York: Atheneum, 1965.

———. *The Making of the President, 1968.* New York: Atheneum, 1969.

———. *The Making of the President, 1972.* New York: Atheneum, 1973.

Wicker, Tom. *One of Us: Richard Nixon and The American Dream.* New York: Random House, 1972.

Wilson, Edward O. *Consilience: The Unity of Knowledge.* New York: Knopf, 1998.

Woodward, Bob. *Shadow: Five Presidents and the Legacy of Watergate.* New York: Simon & Schuster, 1999.

Woodward, Bob, and Scott Armstrong. *The Brethren: Inside the Supreme Court.* New York: Simon & Schuster, 1979.

Woodward, Bob, and Carl Bernstein. *The Final Days.* New York: Simon & Schuster, 1976.

Newspapers, Magazines, and Serials

Austin American–Statesman
Current Biography Yearbook
Discover magazine
Facts on File
Life magazine
Reader's Guide to Periodical Literature
New York Times
Time magazine
Newsweek
Saturday Evening Post
Vanity Fair
Wall Street Journal
Washington Post

Index

—N—